Faulkner and Race
FAULKNER AND YOKNAPATAWPHA
1986

Faulkner and Race

FAULKNER AND YOKNAPATAWPHA, 1986

EDITED BY
DOREEN FOWLER
AND
ANN J. ABADIE

UNIVERSITY PRESS OF MISSISSIPPI
Jackson and London

*This book has been sponsored by the University of Mississippi's
Center for the Study of Southern Culture*

The paper in this book meets the guidelines for permanence and durability of the
Committee on Production Guidelines for Book Longevity of the Council on Library
Resources.

Library of Congress Cataloging-in-Publication Data

Faulkner and Yoknapatawpha Conference (13th : 1986 :
  University of Mississippi)
  Faulkner and race.

  Papers presented at the 13th Annual Faulkner and
Yoknapatawpha Conference at the Oxford campus of
University of Mississippi, 1986.
  Includes index.
    1. Faulkner, William, 1897–1962—Characters—
Afro-Americans—Congresses.   2. Faulkner, William,
1897–1962—Political and social views—Congresses.
3. Afro-Americans in literature—Congresses.   4. Race
in literature—Congresses.   I. Fowler, Doreen.
II. Abadie, Ann J.   III. Title.

Library of Congress Cataloging-in-Publication Data

  PS3511.A86Z7832113   1986   813'.52   87-19004
  ISBN 0-87805-328-X (alk. paper)
  ISBN 0-87805-329-8 (pbk. : alk. paper)

Contents

Introduction

Faulkner is one of America's greatest writers, and one of his central subjects is race. But can Faulkner, a white Southerner, the great-grandson of a slave owner, or, for that matter, can any white man enter a black consciousness or render accurately black lives? Opinions vary. On the one hand, Faulkner has created unforgettable black characters like Dilsey Gibson, Faulkner's own favorite character, whom Faulkner described as "much more brave and honest and generous than me."[1] And, with characters like Joe Christmas, a man who can never be categorized as either black or white, and Charles Bon, a seemingly godlike creature who is admired and beloved by all until his drop of black blood is revealed, Faulkner resolutely has probed the deeply repressed psychological dimensions of race, asking in novel after novel the perplexing question: what does blackness signify in a predominantly white society? On the other hand, Faulkner's public statements on the subject of race have sometimes seemed less than fully enlightened, and some of his black characters, especially in the early fiction, seem to conform to white stereotypical notions of what black men and women are like.

These and related questions are explored in the essays in this volume, which were originally presented by Faulkner scholars, black and white, male and female, at the 1986 Faulkner and Yoknapatawpha Conference, the thirteenth in a series of conferences held on the Oxford campus of the University of Mississippi.

Eric J. Sundquist, author of the text *Faulkner: The House Divided*, opens the collection with an essay that thoughtfully addresses one of the central problems raised by the subject of Faulkner and Race: can the black experience be formulated by a white writer? In "Faulkner, Race, and the Forms of American Fiction" Sundquist claims that "Faulkner's position as one of the most important American writers on the problem of race is secure," but then goes on to add that "there are limitations to [Faulkner's] vision." Accordingly, Sundquist maintains that Faulkner's fiction on race should be read in the context of other authors, black and white, whose works "engage and complete those of Faulkner, giving clearer voice to black lives and to the cultural traditions of race in America." As if in direct response to Sundquist's call for more studies that place Faulkner in the tradition of literature on race, Craig Werner's essay, "Minstrel Nightmares: Black Dreams of Faulkner's Dreams of Blacks," contrasts Faulkner's narrative handling of race in *Intruder in the Dust* with Ernest Gaines's treatment of similar themes in *A Gathering of Old Men* and concludes that while "he rarely distorts observed facts, Faulkner frequently misperceives the underlying dynamic of Afro-American experience."

Is Faulkner's depiction of black lives then flawed? Four essays tackle this question. In "Faulkner's Negroes Twain" noted Afro-Americanist Blyden Jackson argues that "there are two fictive Negroes" in Faulkner's canon, the black characters of the early works, like *Soldiers' Pay* and *Mosquitoes*, who are stereotypes, and the black figures who were created after Faulkner discovered Yoknapatawpha, his own literary domain. These later blacks, Jackson claims, are "a reliable transcript and model of Faulkner's sincerest inner impressions and convictions." Another scholar who identifies two different modes of black characterization in Faulkner's fiction is Thadious M. Davis, author of the critical work *Faulkner's "Negro": Art and the Southern Context*. According to Davis, one of Faulkner's styles of black characterization corresponds to the rhythms of jazz, the other, to the elegiac strains of blues; and, while neither style "is entirely free of the burden of inadequate racial assumptions," blues characterization "magnifies an internal life that is substantially unaffected by the immediacy of the white world." An impulse toward two different modes of black characterization in

Faulkner's fiction is also the theme of Pamela Rhodes's essay. In "Who Killed Simon Strother, and Why? Race and Counterplot in *Flags in the Dust*" Rhodes argues that Simon Strother is rendered in two, variant narrative styles: as a comic stereotype and as a more complexly independent figure who pursues opportunities for self-definition. Thus, concludes Rhodes, Faulkner killed Simon Strother for fear of where the latter, more realistic portrayal might lead. The last essay to deal specifically with black images in Faulkner's fiction is by Walter Taylor, author of *Faulkner's Search for a South*. In "Faulkner's *Reivers*: How to Change the Joke without Slipping the Yoke" Taylor contends that Faulkner's depiction of Ned McCaslin in *The Reivers* "beams the very loud message that Jim Crow was not so bad."

If some scholars suggest that Faulkner's black portraits are perhaps a distortion of black reality, others counter this claim with a forceful defense of Faulkner's treatment of race. For example, Noel Polk, author of *"Requiem for a Nun": A Critical Study*, exhorts scholars to adopt a positive approach in addressing the subject of Faulkner and Race. "I believe," writes Polk, "that we have tried too hard to discover the number and kinds of things that Faulkner *did not* or *could not* write about, and not nearly hard enough to find the profound and perplexing human drama that within his lights—illuminating ones they were indeed—he did draw so convincingly." In line with this positive approach, a number of essayists praise Faulkner's daring and innovative exposition of racial themes. For example, James A. Snead, author of *Figures of Division: William Faulkner's Major Novels*, focuses on Joe Christmas, a Faulknerian protagonist who, by resisting all signification and refusing to be either black or white, embodies "a truth of merging across social barriers that [Faulkner's] contemporaries found unspeakable." Similarly, Philip M. Weinstein credits Faulkner with having understood the crucial role of even seemingly peripheral black characters; for "take away the margin and you have lost the center: it is that outside the center which allows us to conceive of 'center.'" And German scholar Lothar Hönnighausen defends Faulkner's characterization of blacks by identifying the historical matrix that shaped these characterizations. If Faulkner's depiction of blacks "is perhaps not realistic," writes Hönnighausen, it is, however, "in line with an international tendency in modernism—part of an effort to go back and rediscover timeless and essential human values." In this same positive vein, Frederick Karl calls attention to Faulkner's masterful interlocking of race and technique in *Absalom, Absalom!;* and Hoke Perkins commends Faulkner for "a remarkably perceptive view of the way those in positions of authority think of and use black criminals, a psychological pattern grounded . . . in several other modernist writers." Finally, Soviet scholar Sergei Chakovsky measures Faulkner's treatment of race against Twain's formulation of similar themes and finds that unlike Twain, who "admitted defeat and despaired over man's inhumanity to man," Faulkner "refused to 'quit' the race issue . . . and forged ahead" because, for Faulkner, "the black and white parts of humanity had to be artistically (if not immediately socially) integrated."

Taking an unexpected approach to the subject of race, the two subsequent essays uncover hidden connections between racial issues and Faulkner's literary vocation. For example, Michael Grimwood, author of *Heart in Conflict: Faulkner's Struggles with Vocation,* argues that Faulkner always doubted his own ability "to see black people—to penetrate appearances—and then to describe the reality within." This doubt, continues Grimwood, "grew into an anxiety about a writer's power to scrutinize anything" and eventually "helped to precipitate a crisis of confidence from which [Faulkner] never fully recovered." A crisis of confidence is also the subject of Karl Zender's essay, "*Requiem for a Nun* and the Uses of the Imagination." According to Zender, in *Requiem* Faulkner is working through the implications of a recent period of creative blockage and Nancy Mannigoe figures importantly in this meditation: she embodies Faulkner's recurring notion that "wordless black experience may be more authentic than white experience, and that blacks may have access to 'a Oneness with Something somewhere' that is denied to whites."

In addition to the essays collected in this volume, the 1986 Faulkner and Yoknapatawpha Conference also featured a number of special events. To summarize briefly, these events included a dramatic reading of race-related selections from Faulkner's fiction; a workshop, "Black History and Culture in Faulkner's Works," conducted by Sister Thea Bowman; a slide show, "Knowing William Faulkner," narrated by Faulkner's nephew, J. M. Faulkner; guided tours of North Mississippi; discussion sessions led by Oxford residents who knew Faulkner; an exhibit of paintings and drawings of Lafayette County by John McCrady; numerous book exhibits, including an exhibition of Soviet Faulkner scholarship in translation and an exhibition of books, manuscripts, photographs, and memorabilia from the University of Mississippi Faulkner Collection; a picnic served on the grounds of Rowan Oak; a buffet supper served at the home of Mr. and Mrs. William Lewis, Jr.; and parties for conference participants hosted respectively by Dr. and Mrs. C. E. Noyes and Square Books.

In conclusion, the editors thank all the individuals and organizations who support Faulkner and Yoknapatawpha annually; in particular, we wish to express our gratitude to Mr. and Mrs. Richard Howorth, Mr. and Mrs. William Lewis, Jr., Dr. and Mrs. C. E. Noyes, and The Friends of the Performing Arts of Oxford.

Doreen Fowler
The University of Mississippi
Oxford, Mississippi

NOTE

1. *Lion in the Garden: Interviews with William Faulkner, 1926–1962,* ed. James B. Meriwether and Michael Millgate (Lincoln: University of Nebraska Press, 1968), 245.

Faulkner and Race

FAULKNER AND YOKNAPATAWPHA

1986

Faulkner, Race, and the Forms
of American Fiction

ERIC J. SUNDQUIST

"Jazz, like the country which gave it birth, is fecund in its inventiveness, swift and traumatic in its developments and terribly wasteful of its resources. It is an orgiastic art which demands great physical stamina of its practitioners, and many of its most talented creators die young." Ralph Ellison's remarks in his essay on Charlie Christian are pertinent as well to American literature, in particular the literature of race. If the wealth of resources for invention available to both white and black writers in America has not been so clearly wasted, nor claimed such a high personal price, as in the case of music, there is nonetheless little doubt that the volatile subject of race conflict has intimidated or silenced many writers and forced others to mask their work in deceptive forms. It is only in the last several decades that the tradition of black writing, as well as the tradition of white writing on race, has begun to emerge with clarity. Ellison further notes that because jazz, given the improvisatory character of its form, often goes unrecorded before being immediately absorbed into the collective vernacular tradition, each act of improvisation represents a definition of the musician's identity "as individual, as member of the collectivity and as a link in the chain of tradition." This "endless improvisation on traditional materials," in which lost voices are recovered and transmuted into new forms by emulation or critical appropriation ("devoured alive by their imitators," as Ellison puts it), may also be taken to characterize the various fictional improvisations on the problem of race that have worked with one another to create an American literary tradition, one in which William Faulkner occupies a command-ing place.[1]

The example of jazz is important not just because it is preemi-nently a black American art form and has influenced the modern black literary tradition in vital ways but also because the idea of improvisation upon past materials, a means of redeeming a past that threatens to go unrecorded or be lost from memory, is a key to the formation of any literary tradition. More recently, several critics have advanced the notion of "signifying," the black folk metaphor of manipulative or subversive response to a previous text, as a key element in black American culture and its literary history.[2] The trope of signifying would explain the tradition of texts dealing with race in America as a series of responses and counterresponses in which black and white writers critically improvised upon one another, in some cases undermining their "masters" or exposing the enslaving figures and forms with which they have been burdened.

Whether or not such a response to existing forms and themes is entirely conscious, the writer who enters the fictive dialogue on race in America inevitably invokes a tangled, violent history and a literary tradition that is still in need of coherent critical formulation. Any discussion of the canon of American literature will thus need to take account not only of the canon of neglected writers but also of the historical mechanisms of their neglect. Literary traditions are inherently instruments of judgment and segregation; at the same time, they correspond to ideas of cultural division and superiority that are not meaningless but must be examined for their virtues as well as their flaws. Faulkner's position as a modern novelist and as one of the most important American writers on the problem of race is surely secure, but the literary and historical traditions in which we are to place his central novels—*Light in August, Absalom, Ab-salom!*, and *Go Down, Moses*—have received comparatively lit-tle attention. Moreover, the question of fictional form that his works explore serves to remind us that the distinctive feature of our major fictional works on race is their appropriation of complex, often tortuous forms in which history and social conflict are embedded. Although Faulkner's novels bring to a pitch the literary confrontation with race hatred in the early twentieth century, there are, by the same token, limitations to his vision. The fictional forms achieved by other authors, both black and white, in this way engage and complete those of Faulkner, reaching beyond the world of Yoknapatawpha and giving clearer voice to black lives and to the cultural traditions of race in America. The reconstruction of these traditions, their strands of signification and revising improvisations on the past, is today the main question for Faulkner's readers. I would like here to sketch out some elements of that tradition by concentrating on the ways in which the central themes of miscegenation, rebellion, sacrificial justice, and gothic historicism have found expressive form in some key works of fiction that themselves explore the question of canon.

Neither the tradition of classic American literature nor that of Afro-American literature adequately defines the problem of race; like the larger social history that they reflect, the two traditions must be read together for their interactions and conflicts, their revisions of one another. Most of all, they must be read with careful attention to the historical contexts whose pressures have in every case formed them, with or against their will, and often by placing them in a web of reference that simple attention to the text will not uncover. The powerful idea advanced by a number of cultural historians that the recorded history of blacks in America has been largely a history of "the black image in the white mind" could perhaps be said to have its counterpart in the white image recorded in black culture and writing.[3] In the latter instance, however, the "white image" would not so clearly be a phantom to be repressed or a distorted projection but rather an oppressive burden, a field of violence and constraint that most American blacks have found to determine the shape of their lives. While this tradition still awaits clear articulation, in Faulkner's case, as in that of most white writers, it is the consciousness of the problem of race as a white cultural construct that first engages our attention. His treatments of race violence belong in the tradition that dates from the black "nadir" of the Progressivist years when invidious race theory and legal sanctions against the Negro increased exponentially. The classic expression of that era's racism, Thomas Dixon's *The Clansman* (1905), inadvertently exposed the virulent contagion of the black image in the white mind in the remarkable scene in which the retina of the dead Mrs. Lenore retains as evidence the image of her bestial black rapist: "Impressions remain in the brain like words written on paper in invisible ink."[4] The metaphor of invisibility that Ellison would later exploit so brilliantly contained within it both the seldom "invisible" empire of race hatred Dixon chronicled and the visible blackness that often had no legal meaning except in forms of proscription. Faulkner's novels explore the problem of race visibility—a problem centered, as Dixon's novels insisted, in the problem of "blood" and physical violation—by superimposing the twentieth century upon the antebellum years, as Quentin and Shreve rehearse again the agony of Henry Sutpen and Charles Bon; as old Ike McCaslin offers the symbolic hunting horn to the granddaughter of Tennie's Jim; or as Joe Christmas, living in the virtual slave quarters of a ruined big house now occupied by a Yankee spinster, plays out for his community the ritual acts that the fantasy of his mixed blood provokes.

The Dixonian thesis of black degeneration both reflected and furthered the radical arguments for Jim Crow; the graphic popularity of his work, best illustrated in its conversion into *The Birth of a Nation*, played on images of racial subjugation that the press, the courts, and the social sciences conspired to make acceptable to the public. As the literature of passing that proliferates at the turn of the century indicates, the optical illusion of "color" brought forth pyschic disturbances about identity that were grounded in, or took their analogic form from, sexuality. The nineteenth-century fascination with generation and female reproduction that reached new heights with the advent of fears about aliens destroying the "body" of America thus included race as a factor. In its clichéd form of the sanctity of Southern womanhood, the focus on sexuality revealed that the preservation of precariously brittle ideals of paternalism was central to American life: the New Woman and the New Negro were similarly threatening, and along with the problem of massive immigration—a combination that Lothrop Stoddard fixed in his book on *The Rising Tide of Color*—they would need simultaneous consideration in any reassessment of social hierarchies in the period.

The vogue for novels of passing at the turn of the century and after situated the nation's melodrama of color in the arena of publication itself. *Light in August* (1932) is the most significant treatment of the problem of miscegenation in the twentieth century precisely because Faulkner treats the issue indirectly, exposing the central anxieties of the radical thesis and in effect turning it into hallucination. The more conventional treatments of passing in such works as Charles Chesnutt's *The House Behind the Cedars* (1900) or Nella Larsen's *Passing* (1929), as well as the penetrating analysis in James Weldon Johnson's novel of ideas, *The Autobiography of an Ex-Coloured Man* (1912), are subsumed into the texture of *Light in August*. Faulkner, as it were, accepts Johnson's complaint that the black man attempting to better himself in America, or the novel attempting to deal seriously with his life, is "looked upon as a sort of absurd caricature of 'white civilization,'" the black man a potential tragedian condemned by his racist audience to repeat comic minstrel roles.[5] Revising the tradition of plantation fiction and surpassing the more straightforward depictions of lynch law in the fiction of Johnson, Sutton Griggs, Paul Laurence Dunbar, and Walter White, Faulkner pushed them toward caricature in the tragedy of Joe Christmas.[6] Whereas Johnson's protagonist is told by his mother (echoing Twain's Roxy) that he has in him the best blood of the white South—and in the agony of his divided identity ultimately forsakes his black self and chooses the privileges his white "blood" offers—Joe Christmas has no idea what blood is in him. Although it pervades the novel as an emblem of the charged antagonisms of race and sexuality, and sets in motion grotesque ritual violence, his blood is fictional, so to speak, giving specific form to his life and story but remaining invisible itself.

As a number of slave narratives and antebellum works of fiction such as those by Harriet Beecher Stowe, Harriet Jacobs, and Harriet Wilson demonstrate, reproduction and color have been linked from the earliest moments of the literature of race. I would like to consider some more modern works, including Faulkner's, that bring the conjunction of racial and sexual identity into clearer focus but first want to take note of a text that discards altogether the structures of romance in order to expose in satire the ultimate limits of the American melodrama of race. Mark Twain's *Pudd'nhead Wilson* (1894), appearing at the rise of the virulent racism that flanks the turn of the century, employs outright burlesque to subvert the fictions of law and custom that have often made tragedy and comedy indistinguishable in American race relations. The farcical form of Twain's work, with its ineptly extricated story of "Those Extraordinary Twins," has seemed to many critics flawed in the extreme. But there are good reasons to think Twain perceived that the story's inconsistencies and lapses, most of all the utter artifice in his tale of doubling, mimicry, and enslavement to habits of mastery, were the best commentary on a nation still acting out fantasies of antebellum plantation life and indulging in the most irrational forms of racial separation.

As in all satire or parody, the close proximity of truth and fiction is the key to the success of these works. The best index of the meaning of *Pudd'nhead Wilson* and the literature of passing that follows it lies, in fact, in an event of national importance. The Supreme Court ruling in *Plessy* v. *Ferguson* in 1896 conclusively decided the doctrine of "separate but equal" on the basis of a case originating in Louisiana in 1892 when Homer Plessy, a black man who could easily pass for white, deliberately challenged the state's Jim Crow railroad laws. The eventual ruling by the Court's majority ignored Justice John Marshall Harlan's famous dissent in claiming that "if one race be inferior to the other socially, the constitution of the United States cannot put them on the same plane." It also ignored the peculiar brief for Plessy prepared by Albion Tourgée, the Reconstruction judge and author of the satiric novel *A Fool's Errand* (1879), who helped argue the losing case. Tourgée's brief, like Twain's novel, said there was no limit to the absurdities sanctioned by a doctrine of separate but equal: "Why not require every white man's house to be painted white and every colored man's black? . . . Why not require every white business man to use a white sign and every colored man who solicits customers a black one?" As Tourgée noted, in phrases that echo *Pudd'nhead Wilson*, the question is not so much that of social equality but rather of "the right of the State to label one citizen as white and another as colored." In addition to forecasting the extremity of some Jim Crow provisions of the following decades, Tourgée brought forward a more problematic issue in his emphasis on Plessy's white skin, which he argued was part of the "property" that the Jim Crow law had denied him—specifically the "reputation of being white," which is the "most valuable sort of property, being the master-key that unlocks the golden door of opportunity."[7] Tourgée's argument on the basis of color, however strategically sound at the time, had the effect of furthering the absurdity of American racial attitudes, protecting only those who could pass well enough to go undetected as Negroes: well enough, say, to be raised as Tom Driscoll rather than as Valet de Chambre.

I have mentioned *Plessy* v. *Ferguson* in some detail because the case largely determined the parodic "form" of American race relations for the next half century, and did so by defining race as a genetically transmitted, but essentially metaphysical, factor— subject to reproductive, not ocular, laws. Race could not always be seen, but it was there and became a form of biological property. The tragic mulatto, as portrayed for example by Nella Larsen and Judith Peterkin, was typically a character trapped between charges of Negro lasciviousness and middle-class audience expectations of virtue. Her virtue was her property, as the tradition of sentimentality dictated, but in this case its value became a function of color. Likewise, although he ultimately regrets his choice, James Weldon Johnson's protagonist in *The Autobiography of an Ex-Coloured Man* recognizes his whiteness to be the most valuable sort of property, a possession that outweighs the Afro-American traditions to which he is heir but which remain for him elusive, even dangerous. The novel thus has embedded within it an explicit treatment of the problem of establishing and employing the sources of an Afro-American cultural canon. Caught in an immobilizing role of outsider and observer, Johnson's protagonist is so torn between two worlds that he must be jolted from his analytic note-taking on the lost gospel traditions of Afro-American life by a terrifying, inexplicable, but for him enthralling, lynching. The shame that drives him to choose whiteness and marry white does not conceal the greater shame that will haunt him in forsaking his birthright and living as a caricature not just of whiteness but of blackness as well. The novel was Johnson's fantasy, but the violent rebuke of Afro-American life it introspectively contained, rooted in the reproduction of color and the violence it could set in motion, was real enough.

In the novel as in society, sexuality was thus often the vehicle for regulating racial subordination. In the case of Twain's novel, both the real and the false Tom Driscoll define the paradoxical double masquerade miscegenation and the color line could create. As the "imitation nigger" (colored "imitation white") that the real Tom becomes as the slave Roxy's son, he is a parody of himself and of those "blaspheming colors" sported by the freak Siamese twins that were Twain's simulacrum of the psychic and physiological nightmare of the conjoined American races. Like the freak, the mulatto, it was argued by some social theorists, was an unnatural hybrid, destined to die out through a failure of reproduction—a perversion of the natural development toward higher, more pure racial forms. The mulatto, especially the invisible one, as Twain saw, had become the scapegoat for contemporary proslavery apologists, the sign of the master's sin—*his* conjunction of property and reproduction—now transfigured into a degenerate offspring who was not white but "black." The appropriate logic of revenge that appears when the false Tom, disguising himself as a black woman, murders his uncle the Judge (Twain originally made the Judge his actual father) points to an act of black rebellion against slaveholding sexual abuse. Like Faulkner in the characterization of Joe Christmas, however, Twain fused the antebellum and modern worlds by dramatizing the essential reversal in meaning miscegenation underwent after emancipation, whereby the fact of slaveholding miscegenation by white masters and the feared potential for slave rebellion were together transformed into the new specter of black crime and contamination—the Negro as "beast." The imitation white Tom Driscoll, now like a minstrel performer masquerading in the black female disguise that parodies his hidden slave status, becomes in effect the mulatto killer of contemporary race theory. Mirroring the insubstantial artifice of Twain's novel, the "fiction of law and custom" that defines black and white in Dawson's Landing resides in the power of distorting legal form, torn loose from reason and operating in the realm of fantasy.[8]

Although *Pudd'nhead Wilson* is hardly a noncanonical text, it is without question a problematic one; my reason for dwelling on it is to suggest that the range of its most important implications has much more to do with the climate of social and legal thought reflected in the book's obsessive examination of law, custom, evidence, codes, and the like, than with arguments about the unreliability of the text. It is a work that improvises upon the tradition of race in American fiction in the double sense of ridiculing the then popular plantation tradition and also subverting Twain's own more idyllic critique of "setting a free nigger free," as he put it, in *Adventures of Huckleberry Finn*. From the perspective of its wealth of historical implication, rather than its organic coherence as narrative, then, *Pudd'nhead Wilson* may have an equally central place in the canon of American literature. It is only our reluctance to take into account the manifold

contextual pressures working on the text—not the difficulty of unfinished manuscripts, evidence of shoddy revising, and the like—that undermines the "canonical" place of Twain's work.

The significance of the reproductive powers of Twain's own novel is evident in works that it appears to have spawned. A work that improvises upon *Pudd'nhead Wilson* and similarly opens to view the defining forces of racial subordination is Charles Chesnutt's *The Marrow of Tradition* (1901), a novel structured around the 1898 race riot in Wilmington, North Carolina. Like Twain, Chesnutt employed a series of doubled, twinlike black and white characters whose fates are equally entangled, and yet kept carefully separate, by the fictions of law and custom. The domestic and political plots are one for Chesnutt: family honor and the aura of unprofaned genealogy are at the bottom of the ideology of racial suppression; likewise, Olivia Carteret's feminine hysteria, prompted by anxiety about her newborn heir and fueled by the irritating presence of her black half-sister, is the double of her husband's and the town's hysteria about the color line. As in *Pudd'nhead Wilson* and *Light in August*, murder is at the center of the book's ironic subversion of white supremacy. When he kills a white woman during an episode of robbery and murder, the dissipated Tom Delamere, like Twain's Tom, dresses in black-face disguise that makes him the exact twin of the servant Sandy. Tom's skills in mimicking blacks—earlier, for example, in a cakewalk—introduce a double irony into Chesnutt's dry comment on the white community's view of Negroes: "No one could tell at what moment the thin veneer of civilization might peel off and reveal the underlying savage." Of course virtually every action of the white citizens of Wellington exposes their own savagery, most of all the campaign against the black vote that merges with communal outrage over the murder. In the episode of the murder, which raises as well the spectre of violated white womanhood, Chesnutt invented an analogy for the riot's sexual undercurrent that in reality had been provided by Rebecca Latimer Felton's notorious prolynching speeches. In his sarcastic editorial reply to Felton, Wilmington's black journalist Alexander Manly rightly argued that white women had desires of their own and that the problem of rape was largely a hallucination; that is, Manly unmasked the fiction of reproductive purity and deceit that white reactionaries had unleashed in their creation of the black "beast," and Chesnutt unmasked the fictions of the plantation novel that had codified the "beast." Seizing as their pretext the need to "protect the white women of the South against brutal, lascivious, and murderous assaults at the hands of Negro men," the town's leading citizens exploit the "age of crowds" and engineer a race riot in which the savage and the civilized become ironic doubles of one another, mixing in ritual fury.[9]

The novel's complex response to an explosive event critical to the rigidifying of Jim Crow places it at a crossroads of forces—the ascendancy of lynching, the collapse of the Old South in the face of New South expediency, the feminine component of racial hysteria, intra-Negro class antagonisms, and the literary history of black characterization. Chesnutt's intricate use of irony and doubling underscores the novel's self-reflexiveness and its reflection of the historical moment it captures; it is an important "historical" novel not just in its use of actual events but more so in its revealing of the penetration of ideology into aesthetics and, subsequently, into the suppressive forces at work in canon formation.

Twain's Tom and Chesnutt's Tom embody the decay of Southern honor in both family and community, and the two novels' somber contemplation of American race laws puts the two characters, representative of an emerging New South, on trial. Their symbolic role as ironic scapegoats who first efface and then force a reassertion of the color line points forward to *Light in August* and to the bizarre enactment of racial justice carried out in George Schuyler's utopian novel *Black No More* (1931), which depicts the nation in the throes of cultural apocalypse when a newly discovered scientific process of whitening skin threatens to eradicate the sacred color line. Schuyler's satire of bleaching and genealogical hysteria ridicules the subservience of passing literature and the domestic canon it imitated. At the same time, however, Schuyler, himself black, maintained that the search for a coherent Afro-American tradition was a hoax, so bound to white American forms and standards were black artists. Genealogy, which might separate true white from artifice, proves in *Black No More*, as in historical fact, to be of especially dubious value. Driven to flee when their First Family of Virginia ancestors are exposed as tainted by black blood, the Southern Democratic presidential and vice-presidential candidates, Snobbcraft and Buggerie, crash land their plane in backwoods Mississippi. There they are lynched by the True Faith Christ Lovers' Church, a fundamentalist sect that, since the whole country is now bewilderingly white, has been waiting desperately for the Lord to send them a sign in the form a "nigger to lynch." The irony of the incident is doubled here again in the fact that Snobbcraft and Buggerie have disguised themselves in blackface; when they prove to be white, they are momentarily saved, until they are recognized as the polluted Democratic candidates, whereupon they promptly become "black" once again and are mutilated, shot, and burned by the mob—some of whom, of course, are themselves "whitened Negroes" who must ostentatiously "yell and prod the burning bodies" in order to banish "any suspicion that they might not be one-hundred-per-cent Americans."[10] Schuyler's satiric spectacle of whitened blacks lynching aristocratic Southern whites of tainted ancestry takes the hysteria over miscegenation to its limits.

As in Chesnutt and Twain, the mechanisms of justice and farce are here joined together. It is in this context that Faulkner's achievement in *Light in August* has greatest significance, for the novel is a further improvisation on the motif of racial tautology that draws into it the mass of theorizing about Jim Crow and black regression available by the 1930s. Bearing the valuable property of whiteness (like Homer Plessy), but contaminated by an idea, the concept of the "white nigger" that pervaded much current race theory, Joe Christmas is simultaneously white and black. His role is to knit together the stories that surround his own in the novel while taking upon his own body the blood sacrifice the community requires. The form of the novel purposely embeds the story of Christmas's life within other lives, revealing it in brief flashes of significance and defining his hypothetical mixture of blood as the mysterious essence of the community's gravest fears and anxieties.[11] As in *Pudd'nhead Wilson* or *Black No More,* the form gives expression to forces that destroy narrative coherence—disruptive ironies, memories, and family histories strained into tortured shapes. The lives of Joanna Burden, Gail Hightower, Percy Grimm, and Doc Hines are all revealed through the mediating form of Joe Christmas's fragmentary narrative, while Lena Grove's pastoral tale is kept carefully separate—surrounding but never touching that of Christmas with the important exception of the momentary fantasy, introduced by Mrs. Hines, that Lena is Milly and that the "nigger" Christmas has fathered her child. The refusal of the novel fully to integrate Christmas's story into those that surround him is a function of the fact that his life and his story are identified with mechanisms of segregation and exclusion, with violent expulsion both from familial and sexual relationships and from the larger community of human compassion.

With the exception of Lillian Smith, no twentieth-century writer so clearly rendered the psychosexual dimensions of racial antagonism. At the heart of the book's ritual drama, as it is at the heart of Christmas's self, is the symbol of blood with its combined racial, social, and sexual significances. The well-known scene in which Joe Christmas plunges into black life with women in the North, "trying to breathe into himself . . . the dark and inscrutable thinking and being of negroes . . . [and] expel from himself the white blood and the white thinking and being," enacts in his body the conflict we see ritualized in his murder and castration, where the "pent black blood" seems to rush from his loins "like a released breath." And it illuminates the earlier episode of the primitivist slaughter of the sheep, whose bath of blood purges Joe's adolescent horror at the discovery of menstruation.[12] The emblem of blood structures the novel, giving form to familial history and to community action, and placing the question of race within the structure of male sexual fears. Because it partakes of fetishistic impulses to protect the body and the family from danger or contamination, thus yoking together love and violence, "blood" itself crosses the boundaries between the tangible and the fantastic, destroying the forms of racial order that mean to contain it.

Here Faulkner's novel is informed by two other literary treatments of lynching from the surrounding decades, Lillian Smith's *Strange Fruit* (1944) and Jean Toomer's "Blood-Burning Moon" in *Cane* (1923). Smith's novel, with its idiosyncratic interior monologues addressing a "you" who is simultaneously the reader, the character's speaking self, and the community that absorbs him, puts lush sexuality at the center of the race problem. The constant refrain of second-person address projects from each character a fragment of the fatalistic conscience of the South that drives the book toward tragedy, paradoxically joining together the conventions of race hatred and subliminal eruptions of contaminating desire. As in *Light in August* the swamp and the privy are analogues for indulgence in miscegenation, sites drawn from unconscious association with the communal prohibitions Smith analyzed with such precision in *Killers of the Dream:* "Not only Negroes but everything dark, dangerous, evil must be pushed to the rim of one's life," exiled to "the Dark-town of our unconscious." It is only in the context of Smith's essays that the peculiar second-person voice that permeates *Strange Fruit* becomes clear. The association between sexuality and segregation, in fact, borders on the pathological in her recollection of parental instruction: "Now, parts of your body are segregated areas which you must stay away from and keep others away from. . . . In other words, you cannot associate freely with them any more than you can associate freely with colored children. Especially must you be careful about what enters your body. . . . what enters and leaves the doors of your body is the essence of morality." As the drama of miscegenation and lynching in *Strange Fruit* suggests, the "rites of segregation" make the white body a scene of repressed desire and potential contamination and the black body an object of ritual purgation, with castration "a symbol of an unnamed relationship that in his heart each man wants to befoul."[13]

Strange Fruit and *Killers of the Dream*, as Richard King notes,[14] must be read together in order to absorb Smith's intricate sense of the relationship between the sexual body and the moral community, between unconscious desire and conscious segregation, a relationship in both texts held in place by the purifying exercises of the August revival. Her confessional analysis of segregation describes with equal precision the dynamics of *Light in August*, in which the body of Joe Christmas contains the warring fantasies of blood that the South imposes upon him, yet therefore threatens to befoul the communal order through human intimacy and the unleashing of repressed historical demons. In Schuyler's farce the True Faith Christ Lovers' Church, lacking Negroes to lynch, has "nothing left to stimulate them but the old time religion and the clandestine sex orgies that invariably followed the great revival meetings"; for Smith and Faulkner, August releases purgative racial violence fixed upon what Doc Hines, with Calvinist excoriation, calls "abomination and bitchery," "a pollution and a abomination on My earth."[15]

In the case of Toomer, sacrificial violence also assumes a mythic, seasonal character. The form of his novel *Cane*, a text also built around the problem of interracial sexuality, reflects the disintegration of black life Toomer set out to record in the early years of the Harlem Renaissance. In an often-quoted 1922 letter to Waldo Frank, Toomer wrote that "the Negro is in solution, in the process of solution. As an entity, the race is losing its body, and its soul is approaching a common soul."[16] Toomer's own subsequent denial of his race—in fact, his denial of race as an issue—lends further significance to the form of *Cane*, whose intense impressionist style and fragmentary narratives enact the very dissolution under the forces of migration and industrialism Toomer felt he was witnessing in black life. In a story of white murder and black lynching that borrows from Du Bois's "Of the

Coming of John" (as indeed the whole of *Cane* borrows from *The Souls of Black Folk* and *Darkwater*) and prefigures *Strange Fruit*, "Blood-Burning Moon" enacts the dissolution of black life and the decay of the white life of the Old South against the "skeleton stone walls" of an antebellum cotton factory that becomes the scene of the lynching. The mystical, premonitory symbolism of the "red nigger moon, blood-burning moon," explicitly linked to the primitive fecundity of black or mixed-blood women in *Cane*, casts an aura of Greek tragedy over the story. But it suggests as well that black female sexuality and the risk of miscegenation—the cycle of blood embracing reproduction and race—underlie the disintegration of community.[17]

Toomer's focus on sensual, primitivist dramatic scenes of the racial body can be read as a precursor to the eroticism and Africanist mythos evoked by a number of texts of the Harlem Renaissance (by both black and white writers). The mythic sensuality of a story like "Blood-Burning Moon" belongs also to the larger context of race theory (and its violence) in the early part of the century, an impression enforced by the ambiguous poem entitled "Portrait in Georgia" that precedes the story:

Hair—braided chestnut
        coiled like a lyncher's rope,
Eyes—fagots,
Lips—old scars, or the first red blisters,
Breath—the last sweet scent of cane,
And her slim body, white as the ash
        of black flesh after flame.

Just as the smell of distilled cane mixes with the smell of burning flesh in "Blood-Burning Moon," Toomer's imagist poem superimposes the act of lynching upon the act of love that initiates it. Yet the ultimate ambiguity of the woman's race (even though she is figured as "white") leaves it unclear whether the poem forecasts "Blood-Burning Moon," where the contest of love between a white man and a black man (over a black woman) leads to the murder of one and the lynching of the other, or instead imitates the prototypical lynching scenario, the black "beast" hanged and burned to ash for lusting after a white woman.

In either event, the poem's hallucinatory merger of the two bodies puts passion and reactionary violence in heated union. Like Lillian Smith's psychosexual reading of Southern segregation and Joanna Burden's impassioned desire to receive into herself the essence of Christmas as a "Negro," Toomer's treatment of the body renders it emblematic of the community, ironically imprisoning the image of the white woman's sexuality within the image of the black man's disintegrating body. The "rites of segregation" make the white body a scene of repressed desire and potential contamination and the black body an object of ritual purgation.

The canon of American literature, of course, has traditionally done much the same thing with texts of race. Segregation in the canon has been yoked to the ideals of organic coherence, New Critical aestheticism, biographical study, and so on; the canonical body—not to mention Faulkner's own body of work—has often been kept pure, or has accepted the threat of rebellion or contamination only as means of containing or subverting it. Lillian Smith's location of racial anxiety within the sexual unconscious is not, of course, a revolutionary insight; it is particularly suggestive, though, of the "place" from which much of the literature of race in America has been written—a position below, or underneath, traditional social and cultural forms. The literature of the Jazz Age, for example, has canonically suppressed the Harlem Renaissance, much as the white appropriation of the cultural elements of the Renaissance—ragtime, the cult of primitive sensuality, Africa—required their immediate subjugation to the mechanisms of control. Thus, *The Emperor Jones,* with its double movement into the realm of voodoo and mystic sacrifice, combined with a dramatic expression of colonial ridicule of black degeneration and political corruption, is the perfect enactment of those mechanisms. Whatever its author's intentions, O'Neill's play cannot purge itself of Conradian "horror." Like Zora Neale

Hurston, O'Neill opened voodoo to literary examination, but unlike her he imagined it as primitive apocalypse rather than the communal narrative of folk tradition; O'Neill's Caribbean, like Melville's symbolic drama aboard the *San Dominick*, acts out the revelation and sudden repression of black power. Although it appeared at the outset of the Harlem Renaissance, *The Emperor Jones* remains a critique of the vulnerability of the "primitive" to double misunderstanding: the Afro-American recovery of heritage threatened to embrace the very forms of regression that Jim Crow claimed were real; or, as in the case of Du Bois, it risked a Euro-American romanticism that was as much a cliché as the imperialist conception of savagery.

O'Neill and Du Bois imagined something entirely different in the idea of primitivism, yet they inevitably accepted the implications of the gothic naturalism that lay at the heart of both the colonialist mentality and Jim Crow America. Naturalism works by strategies of submersion and the exploration of levels of consciousness or society purportedly below the normal: the economically oppressed; the biologically inferior; the theologically depraved or damned; and the psychologically subconscious, that "darker" part of the self or the community which must be repressed. The issue of race, especially during the black nadir (and arguably up until the simultaneous civil rights movement and African revolutions of the 1950s and 1960s), both motivated and reflected the strategies of naturalist thought, echoing in a new context such nineteenth-century gothic structures as Poe's race nightmares, the haunting of Simon Legree's corrupted big house, or the dreamlike revolt aboard Benito Cereno's *San Dominick*.

The essence of the gothic is the eruption from below of rebellious or unconscious forces and the consequent violation of boundaries, whether racial, sexual, or abstractly moral. The entire form of *Benito Cereno*, for example, represses below the surface of Delano's conscious recognition the actuality of slave revolt and Babo's terrifying mastery of his master, much as the historical and legalistic framework of the tale, by layering the

United States and Caribbean crisis over slavery in the 1850s upon the Haitian revolution of the 1790s, imitates antebellum attempts to "contain" the black man and prevent the spread of his contaminating revolt. For Melville, the gothic was American history and the approaching crisis an eruptive force set in motion by the earliest Columbian enslavements. Similarly, Cassy's terrorizing of Legree in the form of his mother's ghost renders the sentimental form and domestic ideology of _Uncle Tom's Cabin_ an instrument of vengeance against sexual and racial abuse. Legree's decaying mansion is both the darkest of the novel's many homes and a Poe-like emblem of the "House Divided" that Lincoln, himself troubled by the risk of miscegenation and the spread of free black labor, would make the nation's most famous gothic structure. For Stowe, as for a number of slave narrators and antislavery novelists, house and family are structures that reflect the comparatively redeemed or violated bodies that inhabit them.

For the white writer, the identification of the gothic with darkness has fixed the image of the black deep in his subconscious mind, a disruptive or rebellious force to be studied and held at bay. In _The Emperor Jones_ the rational perspective of the white man Smithers frames and contains such an eruptive penetration beyond boundaries as Brutus Jones goes deeper and deeper into the "primitive" history of Afro-American heritage cast by the spell of voodoo and the reverberation of the tom-toms that rises from his own heart. The whole history of cultural and political images of "blackness" has conspired to insure the repetition of the gothic pattern, so much so that the black text that has most successfully entered the canon, _Invisible Man_, is written as an eruption from the underground of American history and culture that begins by invoking gothic racial texts by Melville and Poe.

The central writings on race in American literature time and again fuse the two historical time frames for the obvious reason that form and tradition in the fiction of race reflect the relation between form and tradition in social proscription and historical fact, most of all in matters of human intimacy. Just as Twain cast back to antebellum historical settings to judge the continuing "enslavement" of blacks in his own day, and just as Melville's *Benito Cereno* brought to bear upon the 1850s the entire history of colonial slavery in the Americas, the modern literature of race in America cannot but superimpose upon one another the time frames divided by the watershed of emancipation. In *The Confessions of Nat Turner* (1967), for example, William Styron's imagining of Turner's revolt in terms that included sexual reprisal brought to the fore subtle entanglements between rebellion and desire that Toomer, Faulkner, Wright, and others had already explored; but it did so by revealing that historical record could itself become subject to contaminating desire. Styron's indefensible elision of Nat Turner's family life and his attribution to him of rape fantasies had the effect of making his execution a kind of modern lynching. Yet the novel improvises upon Thomas Gray's fragmented, ventriloquistic account so as to create for Turner an interior life and to represent the racial fears left long in the wake of his outburst of violence and his execution. Other artists have distorted history far more grotesquely than Styron, yet the timing of his work and the manner of its distortion have left it justly vulnerable to sociological dismemberment: perhaps there is no better way to read *The Confessions of Nat Turner* than in conjunction with Daniel Patrick Moynihan's controversial *The Negro Family* (1965), which sought sympathetically to explain the fragmentation of the modern American black family but was widely attacked for depicting matriarchal dependence as pathological. Styron read Nat Turner's "Confessions" through the screens of *Light in August* and *Native Son*. He made history a romance of violation and revenge and, in writing from both above and below at the same time, displayed in nearly confessional form his own liberal fantasies. Styron rigorously *contained* the rebellious potential of Nat Turner—made him safe for the canon—by a paradoxical kind of emasculation: Turner is stripped of reality in order to conform to the deeper, naturalistic "truth" imagined for him by Styron.

In turning to a more explicit consideration of the relationship between gothic form and historical materials, I would like to consider from a different angle the question of justice that Nat Turner's history invokes. In *Pudd'nhead Wilson* justice is rendered ironically, the false Tom being sold down the river; in *The Marrow of Tradition* a rioting mob reestablishes white supremacy; in "Blood-Burning Moon," *Strange Fruit*, and *Light in August* lynching reasserts the color line but does so at the price of love. Yet from the standpoint of literature the problem of communal justice embraces more than the mechanism of suppression. *Light in August* thus shares with Richard Wright's *Native Son* (1940) a sensational focus on the black "beast" figure who, though technically guilty of his crime, is nonetheless a product of sociopsychological forces that move him against his will. Even so, the formal and symbolic means by which those forces are portrayed in each case reach beyond simple environmentalism and anchor the communal act of sacrifice in a tradition of race conflict dating from the institution of slavery.

To take a small example: when Joe Christmas cuts Joanna Burden's throat with a razor, his story alludes not only to the archetypal weapon of the black murderer in popular fiction (and to the actual 1905 crime in Oxford committed by Nelse Patton, who was subsequently lynched) but also by implication to several antebellum texts as well. In Poe's "Murders in the Rue Morgue," an allegorical race fantasy that also may have influenced Dixon's portrait of the black rapist in *The Clansman* and others like it, the orangoutan (itself an allusion to Jefferson's notorious remarks on the Negro's place in the chain of being) escapes the whippings of his master and murders a white woman with a razor, nearly cutting off her head. Frederick Douglass, in *My Bondage and My Freedom,* and Thomas Wentworth Higginson, among other abolitionists, remarked that as often as slaves had a razor or knife near the throats of their masters, it was a wonder more were not murdered; and Melville's Babo, in a magnificent inverted scene of enslavement and torture, turns his shaving of Benito Cereno into a mock execution—an execution once more reversed when the black rebel is later decapitated and his head fixed on a pole in the plaza at Lima. Joe Christmas revises these acts—signifies upon them—transporting nineteenth-century rebellion into a setting of modern race hysteria that, because of his "invisible" color, forces the community to confront the irrationality of its fantasies. Like Nat Turner, like Rider in "Pantaloon in Black" or Bigger Thomas in *Native Son*, Christmas's act stands between murder and revenge, and it likewise precipitates a form of communal revenge (Percy Grimm) that is at once legal and mad. Spilling out of the attempts to order and control it by the mechanisms of justice, Christmas's sacrifice is neither a lynching nor a murder but an act that blurs two spheres of action, much as his entire life blurs careful physical and moral separations.

The rigid naturalistic scheme of *Native Son* clearly diverges from Faulkner's labyrinthine fictive formation of historical consciousness, but Wright's greatest moments in the novel reveal imaginative freedoms consonant with Bigger's own flickering consciousness of escape from the prison of Jim Crow Chicago. James Baldwin's complaint that *Native Son* is in essence disarmed by its strategies of "protest" is relevant here but fails, I think, to give Wright his due for reflecting seriously on the place of his own novel in the tradition—the canon of bestiality defined by Jim Crow sociology and the literary canon of gothic rebellion to which the novel belongs. The maze of the symbolic colors red, white, and black that accompany the murder and its aftermath (giving the Dalton basement and the Chicago landscape a surreal quality); the Poe-like white cat that torments Bigger; and the garish theatricality of the courtroom reconstruction of the murder, complete with bones, furnace, a living model of Mary, and Bessie's corpse brought forth to reenact the murders now as part of the mechanism of justice—these elements among others give *Native Son* a relentless allegorical character that unites the ideological novel and the modern descendant of the gothic, the crime novel, both of which had reached a peak in the 1940s. While the novel no more fully escapes the constraints of ideology than does any work of art, however, it appears deliberately to break out of the mold of Party ideology that the attorney Boris Max would impose upon Bigger's story by conceiving of the murder in hallucinatory terms that have more in them of Poe than of Lenin. "After Marxism has laid bare the skeleton of society," Wright had already remarked in his doctrinaire "Blueprint for Negro Writing" (1938), "there remains the task of the writer to plant flesh upon those bones out of his will to live."[18]

Wright's sense that writing entailed a form of freedom that could be at odds with politics was even greater within a few years. The "heritage of free thought," allowing a man to "redeem himself through his own acts,"[19] that he recorded as taboo among American Communists in his autobiography (and repeated in *The God That Failed*) appears already in *Native Son* not in declared ideology but in the imaginative constructs of Bigger's actions, which Max is horrified to imagine might represent a form of self-discovery and freedom. The meaning of violence in the imagination of black freedom can be made no more clear than by a simple comparison of the inadequate responses to violence and to the ultimate rendering of justice by five white witnesses: Thomas Gray in his record of Nat Turner's confessions, Captain Delano in *Benito Cereno*, Twain's *Pudd'nhead Wilson*, Gavin Stevens in *Light in August*, and Max in *Native Son*. All construct fanciful theories for acts of rebellion or murder but fail to comprehend their ultimate meaning. Their minds represent simplicity and order, whereas the minds of the rebel blacks—Nat Turner, Babo, Roxy, Joe Christmas, Bigger Thomas—represent complexity and searchingly imagined freedom.

In *Native Son*, as in *Light in August*, the element of violence, surprisingly, stands imaginatively separate from Max's ideological explanation of Bigger's crimes. As much of Wright's work indicates, from the stories of *Uncle Tom's Children* (1938) to *The Long Dream* (1958), the white world's existence as a kind of sexual body suffocating the black world while inviting black violation transcended the problem of class. While he thus renders in detail Bigger's own path to execution, the entire novel becoming the machinery of his sacrifice, Wright also inserts into Bigger's tragedy—as though in a moment of unconscious vengeance—an ironic reversal of the novel's communal sacrifice. In doing so he draws upon the representations of domesticity and sacrifice available in such antebellum texts as *Benito Cereno* and *Uncle Tom's Cabin*. In a demonic revision of Uncle Tom in little Eva's ultrawhite bedroom, the wrenching accidental suffocation of Mary in her white bedroom, where Bigger's sexual desires mix with his hatred of the Dalton world, is followed by the crude destruction of her body, decapitated and burned in a furnace that Bigger tends, as Ishmael Reed notes, "like an executioner in a sacrificial rite."[20] It is Mary—white, sexual, liberal, the embodiment of the book's explicitly evocative paternalistic plantation themes—who is sacrificed. The destruction of her body in the furnace (which insures the charge of sexual violation) is a suiting emblem of Wright's sense that the black migration to the industrial North hardly guaranteed equality or economic success. The furnace is both a sign of the labor black migrants were most likely to find and, with the murder of Mary, a sign of criminal rage Wright felt the white North too could produce. Wright's underground scene portrays a classic vision of hell, fusing black mass and factory labor like the Try-Works aboard Ahab's *Pequod*, and perhaps intimating most of all a miniature Holocaust—a reminder of Wright's revelation in "How Bigger Was Born" that he had in mind both the Biggers of Nazi Germany and the Biggers of Chicago who said "that maybe Hitler and Mussolini are all right; that maybe Stalin is all right." Avoiding the desperate implications of such an analogy, both the essay and the novel, like Bigger himself, appear to transcend both environmentalism and the lure of fascism, finding "in the Negro the embodiment of a past tragic enough to appease the spiritual hunger" of a James or a Hawthorne. "And if Poe were alive," Wright concluded, "he would not have to invent horror; horror would invent him."[21] Wright's statement was no less true of American racism than of the world of totalitarian rule poised on the horizon. Indeed, Wright, although he never followed Du Bois in blindly admiring the Soviet example, was driven by the frustrating deterioration of American race relations toward an embrace of totalitarian elements in black and Third World nationalism. Updated, Poe's *Narrative of Arthur Gordon Pym* (1838), a (racist) allegorical fantasy of white imperialism and slave rebellion, might have become a document of modern Pan-African liberation like Du Bois's *Dusk of Dawn* (1940 or Wright's *White Man, Listen!* (1957).

Wright's assault on white liberalism and on Communism as failed allies of the black man implicated both in the remaining plantation structures of modern America. Naturalism, an extension of the gothic into a world of scientific determinism, could participate in a specific critique of the plantation novel, but its strategies nonetheless remained rooted in a world of racial division and hierarchies. For Faulkner, the plantation tale survived only in remnants—Popeye's world at Frenchman's Bend, Joe Christmas's cabin and food, the legend of Thomas Sutpen, the hunts of *Go Down, Moses,* the black mammies. Naturalism, after the virtual deadend of Popeye's farcical psychobiography and Temple's nymphomania in *Sanctuary,* was channeled into a gothic nightmare in which biology was sexuality and race, which in turn comprised nothing less than the history of social forms, irreducible to simple physiology or Marxist dogma. If Faulkner never found a clear way to articulate the links between midcentury international politics and American race relations (both Ike McCaslin and Gavin Stevens appear to have only rudimentary ideas), he nonetheless intuited the power of allegorical form to reveal the historical forces at play in a provincial moment or event. *Sanctuary,* for example, places misogyny and racism in a broader climate of brutality. The hard, glassy surface of the novel, terrible in its perversion both of sexuality and of justice, prefigures some elements in *Native Son* but more resembles the detective novels of Dashiell Hammett or, among Afro-American fiction, Chester Himes's *If He Hollers Let Him Go* (1945). Himes's novel, like *Sanctuary,* is formally methodical, employing the rigid grid of the Los Angeles road system and the prisonlike shipyard where Bob Jones works to simulate the novel's emotional pain. But—here again like *Sanctuary*—Bob's fights with white Southern workers and his entrapment on a rape charge by a Texas "cracker bitch" (as he calls her) superimpose upon wartime Los Angeles echoes of the past: the yard becomes a kind of plantation, and the Kafka-like ship at times seems a slave ship. Indeed, Himes wrote in a 1943 essay on the Zoot Suit riots that "the South has won Los Angeles," recreating there a Klan mentality and the racial geography of the actual South.[22]

Like *Native Son* or Ann Petry's *The Street* (1946), Himes's novel revises the plantation tale, carefully delineating black (slave) quarters and the house, territory, and rights of the master in the world of urban naturalism. In Faulkner's mind, *Sanctuary* led directly to *Light in August*, the pure text of sexual naturalism to the pure text of racial naturalism. Faulkner's discovery that gothicism and naturalism were entwined in the American tradition thus places him at the center of modern writing on race. Of what was Faulkner writing in *Absalom, Absalom!* and *Go Down, Moses* but the haunted mind of the South—and of the nation—its house still divided by racial nightmares? And what form did he choose but intimate crimes of blood in which incest and miscegenation were joined in the ultimate violation of social taboo, yet figured still as "repressed" forces by the formal surveillance of the novel, as its narrative screens and convolutions of memory work to bury the image of the black man deep in the white mind? When Faulkner turned from *Light in August* to *Absalom, Absalom!*, a new exploration of the race nightmare, he chose a tale steeped in antebellum history and, like *Benito Cereno*, anchored through Sutpen's so-called mistake in the revolt of Haitian slaves that became the central emblem of insurrectionary terror in the slaveholding South. As in *Light in August*, he once again began with the working title of "Dark House," and the novel he produced—both a mystery story and an elaborate crime novel—utilized the most gothic materials of

American social history. His excavation of America's unconscious revealed history itself to be a slave ship, a dungeon still holding captives nearly a hundred years after the end of slavery. But it revealed, too, his authorial mastery of such rebellious materials.

Faulkner revised his own earlier exploration of Quentin Compson's family trauma, making his psyche a personification of the South and the novel a "condensation" of its racial situation.[23] The novel's narrative screens and convolutions, which alternately hide and reveal the secret of Charles Bon's "blood," support the story's fragile, expressionistic containment of repressed memories disturbing the psyche, its threat of violated racial and sexual boundaries. Faulkner's design, like that of Sutpen himself, exists at a point of crisis; and the heroic narrative efforts of Quentin and Shreve—their "happy marriage of speaking and hearing" that passes over inconsistencies and denial in searching out the buried love of Bon and Judith, Bon and Henry, Bon and Clytie, Bon and Rosa—must mend and complete the flawed design of Sutpen himself. That is, Faulkner's novel must work through—as in an analytic session—possible plots and historical scenarios in order to create and redeem the beautifully imagined catastrophe of Sutpen's refusal of his first son on the field of retreat in Carolina: "Then for the second time [Bon] looked at the expressionless and rocklike face, at the pale boring eyes in which there was no flicker, nothing, the face in which he saw his own features, in which he saw recognition, and that was all."[24] Superimposing Quentin's discovery of Clytie's secret upon Henry's final confrontation of Bon, Faulkner enters Sutpen's ruined dark house in order to marry past and present, bringing to light the mystery that will explicate, if not expiate, the sins that have lived from the Civil War on into the present. That Faulkner himself later voiced careful hesitations about the wisdom of swift desegregation underscores the fact that in his fiction, as only the freedom of the imagination would permit, he went further in courage and in vision than virtually any writer, historian, or politician of his day—but still could not escape the nightmare any more than could Quentin Compson.

For the black writer, the white man's identification of the black man's racial self with evil or with submerged, rebellious life has even more obviously posed formal as well as social problems. For him, what is submerged or suppressed is not an idea, even a nightmare, but freedoms of expression and action critical to life itself. Thus in Toomer's "Kabnis," Father John, the community's fragile link to its slave past, lives as a "Father of hell" in a cellar called "The Hole"—a "dead blind father of a muted folk who feel their way upward to a life that crushes or absorbs them."[25] Trapped with Madge in an iron box of a room aboard the ship where he is still the white man's slave, Himes's hero, falsely charged with assaulting her, exists symbolically in the "hole" of Jim Crow America. Like the furnace room of the Dalton home, Wright's famous story "The Man Who Lived Underground" is a Dostoevskian expression of life in "the hole," as is the novel it influenced, Ellison's *Invisible Man*. Wright's conception is echoed as well in Ann Petry's *The Street* (1946), where Jones, the tenement super, is driven to madness and sexual violence by his life in various cellars. The history of positions beneath or within America's conscious ideological convictions and its diverse modern extensions of slavery's paternalistic structures are summed up by Ellison's great midcentury novel, which coincided with the nation's shift toward racial justice and at the same time appeared as an undercurrent of the canon that Ellison quite clearly hoped to join.

Given that his novel recapitulates the history of black American life in the first half of the twentieth century—and by its manipulation of such symbols as Trueblood's dream and Tarp's chain reaches back into the history of slavery—it is fitting that Invisible Man writes to us from an underground "hole," plunging outside of history (like the subway hipsters) to narrate the submerged story of black life in the United States. Invisible Man's underground hibernation revises the hold of the slave ship (perhaps specifically the cuddy of Melville's *San Dominick*, to which the novel's first epigraph refers us) and the gothic dungeon (perhaps specifically Father John's underground cell of

slave history). Like Harlem itself, Invisible Man's buried space is
in the "very bowels of the city"; it is "nowhere" but for that very
reason may represent "an underground extension of democracy." Ellison's essay, "Harlem Is Nowhere," which I am citing,
delineates a phantasmagoric black world of brilliant madness "in
which the major energy of the imagination goes not into creating
works of art, but to overcome the frustrations of social discrimination."[26] Life in Ellison's Harlem, as in *Invisible Man* itself, is a
masquerade and a search for that identity everywhere buried
beneath the available structures of power and enterprise in mid-
century white America.

The novel finds identity in the protagonist's acceptance of
black life—his family, his region, and his race. But for Ellison,
even a decade after *Brown* v. *Board of Education*, black identity
was still at risk. Writing at the crest of the civil rights movement
in 1965 in an essay entitled "Tell It Like It Is, Baby," Ellison
described a personal nightmare dating from 1956 and displaying
all the signs of compelling gothic fiction. In the dream his own
dead father merged with the body of Abraham Lincoln, and
Ellison, "fallen out of time into chaos," took on the role of a
young slave powerless to stop a white mob from its carnivalesque
desecration of the corpse of the president, "the old coon."[27]
Provoked by the campaign against *Brown* by Southern con-
gressmen, the dream imposed past upon present and drove the
dream of black freedom back underground, but did so by an
eruption out of Ellison's—as though out of the nation's—unconscious. From Ellison's point of view—in direct counterpoint to
Faulkner's equally impassioned and searching apologies for
Southern resistance to desegregation during the 1950s—the
nightmare was alive, and history's march toward freedom, like
Lincoln's corpse, was again in jeopardy of being lynched.

If black writing itself must reflect the submerged trauma of
the American dream, implicitly critical and subversive beneath
its masking images, the absorption of both history and the tradition of the literature of race in satire may represent its most
significant improvisation. Ishmael Reed's *Flight to Canada* (1976)

burlesques the slave narrative, the antislavery novel, the plantation story, and Lincoln's legend, merging the 1850s and the
twentieth century in a kaleidoscope of jokes and masquerade.
Like Frederick Douglass, Reed's slave author, Raven Quickskill,
writes a letter to his old master, the sadomasochist Arthur
Swille, in the form of the poem "Flight to Canada," and the
novel builds on Quickskill's personal signifying to construct a
signifying improvisation upon the whole history of American
race relations. As though written out of the novel's Slave Hole
Café in Emancipation City, *Flight to Canada* re-creates the underground source of black history and writing as a nightclub riff
on the central legends of bondage and emancipation. Revising
Ellison's actual nightmare and what Toomer calls the "godam
nightmare" of the black artist's soul, the "twisted awful thing that
crept in from a dream" and lives, according to Kabnis, on "mis-
shapen, split-gut, tortured, twisted words," Reed's novel testi-
fies to Quickskill's dictum that "words built the world and words
can destroy the world."[28] Words signify in the sense that they
mean; but they signify in the further sense that they revise and
subvert words that have come before, destroying one world—
say, the world of white racism—and replacing it with another
that remakes it in a new image.

If we may briefly return now to Ellison's remarks on Charlie
Christian, it can be said that the black tradition, like jazz, has
itself often gone unrecorded, running a submerged course until
it could at last rise up into an individual consciousness and
public voice. In doing so, it has taken various forms, but in all
cases has striven for that condition of storytelling tradition described by Zora Neale Hurston in *Their Eyes Were Watching
God* (1937) and brilliantly reflected in the novel itself: "words
walking without masters; walking altogether like harmony in a
song."[29] Hurston's novel, like her essay "Characteristics of
Negro Expression," discovers in dialect and the highly figurative
language of Afro-America the central tropes, not of bondage and
naturalistic submersion below the civilized, but rather of adorn-

ment, rebellious creativity, and freedom from imprisoning forms. As the examples of Hurston, Ellison, and Reed suggest, the mastery and power of the word is critical not only to a black tradition that conceives of itself apart from the white world but even more so to a black tradition that would prevail in combat and union with a white world. Thus a felt urgency to record the vanishing stories of her literal and figurative mothers lies behind the fiction of Alice Walker. "For these grandmothers and mothers of ours were not Saints, but Artists," she writes, "driven to a numb and bleeding madness by the springs of creativity in them for which there was no release." Her intention, as she phrases it on another occasion, is to write "all the things I should have· been able to read." The "spiritual waste" of resources that Walker seeks to redress thus belongs both to her silenced black mothers and to the traditional images in the white mind to which she responds.[30]

From this point of view, *The Color Purple* (1982) does something more than recapitulate and revise the slave narrative and the plantation tale, superimposing modern experience upon an antebellum model while invoking the thousands of lives, particularly those of women, that destroyed letters or illiteracy itself buries in the past. It also implicitly alludes to recent texts in creating the tradition that Walker "should have been able to read." In addition to *Their Eyes Were Watching God*, which has been Walker's most evident inspiration, one might say that *The Color Purple* recasts the classic tradition represented by *The Sound and the Fury* (1929) and *Go Down, Moses* (1942), exploring the pathology and eventual triumph of a *black* Southern family and giving to Dilsey Gibson or to Tomasina McCaslin the clear narrative voice that Faulkner was unable to give them. Without granting that *The Color Purple* is an entirely successful novel, who would not agree that Celie is as strong a character, and perhaps in some respects as powerful a storyteller, as Quentin Compson or Ike McCaslin?

Walker's novel, like much of Faulkner's work, employs storytelling letters to delve into familial, ancestral mysteries and to search out lost passion. In *The Color Purple* family integrity and love triumph over sexual abuse and a form of incest that is barely less frightening for turning out to be only symbolic—surely as frightening, if not worked out with such psychological or historical complexity, as Quentin Compson's fantasies of Caddy or Charles Bon's proposal of marriage to Judith. The epistolary form, with the separate narrative lines of Celie's and Nettie's letters, reflects the family's fragmentation and its repair, much as the convolutions of narrative form epitomized by the ancestral ledgers reflect the fragmentation of Ike McCaslin's family, whose sins he would expiate through acts of sacrifice. Like *The Color Purple*, *Go Down, Moses* attempts precariously to override racial and sexual violence—the combined incest and miscegenation that Faulkner fixed as its emblem at the heart of Ike McCaslin's heritage—to knit together a disintegrating family and redeem the broken promise of familial love.

The form of Walker's novel calls attention to the special symbolic significance of literacy in the black American cultural tradition, running from Phillis Wheatley's testimony to the authenticity of her own poems to Malcolm X's verbatim copying of the dictionary in prison. At the same time, the novel subverts, by critically revising—or improvising upon—the white tradition that has held "letters" and the laws they embody to be privileged property, signs of power of the kind exercised in the court depositions in *Benito Cereno*, which contain and repress the rebellious explosiveness of Melville's imagination; or by Huck Finn, who in moments of deep compassion decides to go to hell rather than send the letter naming Jim as a runaway, but nevertheless signs off his narrative, full of ambiguously cruel treatment of Jim, in the form of a letter; or in the haunted documents of Ike McCaslin's inheritance: "*Eunice Bought By Father in New Orleans 1807 $650. dolars. Marrid to Thucydus 1809 Drownd in Crick Cristmas Day 1832.*" "*But there must have been love,*" Ike imagines. "*Some sort of love.*"[31]

The relation between love and literacy is a less conventional way to conceive of the thematic problem of the family, which is central to the American literature of race and repeatedly lies at the heart of the issue of fictional form. In both *Absalom, Absalom!* and *Go Down, Moses*, Faulkner's deepest penetrations into the heart of the American race trauma, storytelling and intimate family documents bear the burden of revealing a love that may never have existed except in the forms into which it is now cast by acts of imagination at once desperate and compassionate. Like the issue of miscegenation, which often renders it tragic, or the survival in modern consciousness of historical forms of slavery, which contains its gothic prototypes, the relation between love and literacy in Faulkner's texts as in others may tell us much about the history of American race relations, not least because our greatest writers have found their own freedom in its expressive forms.[32]

NOTES

1. Ralph Ellison, "The Charlie Christian Story," *Shadow and Act* (New York: Random House, Vintage Books, 1972), 233–34.

2. See, for example, Henry Louis Gates, Jr., "The Blackness of Blackness: A Critique of the Sign and the Signifying Monkey," in Gates, ed., *Black Literature and Black Theory* (New York: Methuen, 1984), 285–321.

3. See, for example, George Fredrickson, *The Black Image in the White Mind: The Debate on Afro-American Character and Destiny, 1817–1914* (New York: Harper and Row, 1971) and Joel Williamson, *The Crucible of Race: Black-White Relations in the American South Since Emancipation* (New York: Oxford University Press, 1984).

4. Thomas Dixon, *The Clansman: An Historical Romance of the Ku Klux Klan* (New York: A. Wessels, 1917), 313.

5. James Weldon Johnson, *The Autobiography of an Ex-Coloured Man* (New York: Hill and Wang, 1960), 167–68.

6. A discussion of lynching and its appearance in black fiction is available in Trudier Harris, *Exorcising Blackness: Historical and Literary Lynching and Burning Rituals* (Bloomington: Indiana University Press, 1984).

7. The court's ruling and Tourgée's brief are quoted in C. Vann Woodward, "The National Decision Against Equality," *American Counterpoint: Slavery and Racism in the North-South Dialogue* (Boston: Little, Brown, 1971), 224–29.

8. Mark Twain, *Pudd'nhead Wilson and Those Extraordinary Twins* (Baltimore: Penguin, 1969), 103, 240, 64. On the evolution of race theory in this period, see I. A. Newby, *Jim Crow's Defense: Anti-Negro Thought in America, 1900–1930* (Baton Rouge: Louisiana State University Press, 1965). On miscegenation and mulattoes, see also Joel Williamson, *New People: Miscegenation and Mulattoes in the United States* (New York: The Free Press, 1980) and James Kinney, *Amalgamation!: Race, Sex, and Rhetoric in the Nineteenth-Century American Novel* (Westport, Conn.: Greenwood Press, 1985).

9. Charles Chesnutt, *The Marrow of Tradition* (Ann Arbor: University of Michigan Press, 1969), 119, 185, 81.

10. George S. Schuyler, *Black No More* (New York: Collier Books, 1971), 203–18.

11. On the problem of form in its relation to race and contemporary race theory in Faulkner's novels, see the longer account in my *Faulkner: The House Divided* (Baltimore: Johns Hopkins University Press, 1983).

12. William Faulkner, *Light in August* (New York: Modern Library, 1968), 212, 440, 174.

13. Lillian Smith, *Killers of the Dream* (New York: Norton, 1961), 87–90, 122, 162.

14. Richard H. King, *A Southern Renaissance: The Cultural Awakening of the American South, 1930–1955* (New York: Oxford University Press, 1980), 173–93.

15. Schuyler, *Black No More*, 205; Smith, *Killers of the Dream*, 101–108; Faulkner, *Light in August*, 341, 365.

16. Toomer quoted in Brian Joseph Benson and Mabel Mayle Dillard, *Jean Toomer* (Boston: Twayne, 1980), 26.

17. Jean Toomer, *Cane* (New York: Liveright, 1975), 51–67.

18. Richard Wright, "Blueprint for Negro Writing," in *Richard Wright Reader*, ed. Ellen Wright and Michael Fabre (New York: Harper and Row, 1978), 44.

19. Richard Wright, *American Hunger* (New York: Harper and Row, Perrenial Library, 1979), 120. *American Hunger*, the second half of Wright's autobiography, was written at the same time as *Black Boy* (1945), but not published until 1977, although Wright's portrait of his experience with the Communist party appeared as one among six essays by various intellectuals in the volume *The God That Failed: Six Studies in Communism* (1950).

20. Ishmael Reed, *Shrovetide in Old New Orleans* (1978: rpt. New York: Avon, 1979), 53.

21. Wright, "How Bigger Was Born," *Native Son* (New York: Harper and Row, Perrenial Library, 1966), xiv–xix, xxxiv.

22. Chester Himes, "Zoot Suit Riots Are Race Riots," in *Black on Black* (Garden City, New York: Doubleday, 1973), 220–25.

23. *Faulkner in the University: Class Conferences at the University of Virginia, 1957–1958*, ed. Frederick L. Gwynn and Joseph L. Blotner (Charlottesville: University of Virginia Press, 1959), 94.

24. Faulkner, *Absalom, Absalom!* (New York: Random House, 1972), 316, 348.

25. Toomer, *Cane*, 212, 195, 233. The idea of the "black hole" as a figure in black writing is developed in a different fashion by Houston Baker in *Blues, Ideology, and Afro-American Literature: A Vernacular Theory* (Chicago: University of Chicago Press, 1984), 144–57.

26. Ellison, "Harlem Is Nowhere," *Shadow and Act*, 294–302.

27. Ellison, "Tell It Like It Is, Baby," *The Nation*, September 20, 1965, 129–36.

28. Reed, *Flight to Canada* (New York: Avon, 1977), 92.

29. Zora Neale Hurston, *Their Eyes Were Watching God* (Urbana: University of Illinois Press, 1978), 10.

30. Alice Walker, *In Search of Our Mothers' Gardens* (San Diego: Harcourt, Brace, Jovanovitch, 1983), 233–40, 13.

31. Faulkner, *Go Down, Moses* (New York: Modern Library, 1955), 267–70.

32. For valuable suggestions about this essay I would like to thank Professor Robert Coleman of Sonoma State University and Professor Wayne Mixon of Mercer University.

Minstrel Nightmares:
Black Dreams of Faulkner's Dreams of Blacks

CRAIG WERNER

Each generation, of course, re-creates great writers in its own image. This is partly a matter of critical response, more profoundly a matter of literary impact. What I want to argue is that the Afro-American literary response to Faulkner, like Faulkner's greatest works themselves, pushes us to excavate the premises of our history, to focus not on the "eternal verities" that can be carved on the walls of libraries but on those aspects of our experience that we least understand.[1] The irony here is that if Faulkner understood something adequately, the next generation can simply incorporate that understanding into its conceptual vocabulary and move on to wherever the game is actually being played. Unfair, certainly. But one mark of Faulkner's greatness is the extent to which contemporary writers, including an increasing number of Afro-American writers, continue to find him worth arguing with. While travelling to Oxford, I was reminded of just how pressing and complex the issues involved in this argument—the issues at the center of this conference—are. As I read Nicholas Lemann's article "The Origins of the Underclass" in the most recent issue of *The Atlantic,* I was in roughly equal parts stimulated and enraged.[2] Lemann offers some real insights into contemporary racial problems when he points out that the exodus of the Afro-American middle classes from the inner cities, especially the projects, is effectively condemning many blacks to life in a single class society. This cuts off many younger blacks from contact with the *real* role models with whom they would have had contact in the past. This complex of problems has a number of implications. On the one hand, it places tremendous pressure on the older residents of the inner cities, who have all too often been driven into effective withdrawal. Speaking at a celebratory gathering in Chicago in February 1985, Gwendolyn Brooks related an anecdote emphasizing just this point. During the 1960s she met Don L. Lee, now known as Haki Madhubuti, when he literally knocked on her door in the middle of the night. The contact both sparked Madhubuti's poetic career and led to Brooks's involvement with a number of cultural programs among the Chicago gangs.[3] Sadly, but entirely understandably, she told the audience gathered at the Museum of Science and Industry located on Chicago's predominantly black South Side, that she would no longer even think about coming to the door. In addition to this breakdown in contact between classes and generations within the Afro-American community, the decline in inner city conditions has had a horrifying impact on the position of black women. This is particularly evident in the cycle of teenage pregnancy—well-documented but inadequately understood—which makes escape from the triple jeopardy of racial, gender-based, and economic oppression effectively impossible. Even as I acknowledge the validity of some of Lemann's points, however, I feel a profound frustration with his article, which exhibits a horrifying lack of context, of history, of the depth of understanding which might make the problems he describes comprehensible. This lack has afflicted white approaches to Afro-American culture—neoconservative, paleoliberal, protomarxist—from Henry David Thoreau through Daniel Moynihan's half-digested appropriation of Kenneth Clark to Bill Moyers's recent television documentary cum slander. The lack of context makes many blacks—and white Afro-Americanists like myself—feel like saying the hell with it all and either denying or whitewashing the very real problems.

It is against this background that the dialog between Faulkner and Afro-American culture takes on a very real, and largely extraliterary, importance. In regard to this complex of problems, Faulkner has much to offer, particularly in *Absalom, Absalom!*

For Euro-Americans, his insistence that the "past isn't dead, it isn't even past" articulates the simple, but all too often ignored, knowledge that the excavation of history is an absolute necessity if we are to make any sense of the present. For Afro-American culture, Sutpen—or more precisely Quentin's imagination of Sutpen—has something to say about the costs of leaving one's roots behind. In addition, *Absalom, Absalom!* intimates the connection between racial and sexual oppression visible in the inner city today.

Faulkner's relevance to Afro-American society has not always been clear, or even marginally accessible, in part because of his problematic public stances.[4] The first stage of the Afro-American response to his work consisted largely of correcting Faulkner's misconceptions. This stage resulted in what I think is a fairly clear consensus that, while Faulkner was a good observer, he consistently interpreted Afro-American behavior in static rather than kinetic terms, substituting "endurance" for "ascent" and "immersion," concepts to which I'll return. In essence, Faulkner fails to excavate Afro-American history as thoroughly as he excavates Euro-American male history. Nonetheless, a new stage of Afro-American response to Faulkner appears to have begun opening over the last decade. In this stage, Afro-American writers both draw on Faulkner for insight into their own cultural situation and contribute important insights to the excavation which he began. Rereading Faulkner through the works of Leon Forrest, Ernest Gaines, Gloria Naylor, Sherley Anne Williams, and David Bradley clarifies why Euro-American culture, collectively, and in most cases individually, has been unable to get beyond—to adapt John Irwin's terms—the patterns of revenge and repetition, or at best endurance and moral repudiation, characteristic of Faulkner's most aware protagonists.[5] Specifically, Afro-American writers bring the implications of *Absalom, Absalom!* closer to light, focusing on the cost of excluding "others"—either racial or sexual—from *active* participation in the dialog necessary to the excavation of history. Tapping the call-and-response dynamic of Afro-American expression as a way of mediating between individual and communal values, they present images of more comprehensive dialog/excavations. These are presented not as a series of simplistic acceptances of the other but as attempts to conceive a process capable of carrying out our own extraliterary stage of the process. The emerging consensus on the dynamic of this revised process stresses the need for (1) an awareness of Quentin's—and I suspect they are to some extent Faulkner's—shortcomings, particularly his inability to accept the complexity and participation of the other; (2) a determination to avoid simplistic applications and to seek out our own analogous blindnesses; and (3) a commitment to putting the resulting insights to use in the world.

Essentially I'm suggesting that resisting the realistic significance of either Faulkner's insight or his blindness dooms us to a simplified excavation with suicidal implications for Sutpen, for Quentin, for the forty-five-year-old great-grandmothers in Cabrini Green or the Mississippi Delta. What this means is that I will not be concerned with either refuting or upholding Harold Bloom's *The Anxiety of Influence,* a parlor game with diminishing returns. Nor will I be attempting to prove that a novel is "Faulknerian." "Faulknerian," by the way, is a term I understand to mean any story with long sentences, two narrators, italics, and incest, which is superficially more difficult to comprehend than the feature section of *USA Today.* If it is a second novel set in the same fictional county as the author's first, or involves the killing of a large nonaquatic animal, any two of the preceding provisions may be waived. All novels concerning Mississippi, of course, are automatically Faulknerian. As a critic concerned with tradition, I've done my share of such defining and I no doubt will do so again. But now I don't even much care whether the writers I'm considering were concerned at all with Faulkner, though it's fairly easy to demonstrate that most were. Rather, I think of what I'm doing as part of an ongoing literary minstrel show. Prior to Walter Taylor's use of the image at this conference, the image of the minstrel show had been used most recently in Faulkner criticism by Eric J. Sundquist who writes:

"The gothicism of *Absalom, Absalom!* is not by any means the sentimentality of a minstrel show—not the benign dream in which 'all coons look alike'—but the nightmare in which black *and* white look all too hauntingly alike."[6] While I agree thoroughly with Sundquist's observations concerning *Absalom, Absalom!* I differ with him to the extent that I think the similarity of black and white is exactly what makes *Absalom* into a minstrel show. This view of the minstrel show, derived from the work of Ralph Ellison, John Toll, Charles Sanders, and particularly Berndt Ostendorf's *Black Literature in White America*, emphasizes that parody, travesty, and misunderstanding are as central to intercultural communication and the development of a democratic or pluralistic sensibility as are more conscious approaches.[7] Ostendorf stresses that minstrelsy entailed the "blackening of America." Even though the white minstrels presented their burlesques as simple fun, they tacitly acknowledged something in Afro-American culture worthy of imitation. Ellison articulates the importance of the minstrel dynamic when he describes his response to a stage production of Erskine Caldwell's *Tobacco Road:* "It was as though I had plunged through the wacky mirrors of a fun house, to discover on the other side a weird distortion of perspective which made for a painful but redeeming rectification of vision."[8] Blacks and whites can move closer to mutual understanding by approximating versions of one another. Faulkner imitates blacks in his fiction; black writers imitate Faulkner's forms. Each broadens his/her knowledge and communicates, if obliquely, to his/her audience, creating a more synthetic base for the next act of the minstrel show.

The dialog between Faulkner and Afro-American culture involves several levels of distortion and rectification grounded as much in the wider cultural context as in the content of a particular work or works. The early response of black writers to Faulkner was surprisingly—given some later developments—positive, in large part because he was quite correctly understood in relation to the virulent racism of Bilbo and Vardaman. Sterling Brown's pioneering study *The Negro in American Fiction* (1937) contrasts Faulkner's accurate observations of "the bitter life [black Mississippians] are condemned to live" with the "happy-go-lucky comics" common in fiction of the era and concludes that while Faulkner "does not write social protest . . . he is fiercely intent upon the truth."9 This sounds most of the major elements of the positive Afro-American response to Faulkner, which has been reiterated—with varying degrees of enthusiasm—by Ernest Gaines, Melvin B. Tolson, Leon Forrest, and Toni Morrison. Faulkner has been repeatedly praised as an excellent observer who, despite the limitations of his vision, refuses to lie about the realities of the Southern past or present. His use of black folklore in works such as *Sartoris* (one of the first novels to describe the blues), "That Evening Sun," and "Pantaloon in Black" ratifies Alain Locke's prediction in "The New Negro" (1925) that in the immediate future white writers would begin to recognize a deeper level of power in black culture than they had previously.10 Even when he fails to comprehend fully the nature of Afro-American signifying—to use a term common in both black folklore and critical theory11—Faulkner provides images capable of deconstructing the binary oppositions on which racial privilege depends. Among the most powerful of these images are Sutpen's fights with the slaves, Chick Mallison's initiation in *Intruder in the Dust,* and the eloquent silence of Lucas Beauchamp's gold toothpick in *Go Down, Moses.* Like many of the writers sympathetic to Faulkner, Ellison celebrates his individual heroism: "If you would find the imaginative equivalents of certain civil rights figures in American writing, Rosa Parks and James Meredith, say, you don't go to most fiction by Negroes, but to Faulkner."12

In a more ambivalent moment, Ellison tempers his enthusiasm, describing Faulkner as "a writer who has confronted Negroes with such mixed motives that he has presented them in terms of both the 'good nigger' and the 'bad nigger' stereotypes, and who yet has explored perhaps more successfully than anyone else, either white or black, certain forms of Negro humanity."13 Most of the Afro-American writers who have expressed serious

reservations about Faulkner—among them James Baldwin, Alice
Walker, and John A. Williams—emphasize Faulkner's mixed
motives, especially as expressed in his public statements. If
Faulkner comprehends the Southern past, they emphasize, he is
blind to its future and a large part of its present. In his essay
"Faulkner and Desegregation" and his book *No Name in the
Street*, and through the character Faulkner Grey in *Just Above
My Head*, Baldwin repeatedly criticizes Faulkner for under-
estimating the realistic impact of his argument that change
would come to the South through moral transformation rather
than political action. Arguing that "Faulkner could see Negroes
only as they related to him, not as they related to each other,"
Baldwin repudiates Ellison's individualistic emphasis: "the
cultural pretensions of history are revealed as nothing less than a
mask for power, and thus it happens that, in order to be rid of
Shell, Texaco, Coca-Cola, the Sixth Fleet, and the friendly
American soldier whose mission it is to protect these invest-
ments, one finally throws Balzac and Shakespeare—and
Faulkner and Camus—out with them. Later, of course, one may
welcome them back, but on one's own terms, and, absolutely, on
one's own land."[14] A similar current informs Alice Walker's comment that "unlike Tolstoy, Faulkner was not prepared to struggle
to change the structure of the society he was born in. One might
concede that in his fiction he did seek to examine the reasons for
its decay, but unfortunately, as I have learned while trying to
teach Faulkner to black students, it is not possible, from so short
a range, to separate the man from his works."[15] In another essay,
Walker writes "that in Mississippi no one even remembers
where Richard Wright lived, while Faulkner's house is maintained by a black caretaker," and that as a result of the contextual
injustice "for a long time I will feel Faulkner's house, O'Connor's
house, crushing me. To fight back will require a certain amount
of energy, energy better used doing something else."[16]

It should be noted that both Baldwin and Walker were writing
in the mid-1970s and that some things have changed since then,
including a degree of recognition for Wright represented by a

Richard Wright symposium here at Old Miss last November.[17]
Nonetheless, a great deal of energy has been spent responding
to the distortions of Faulkner's visions of blacks; as a result, more
black writers now seem willing to welcome Faulkner back.[18] The
preceding stage of the Afro-American response reveals a consensus that, while he rarely distorts observed facts, Faulkner
frequently misperceives the underlying dynamic of Afro-American experience. Robert Stepto has identified two constituting
patterns in Afro-American narrative from the slave narratives to
Invisible Man. The first is the narrative of ascent, in which the
protagonist progresses toward literacy (understood in Euro-
American terms) and freedom, usually in the North. The cost of
ascent for the "articulate survivor" is a degree of alienation and
isolation within the white world. The second pattern is the
narrative of immersion in which the protagonist returns to his/
her cultural roots and reintegrates him/herself with the community, usually in the South. The cost of immersion for the
"articulate kinsman" is the loss of a certain degree of individual
mobility and freedom.[19] Although they differ markedly in many
ways, the revoicing of Faulknerian motifs and themes in Afro-
American novels including Gayl Jones's *Corregidora*, William
Melvin Kelley's *A Different Drummer*, Ernest Gaines's *The Autobiography of Miss Jane Pittman*, and Ellison's *Invisible Man*
highlights Faulkner's failure to interpret Afro-American experience in relation to ascent or immersion, both of which emphasize future movement as the key to understanding present
action. Rather, he substitutes a narrative of endurance, a static,
past-oriented framework which replaces the articulate heroes
with the "enduring saint." Physically enslaved but spiritually
free, this figure places little value on articulation, which may
interfere with moral clarity. Rather, he/she is primarily committed to the salvation of both blacks and whites in the next world.
Following Stowe's Uncle Tom, Faulkner's Dilsey is the archetypal enduring saint. Other Faulkner blacks share her characteristics to varying degrees, but almost none—Molly in *Go Down,
Moses*, Lucas in *Intruder in the Dust*—possess a kinetic frame for

their actions. If they move, their movement is aimless, like that of Rider in "Pantaloon in Black" or Joe Christmas in *Light in August*, or destructive. Several characters in *Go Down, Moses* are destroyed by their attempts at ascent.

Although it will no doubt continue to inform Afro-American responses to Faulkner for some time, the argument over endurance no longer seems central. In fact, Gaines's recent novel *A Gathering of Old Men* seems something of a requiem for the entire debate. Set in Gaines's Bayonne county, which Michel Fabre has discussed at length as a revoicing of Yoknapatawpha,[20] *A Gathering of Old Men*, composed of monologs similar to those of *As I Lay Dying*, is quite clearly a response to the vision of the "new South" presented in *Intruder in the Dust*. Both novels concern the murder of the son of a powerful but distinctly unaristocratic white family; both focus on the presumed guilt of an aging and somewhat aloof black man (Gaines's Mathu and Faulkner's Lucas) who has earned the grudging respect of his community by refusing to surrender his dignity to an oppressive social system and who says very little in his own defense; both generate a vision of salvation based on interracial cooperation. But, where Faulkner emphasizes the role of whites able to maintain some sense of moral vision (his saviors are a young white boy, his black companion, and an elderly white woman), Gaines emphasizes the need for Afro-American self-assertion. Gaines certainly acknowledges the need for white participation in the metaphorical salvation of the Southern soul: Candy, the young heiress to the Marshall plantation where the killing takes place, sets in motion the machinery leading to salvation because of her deep, if paternalistic, love for Mathu; Lou Dimes, a Baton Rouge journalist and frustrated suitor of Candy, is perceptive, but his insights, like those of Gavin Stevens, are rendered nearly useless by his inability to take action; Mapes, a Southern sheriff in the mode of Faulkner's Hope Hampton, respects Mathu's dignity and, despite his personal racism, does everything in his power to prevent violence against the black community. Mapes, ironically, serves as something of a spokesman for Gaines when he criticizes Candy for her inability to conceive of blacks acting or speaking for themselves: "you want to keep them slaves the rest of their lives. . . . At least your people let them talk. . . . Now you're trying to take that away from them."[21]

The real focus of Gaines's response is on the complex eloquence of the black community, an eloquence that profoundly contradicts paternalistic assumptions. A Gathering of Old Men focuses on the group of about fifteen black men, all past seventy, who gather at the scene of the murder when summoned by Candy, who claims to have killed the victim, Beau Boutan, herself. Each arrives with a shotgun and discharged shells. When Mapes arrives, each claims responsibility for the killing. Both the collective action and the presence of the guns assert a much more active response to racism than anything Faulkner conceived in Intruder. As in Intruder, Mathu is actually innocent. In Gathering, however, the real killer is not a white, but another black: Charlie Biggs, a fifty-year-old plantation hand who despite a huge body has spent his entire life running away from confrontations. Although several of the characters comment briefly on Charlie's absence when they arrive at Marshall, all assume he has simply run away until, as Mapes prepares to take Mathu into custody, Charlie reappears to admit his guilt and reclaim the dignity he first earned by resisting Beau and then forfeited by asking Mathu to accept the consequences. A direct literary descendant of Richard Wright's Big Boy (from "Big Boy Leaves Home") and Bigger Thomas (from Native Son), both of whom ran after killing a white person, Charlie infuses Faulknerian Bayonne with a central motif from the Afro-American tradition. Claiming responsibility for his actions, like Bigger on the last pages of Native Son, Charlie earns the right to be addressed as "Mister Biggs." Like Bigger, Charlie dies. But Gaines presents his death—using a number of images recalling the death of Old Ben in "The Bear"—as an emblem of the destruction of the Old South.[22] Where Faulkner laments the passing of the Old South, Gaines insists that even its real values were inextricably involved with denial of the Afro-American other. Where Faulkner's vision of the New South, as expressed in *Intruder*, rests on black silence—on endurance—and on the ability of whites to transform their heritage, Gaines's vision emphasizes collective black assertion, expressed both verbally and through physical actions.

Although Gaines's presentation of the family of the Cajun "victim" is somewhat unconvincing, it is significant that he includes it in his consideration. This type of expanded dialog has become increasingly central as the Afro-American dialog with Faulkner moves beyond the focus on endurance. Discussing the hilarity and shock he felt upon recognizing his deep sympathy with the poor whites portrayed in Caldwell's *Tobacco Road*, Ellison offers an observation applicable to many aspects of the American literary minstrel show: "In the Lear-like drama of white supremacy Negroes [substitute Cajuns, white trash, women, Republicans, fundamentalists, New York Yankees— whatever group you like least] were designated both clowns and fools, but they 'fooled' by way of maintaining their own sense of rational order, no matter how they were perceived by whites. For it was far better to be looked down upon as 'niggers' than to lose themselves in a world rendered surreal through an excess of racial pride. Their challenge was to endure while imposing their claim upon America's conscience and consciousness, just as they had imposed their style upon its culture. Forced to be wary observers, they recognized that American life is of a whole, and that what happens to blacks will accrue eventually, one way or another, to the nation as a whole."[23] This certainly parallels Sundquist's description of the "nightmare in which black and white look all too hauntingly alike."

Although I find Faulkner's overall treatment of race most nearly satisfactory in *Go Down, Moses*, his most intense confrontation with this particular issue is *Absalom, Absalom!* As Thadious Davis and Eric Sundquist have noted, the relationship between Clytie, Judith, and Rosa revolves around the difficulty of acknowledging likeness. The moment when Clytie grabs Rosa's arm to restrain her from climbing the stair is perhaps the

most intense confrontation with racial likeness in Faulkner's work. Elsewhere in *Absalom, Absalom!* Faulkner presents similarly compressed images which intimate a great deal concerning the connection between racial and sexual otherness, an issue which has been crucial to the ways Afro-American novelists have pursued their excavation. Two passages stand out. One is Quentin's speculation on Sutpen and the "monkey nigger" who puts the poor white boy in his place. The passage concludes: "he never even remembered what the nigger said, how it was the nigger told him, even before he had had time to say what he came for, never to come to the front door again but to go around to the back."[24] Forced to assume the role of the "nigger," Sutpen—curiously resembling the protagonists of Afro-American "passing narratives," a version of the ascent narrative in which the protagonist severs all connection with his/her roots—responds by creating and enforcing a vision of himself as a kind of minstrel show aristocrat. What is particularly striking about Quentin's speculation, however, is the emphasis on Sutpen's inability to speak—"even before he had had time to say what he came for"—and his subsequent silencing of the black voice—"he never even remembered what the nigger said." Although Faulkner never really pursues the implications, this seems to imply an awareness that the silencing of the "other's" voice—his own and that of the "monkey nigger"—is crucial to Sutpen's consciousness. It is important to remember that much of what we know of Sutpen's "poor white" past is based on the fact that his performance as an aristocrat is not entirely convincing. From the perspective of white Jefferson, he is more minstrel parodist than accomplished actor; his failure to play an appropriate role attracts a great deal of resistance. It is certainly consistent with the minstrel dynamic of parody and burlesque that Quentin imagines the silence being enforced on Sutpen by yet another despised "other." The minstrel dynamic—a socially significant manifestation of what the theorists call "intertextuality," the dependence of one representation upon previous representations—is extended when Henry attempts to imitate Charles

Bon. Mr. Compson says, "Henry aped his clothing and speech, caricatured rather, perhaps" (102). The "black" son, in the eyes of the "white" son (the use of "black" and "white" reiterates James A. Snead's point concerning the rhetoric of division[25]), is a better aristocrat than the father who derived his idea of aristocracy from the black imitation of a white who, according to W. J. Cash, was probably a criminal in the first place.[26] The deconstructive regression does not end, it merely fades into the mind of the South.

The second passage I want to emphasize is the one in which Mr. Compson tells Quentin "the other sex is separated into three sharp divisions, separated (two of them) by a chasm which could be crossed but one time and in but one direction—ladies, women, females—the virgins whom gentlemen someday married, the courtesans to whom they went while on sabbaticals to the cities, the slave girls and women upon whom that first caste rested" (109). Sutpen's treatment of Rosa Coldfield and Milly Jones violates these distinctions. Faulkner certainly suggests that the gender codes are as arbitrary and destructive as the racial codes which, in Mr. Compson's words, "declare that one eighth of a specified kind of blood shall outweigh seven eights of another kind" (115). Sutpen's attempt to manipulate the codes, which leads to his destruction by the poor white class he should have understood most clearly, reveals not so much his personal corruption as the absurdity of the codes. Yet the silences, the gaps in Quentin's excavation—and I suspect in this he shares much with his creator—reflect an unwillingness or inability to apply the implications of the connection between race and sex to his own process and admit the other into active dialog. Like the blackface minstrels, Faulkner suggests a profound connection between racial and sexual insecurities; female impersonators and black face banjo players share the same dressing room in the white male mind. Unlike the minstrel shows, however, Faulkner does not try to dismiss the tensions he articulates with facile humor. As Walter Taylor demonstrates, his "Hee Hee Hee" is deadly serious.[27]

The reason Faulkner's vision in *Absalom, Absalom!* continues to attract the attention of Afro-American writers rests in large part on his tentative recognition that Sutpen's tragedy is largely social, that he re-creates rather than resists the sources of his own past dehumanization and that his inability to conceive an alternative is in large part responsible for his downfall. Further, Faulkner seems aware that coming to terms with these partially understood patterns requires a collective process, a dialog incorporating numerous perspectives and sensibilities. Unfortunately, in *Absalom, Absalom!*, as in *Go Down, Moses* where Faulkner grants no voice to either Eunice or Tomasina, the actual presence of the "other" is extremely limited. Quentin, Mr. Compson, Shreve—the primary voices are those of white males. Eulalia Bon, Judith, Clytie—all are silent. The only significant female voice—there are no black voices of importance—belongs to Rosa. And she remains a comparatively static figure, bearing a resemblance to the enduring saint, which is at once surprising and, given the limitations of Faulkner's vision, not at all surprising. As she tells Quentin, "I waited not for light but for that doom which we call female victory which is: endure and then endure, without rhyme or reason or hope of reward—and then endure" (144).

Concerned less with refuting Faulkner's vision of endurance than with pursuing his possibilities, novelists such as Leon Forrest, Gloria Naylor, Sherley Anne Williams, and David Bradley—all of whom build on aspects of earlier works by Morrison and Ellison—explore the applicability of Faulkner's insights, particularly concerning the nexus of race and sex, to the Afro-American community. Of this group, Forrest—former managing editor of the Nation of Islam newspaper *Muhammad Speaks* and now Professor of Afro-American Studies at Northwestern University—is the most explicitly concerned with revoicing Faulknerian motifs. One of the crucial incidents in his first novel, *There Is a Tree More Ancient Than Eden* (1973), concerns Jamestown Fishbond, a friend of the narrator Nathaniel Turner Witherspoon. As a young boy, Jamestown experiences a rejection similar to the one Quentin imagines for Sutpen. When Jamestown comes to the back door of what Forrest calls a "mulatto purity party," Nat's Uncle DuPont slams the door in his face, precipitating an argument with his wife that highlights the connection between color prejudice and sexual insecurity in the black bourgeois community: "and aunt dupont . . . saying you dirty motherless crap-eater you could let the little black bastard in his black wasn't going to rub off on your yellow white passing ass take this—and she smashed the white frosted chocolate cake into his high-creamy-yellow face even though when she was sober she hated dark people more than anyone. . . . why you shit-colored bitch i believe you love black men after all."[28] When, years later, Jamestown throws a canteloupe at him, Uncle DuPont has no memory of the original incident. He renders Jamestown invisible in the same way whites render him invisible: "Why I never saw that black sonofabitch before, what the hell would he with his evil black ass have against me anyway?" (59). The black bourgeois community repeats with disturbing exactness the patterns which doomed Thomas Sutpen. By perpetuating what James A. Snead called the "rhetoric of division," by resisting the merging which is even clearer in relation to them than to Joe Christmas, they implicate themselves profoundly in their own oppression. After a second novel, *The Bloodworth Orphans* (1977), which recovers much of the interracially incestuous ground Faulkner explored in *Go Down, Moses,* Forrest returned to *Absalom, Absalom!* in *Two Wings to Veil My Face* (1983), one of the finest, albeit largely unknown, works of recent American fiction. Again narrated by Nat Turner Witherspoon, Forrest's equivalent of Quentin Compson, *Two Wings to Veil My Face* focuses on the relationship between the near legendary black patriarch and juror Jericho Witherspoon and his long estranged wife Great-Momma Sweetie Reed. Superficially Jericho occupies a position much like that of Sutpen or Old Carothers McCaslin; Sweetie, one reminiscent of both Rosa Coldfield and Dilsey. While the unravelling of the relationship is worthy of extended discussion, the process through which Nat—and Forrest—comes to understand it is of paramount interest in relation to the dialog with Faulkner. Like Rosa, Sweetie Reed—at age ninety-one—summons the young Nat to explain an aspect of his past history. Unlike Faulkner, however, Forrest grants Sweetie Reed a fully complex voice. Not only does she initiate his excavation, her own excavation of her relationship with her father and mother provides the model for Nat's process. The women's experiences and voices are as vital as those of Nat's father or any other male. This is particularly important since part of what Nat must come to understand is that black women's apparent acceptance of endurance reflects their complex—and complexly understood—experience of forces of which most black men remain unaware. In effect, Nat comes to understand and experience the complexity of the "other" much more fully and directly than does Quentin Compson. The process of excavation confronts Nat with the uncomfortable knowledge that he is not in fact a physical descendant of Jericho or Sweetie, that his family's legend is based on a deception. More importantly, the excavation leads Sweetie Reed—and by extension Nat—to comprehend the complexity of the behavior of others: her father, I. V. Reed, apparently a loyal darky in the standard Plantation Tradition mode, whose behavior is explained in part by the fact that he is doing penance—imposed by a conjure woman—for an attempt to kill his master; and Jericho—the secular "other" to her own sacred self.

The increased understanding of the "other" and the necessity of including women's voices in any successful excavation recur as central motifs in Naylor's *Linden Hills*. Framing her story with the relationship between two young black men—the darkskinned, streetwise Willie "Shit" Mason and the light-skinned, bourgeois Lester Tilson—Naylor excavates the history of five generations of the Nedeed family. The patriarchs of the Nedeed clan create a financial empire based in large part on their exploitation of the light-skinned women who, like Sutpen, they perceive as means of furthering their grand design. An explicitly feminist revoicing of Faulknerian concerns, Naylor's book revolves around

Willa Prescott Nedeed, the wife whom the youngest Luther Nedeed entombs along with their dead child in the basement of his funeral home as punishment for her failure to bear him an heir. The key to Willa's self-understanding, and to Naylor's excavation, lies in a diary sewed by a previous Nedeed wife into the pages of a family Bible. Like Forrest, Naylor insists that women's experience can be understood only through recognition of the repeated historical pattern, usually invisible from a male perspective, in which black women are entombed in "otherness." Given the tendency to respond to oppression by becoming an oppressor, the frame of *Linden Hills* is particularly significant. Not only does Naylor—who has been accused (quite unjustly I would say) of reverse sexism for the portrayal of men in her first book, *The Women of Brewster Place*—recognize the complexity of black males, she also makes it clear that light- and dark-skinned blacks, lower and middle classes, men and women, are capable of reducing one another to symbolic "others." Failure to recognize and counter this tendency leads inextricably (as it does in *Absalom, Absalom!*) to the final destruction of the Nedeeds' grand design. The family house burns to the ground while the black community looks on with apathy or pleasure.

Responding directly to William Styron's *The Confessions of Nat Turner*, a novel that most black critics would argue has learned very little from Faulkner's heroic excavations, Sherley Anne Williams's *Dessa Rose* juxtaposes three distinct approaches to its historical materials. The first section is written primarily from the perspective of Nehemiah, a white man interviewing Dessa, a black woman who has been condemned to death for her part in a slave rebellion. As he gathers information for a book on the causes of slave uprisings, Nehemiah has access to most of the material necessary for a successful excavation. But he is unable to accept the simple premise that Dessa is as complex a human being as he is; as a result, he can make no sense of her words. After her escape, he descends into an obsessive desire to recapture her, to reduce her again to the role of enduring "other." In a wonderful passage near the end of the book, Williams describes the cost of Nehemiah's obsession. His notes on his conversations with Dessa, which he presents as evidence to a sheriff he is trying to convince to imprison her, are totally devoid of meaning: "'Nemi, ain't nothing but some scribbling on here,' sheriff say. 'Can't no one read this.' Miz Lady was turning over the papers in her hand. 'And these is blank, sheriff,' she say. 'What?' Nemi say, still on his knees. 'Naw, it's all here.'"[29] Devoid of context and cut off from dialog with the "other," the white male excavation in effect self-deconstructs. Equally important in Williams's alternative excavation is her treatment of the relationship between Dessa and the white woman Ruth (the "Miz Lady" of the previous passage) who for complex reasons harbors a community of fugitive slaves on her plantation. Although Dessa at first repudiates the humanity of the white "other"—a repudiation which becomes violent when Ruth sleeps with one of the black men—she eventually comes to understand that, despite Ruth's racist responses—and it is vital that Williams does nothing to romanticize her characters' racial attitudes—Ruth is as human, as complex, as the "people."

For Williams the significance of recognizing the "other" is not abstract. Rather, it exerts a powerful influence over our way of acting in the world, helping to expand our sense of possibility. When Dessa describes Ruth's role in the westward escape of the fugitives to a group of young blacks—the actual image of dialog/ excavation in the novel—Williams provides an image of black-white cooperation much more convincing than those in Howard Fast's *Freedom Road* or Richard Wright's "Fire and Cloud."

Treating a similar set of thematic concerns, Bradley's *The Chaneysville Incident* images the excavation of John Washington, clearly misogynist, partly racist (against both blacks and whites), a black historian of middle-class origin who is living with a white woman whom he emotionally abuses. Ultimately, Washington realizes that the understanding of history depends on constructive use of the imagination rather than on pure facts, a point reiterated by most Faulkner critics. What is unique in Bradley's treatment is the fact that his narrator, reluctantly forced to admit his mother's perspective into his excavation, comes to understand that he has imposed categories on women equivalent to those imposed on blacks. Finally Washington is able to imagine a version of history in which a black woman—his great-grandmother—assumes the traditionally masculine heroic role. What makes Bradley's novel so powerful—and I think it is the single most effective confrontation with gender ever written by an American male, a claim I make with full awareness of Bradley's problematic (I'm tempted to say Faulknerian) public comments on sexual/literary politics[30]—is Bradley's refusal to simplify any aspect of reality he perceives, even when it entails surrendering his privileged position in relation to the other. The point seems simple, but it is not. Simply admitting the perspective of the "other" into a text is rare enough in American literature. Treating it in relationship to structures of thought other than one's own is even rarer; I think this is where Styron fails. Granting it a complexity equivalent to one's own—admitting the underlying likeness without denying the actual difference—is extremely rare. Figuring out what to do with the likeness is nearly unheard of. But it seems to me to be precisely the point of the continuing Afro-American dialog with Faulkner.

In conclusion, I'd like to comment briefly on some of the implications of what I've suggested in this paper. First, an expanded sense of dialog contributes to the re-creation of Faulkner by and for a new generation. Rereading Faulkner through the Afro-American responses to his work highlights the fact that his work is grounded in social, specifically racial, realities. This makes it difficult to accept a rhetoric of division separating narrative and social discourses. While I have no desire to deny the power or significance of *The Sound and the Fury* or *As I Lay Dying*—the books that were presented to me along with "universalist" versions of *Absalom, Absalom!* and *Light in August* as the "great" Faulkner during my graduate education—I think that recognizing the importance of race suggests canon adjustments with implications for college reading lists. In addition to recognizing the social nature of Sutpen's tragedy, racially aware

Faulkner criticism deepens our appreciation of *Light in August* and *Go Down, Moses*. Underlying this adjustment of the canon is a shift in emphasis from the primarily psychological books to the books that present models of the dialog necessary for excavation. I would suspect that recognizing the connection between race and sex, particularly in the dialog works which actively explore the relationship of the spoken and the written word, will also help articulate the importance of the Snopes trilogy in Faulkner's overall development.

Second, the dialog has implications in regard to our understanding of Afro-American literature. Many Afro-American novelists seem now to believe that a point has been reached, aesthetically if not yet socially, where it is possible, to revise Baldwin's formulation, to "welcome Faulkner back on one's own terms." No longer forced to expend a great deal of energy correcting Faulkner's obvious limitations, black writers can now explore more fully the uses of his work in relation to their own concerns. On one level, this may involve the kind of "applications" of Faulknerian concepts to black bourgeois-working class or male-female relationships carried out by Forrest and Naylor. In essence, this entails a revision of Stepto's ascent and immersion paradigms to account more fully for the internal diversity of the black community. On another level, it may suggest ways of coming to terms with the white "other" as in Bradley and Williams. In addition, reengaging Faulkner on different premises can help clarify the nature of the relationship between the spoken and written word—a crucial element of a literary tradition grounded in the blues, in folk expression, in sermons. The spoken word, particularly the call-and-response dynamic, has been recognized by critics from W. E. B. Du Bois and Zora Neale Hurston to Robert Stepto and Williams as central to the Afro-American literary tradition. One of the ongoing problems, however, has been finding a way of translating into relatively static written forms the oral dynamic that admits both self (the leader) and other (the congregation, the respondants) into the dialog as equals. What I would suggest—and I think that Forrest's work provides a first strong intimation of the possibility—is that the Faulknerian sentence, what Irving Howe called his "stream of eloquence" style, suggests one way of solving the problem. Incorporating multiple perspectives, dictions, traditions, Faulkner's sentences—particularly in *Absalom* and part 4 of "The Bear"—carry on a dialog with themselves. Similarly, passages such as part 4 of "The Bear" intimate ways of expressing the silence of writing through dialog rendered back into writing with an awareness of its silences. Combined with the expanded sense of the "other" and conceived as an extension of the call-and-response dynamic, the Faulknerian style—far from being an archaic or idiosyncratic expression of Euro-American solipsism—can be reconstituted as an aesthetic-social instrument of profound significance.

Finally, the dialog between Faulkner and Afro-American culture implies a sense of literature as a collective process, as an engagement with social realities. There's a moment in Gaines's novel *The Autobiography of Miss Jane Pittman* where Jane and the white Jules Raynard sit discussing a tragic death precipitated by Bayonne's racial codes. Alone, neither Jane nor Jules can do more than speculate on the truth. As Jules says, "It would be specalatin if two white people was sitting here talking." Jane says, "But it's us," and Jules answers, "And that makes it gospel truth."[31] In this version of history no one need be, or can be, ignored as "other." Extending this principle, the black dialog with Faulkner heightens, or should heighten, our Faulknerian awareness of the need to be conscious of who's speaking and, equally importantly, of who isn't. The dialog, the excavation of America's psychic landscape, progresses—in works by white writers such as Lee Smith's *Oral History* and Harry Crews's *A Childhood* and books by "other" writers such as Audre Lorde's *Zami,* John Wideman's *Damballah,* and Louise Erdrich's *Love Medicine*. All of these texts share an awareness of literature as a dialog; all attempt to admit the voices of excluded "others." As for Faulkner's role in the dialog with Afro-American writers, he may not have prevailed, but he has certainly endured. As for the rest of us, I suspect that we're stuck in the minstrel show but, with the help of Forrest and Williams, of Naylor and Faulkner, we can at least come to a deeper understanding of the roles we play.

NOTES

1. A brief apologia by way of a preface. The following paper is more a speaking script than a scholarly paper in the traditional sense. I decided to let the original script stand largely unedited in part because the focus of the paper was determined in part by the dynamics and demographics of the Faulkner and Yoknapatawpha Conference at which it was delivered. I hope the paper intimates the problematic exhilaration I felt throughout the conference. The exhilaration stemmed from the extremely stimulating papers delivered throughout the week. Prior to delivering this talk, I rewrote the introductory pages and parts of the main discussion frequently in response to papers by and talks with James Snead, Thadious Davis, Walter Taylor, Frederick Karl, and Eric Sundquist. Several papers delivered after I had spoken—most notably those by Philip Weinstein, Blyden Jackson, and Noel Polk—would have resulted in further revisions. Both the content and the dynamic of the ongoing dialog strengthened my sense that reading Faulkner with an emphasis on race offers something of large importance to a process that is at once literary and social. As a white male—there are thirteen of us among the seventeen speakers listed on the program—I'm deeply aware that my perspective has been in some sense privileged in the dialog on Faulkner and Race. The books that have been most important to the development of my understanding of Faulkner's treatment of race are Davis's *Faulkner's "Negro" Art and the Southern Context* (Baton Rouge: Louisiana State University Press, 1983); Taylor's *Faulkner's Search for a South* (Urbana: University of Illinois Press, 1983); and Sundquist's *Faulkner: The House Divided* (Baltimore: Johns Hopkins University Press, 1983). See also the other essays in this volume, particularly James Snead's *"Light in August* and the Rhetorics of Racial Division,"* based on his *Figures of Division: William Faulkner's Major Novels* (New York: Methuen, 1986).

2. Nicholas Lemann, "The Origins of the Underclass," *The Atlantic*, 258 (1986), 54–68.

3. For Brooks's discussion of this period of her career, see her autobiographical volume *Report from Part One* (Detroit: Broadside Press, 1972).

4. See Noel Polk's essay elsewhere in this volume for the clearest discussion of the complexities of Faulkner's public stance.

5. See Irwin's *Doubling and Incest/Repetition and Revenge* (Baltimore: Johns Hopkins University Press, 1975).

6. Sundquist, 99. See Walter Taylor's illuminating discussion of *The Rivers* as a minstrel show elsewhere in this volume.

7. See Ellison's essays "Change the Joke and Slip the Yoke" in *Shadow and Act* (New York: Random House, 1964) and "An Extravagance of Laughter" in *Going to the Territory* (New York: Random House, 1986); Toll's *Blacking Up* (London: Oxford University Press, 1974); Sanders's *The Waste Land:* The Last Minstrel Show?," *Journal of Modern Literature*, 8 (1980), 23–38; and Ostendorf's chapter "Minstrelsy: Imitation, Parody and Travesty in Black-White Interaction Rituals 1830–1920" in *Black Literature in White America* (Totowa, N.J.: Barnes and Noble, 1982).

8. Ellison, *Territory*, 194.

9. Sterling Brown, *The Negro in American Fiction* (New York: Atheneum, 1969), 177–79. This seminal work of Afro-American literary scholarship was originally published in 1937.

10. Alain Locke, "The New Negro," in *Black Writers of America*, ed. Richard Barksdale and Keneth Kinnamon (New York: Macmillan, 1972), 580.

11. For discussion of the intriguing relationship between Afro-American folk expression and insights into the nature of normally credited to poststructuralist theory, see Henry Louis Gates, Jr.'s "'The Blackness of Blackness': A Critique of the Sign and the Signifying Monkey," *Studies in Black American Literature*, 1 (1984), 129–82. I discuss one literary manifestation of the relationship in "The Framing of Charles Chesnutt: Practical Deconstruction in the Afro-American Tradition," forthcoming in *Southern Literature and Literary Theory*, ed. Jefferson Humphries (Athens: University of Georgia Press, 1987).

12. Ellison, *Territory*, 302.

13. Ellison, *Shadow*, 47.

14. Baldwin, "No Name in the Street," in *The Price of the Ticket* (New York: St. Martin's/Marek, 1985), 472–74.

15. Walker, *In Search of Our Mothers' Gardens* (New York: Harcourt Brace Jovanovich, 1983), 20.

16. Ibid., 58.

17. Although, as a white Ole Miss graduate, Karen Hinton—now teaching in the predominantly black public schools of Washington County, Mississippi—said during a question period at that symposium (21–23 November 1985), very little is being done to alter the conditions which create new Bigger Thomases.

18. I have discussed the first stage of the response, summarized below, in greater detail in "Tell Old Pharaoh: The Afro-American Response to Faulkner," *The Southern Review*, 19 (1983), 711–35.

19. See Stepto's *From Behind the Veil: A Study of Afro-American Narrative* (Urbana: University of Illinois Press, 1979).

20. Michel Fabre, "Bayonne or the Yoknapatawpha of Ernest Gaines," *Callaloo*, 1 (1978), 110–24.

21. Gaines, *A Gathering of Old Men* (New York: Alfred A. Knopf, 1983), 174. All quotations refer to this edition and will be noted parenthetically in the text.

22. For a more complete list of Faulknerian motifs in *A Gathering of Old Men* see my essay-review in *Magill's Literary Annual 1984* (Englewood Cliffs, N.J.: Salem Press, 1984), 323–29.

23. Ellison, *Territory*, 185–86.

24. Faulkner, *Absalom, Absalom!* (New York: Random House, 1936), 232. All quotations refer to this edition and will be noted parenthetically in the text.

25. See James A. Snead's essay elsewhere in this volume.

26. W. J. Cash, *The Mind of the South* (New York: Alfred A. Knopf, 1941).

27. See Walter Taylor's essay elsewhere in this volume.

28. Forrest, *There Is a Tree More Ancient Than Eden* (New York: Random House, 1973), 54. All quotations refer to this edition and are noted parenthetically in the text.

29. Williams, *Dessa Rose* (New York: William Morrow, 1986), 232.

30. See Bradley's lengthy discussion of the literary world's response to black women writers in *The New York Times Magazine*, which added substantially to the unfortunate and misdirected controversy pitting black male and black female novelists against one another in the wake of *The Color Purple*. Recently, Bradley has adopted a more moderate tone in his public statements. Shortly after I delivered this paper, his very favorable review of Williams's *Dessa Rose* was published in *The New York Times Book Review*.

31. Gaines, *The Autobiography of Miss Jane Pittman* (New York: Bantam, 1971), 194–95.

Faulkner's Negroes Twain

BLYDEN JACKSON

It is anything but an environmental fallacy to attribute to Faulkner, in his conception of the South and its inhabitants, a decided impact from the Mississippi of his youth. He was born, as all serious Faulknerians know, in 1897. The War Between the States, to use a now no longer widely vaunted phrase, was then still very much alive, even unto the presence in the flesh of Confederate veterans who had yet to join, within a warriors' Valhalla, their already vanished comrades-in-arms. There was then, also, a version of the Old South, as fine a civilization (according to its entranced proponents) as ever was, which it was a point of honor for white Mississippians to cherish and to maintain. And there was, above all, a white man's concordat, both of action and of thought, regarding Negroes that it was virtually worth a white Mississippian's life not to embrace with all his mind and heart.

For the significance of this Mississippi to Faulkner the careful analyst can begin with Faulkner's sense of his own genealogy. Faulkner's ancestors, Faulkner was taught, through lines of descent both paternal and maternal, had come from the Scottish highlands, whence Popishly inclined friends and neighbors of theirs had risen to join, in the 1740s, the ill-starred last of the Stuart Pretenders to fight on British soil. Faulkner's great-grandfather, author of the commercially successful novel *The White Rose of Memphis*, and the true scion of the Mississippi Faulkners, had commanded a Southern regiment at Bull Run and, some years later, been no less determined, and hardly less violent, in his opposition to Negro suffrage than, in 1861, he had been to the invasion of Virginia by Northern troops. The American history Faulkner learned, very much as if from Sinai, in the public schools of Oxford accommodated itself to interpretations of the American past of which an Ulrich B. Phillips, for example, was a resolute and an accomplished spokesman. One of Faulkner's grandmothers was, for a term, president of the Oxford chapter of the United Daughters of the Confederacy, and it was in an Oxford elementary-school classroom that Faulkner first heard the eulogistic poem "Pickett's Charge," although some Oxonians would swear upon their mothers' graves that the University Greys, composed exclusively of Ole Miss students, had struggled forty-seven yards farther north than any other of Marse Robert's men. Outside Oxford's academic precincts lessons in citizenship included an occasional lynching of a Negro, always (of course) by a person, or persons, unknown, despite the fact that no dearth existed among white Oxonians, or the lynchers themselves, of those who could refer reverently to their sacred Anglo-Saxon heritage of respect for law.

In Faulkner's youth there were members of his family who supported James Kimble Vardaman, white supremacist unrivalled in the venom of his denunciation of Negroes, and Vardaman's successor, the noxious Theodore Bilbo. A classic Negro mammy helped to raise Faulkner and his brothers. Of Faulkner's early environment racially only one conclusion is possible. It was designed to present Negroes in a most unfavorable light. According to it, every Negro in Faulkner's fiction should have been, if not an incorrigibly childlike creature unable to cope with sophisticated white culture, then, a monster, an opprobrious and lecherous Caliban, too degraded to be civilized, yet with brutal instincts of such strength as to constitute him a danger to the social order of America and a stench in the nostrils of every right-thinking human being.

But the Negroes in Faulkner's fiction cannot be so summarily categorized and dismissed. There are, incidentally, many of them. Faulkner is no Ellen Glasgow or James Branch Cabell. The South without Negroes is no South at all to him. Nevertheless, the Negroes in Faulkner's fiction undergo a change. They do not begin as much of anything. To *Soldiers' Pay* and *Mosquitoes*, Faulkner's first two published novels, they contribute nothing that either story could not do without. The action of *Soldiers' Pay*, set mostly in Georgia in the era of World War I, like the action of *Mosquitoes*, which moves from New Orleans to the northern shore of Lake Pontchartrain and back to New Orleans, owes not one whit of either its impetus or its direction to a single word or deed originated by a Negro. Moreover, the Negroes who do occur in *Soldiers' Pay* and *Mosquitoes*, especially in relation to their number in later Faulkner fiction, are scarce. They are scarce, too, in comparison with their genuine profusion in Georgia and Louisiana during the historic periods represented by Faulkner either in *Soldiers' Pay* or *Mosquitoes*— periods which, it might be added, almost coincide. Indeed, both before and after 1920, a date within less than ten years of the simulated week, and more, of action in both novels, three out of every seven Georgians and seven out of every seventeen Louisianians were black. No corresponding fraction of the words even remotely in either novel is devoted to blackness or black people. So, in both novels Negroes are only faintly background figures. Their visibility, in both novels, barely escapes the nebulousness of shadows. And of them something else important may be said. They seem not so much Faulkner's Negroes, creatures representative of his independent thought, as hasty expedients jerry-built out of borrowings from people other than Faulkner. To a great extent, moreover, they seem to be stereotypes and rather racist stereotypes at that. The influence of Sherwood Anderson's Negroes probably may be detected in the Negroes of *Soldiers' Pay*, especially in references there by Faulkner to Negro laughter. But in the main the Negroes of *Mosquitoes* and *Soldiers' Pay* conform to a long-standing determination by American majority opinion, in the days of the composition of *Mosquitoes* and *Soldiers' Pay*, of what Negroes ought to be. They are the Negroes of countless writers of minstrel shows as well as of literary artists like Thomas Nelson Page.

Finally, here, a catalytic effect deriving from the very anatomy of Faulkner's art and his normal discipline of his supposedly creative energies during his early maturity conceivably aided and abetted the imitativeness of his Negro characters in his early fiction.

For Faulkner proceeded into what might well be called his own kingdom in the medium of artistic expression he sought to make his own as do most, if not all, artists who eventually, in their careers, establish a distinctive dwelling peculiar to themselves in the elevated eyries of high artistic achievement. The apprentice artist in every art tends universally to ape his predecessors. Even Shakespeare is not the same artist in *Twelfth Night* that he was in *The Comedy of Errors* or in his later tragedies that he was in *Titus Andronicus* and *Romeo and Juliet*. Faulkner started out to be a poet, a poet steeped in the styles of many other poets before him. He published a book of poetry, *The Marble Faun*, before he published any novel. *The Marble Faun* wears its coat of many colors, its garment contrived from a multiplicity of wardrobes in authorial tastes, as do *Soldiers' Pay* and *Mosquitoes*. But by the time in his own odyssey as an artist when he addressed himself to *Flags in the Dust*, with its ultimate translation into *Sartoris*, Faulkner had embarked upon a journey that carried him, as a writer of fiction, across a great divide. He had envisioned Yoknapatawpha and dedicated himself to making it, in the only sense that mattered, the imaginative sense, a dream come true. This was his great divide and his negotiation of it meant for him no less than the Americanization of many of the immigrants who passed through Ellis Island between 1870 and the killing at Sarajevo meant to those former Europeans. With Yoknapatawpha he ceased to worry overmuch about other men's literary domains. Now he had his own rich and private literary empire on which to lavish all the powers of the literary art he could summon to do his bidding and to gratify his instinct for truth. He did base Yoknapatawpha on a very tangible figment of reality, the bit of actual earth, with the animate and inanimate objects upon it, and whatever he said it had experienced before he was himself a part of it, which he could follow Sherwood Anderson's lead in designating as his "little postage stamp of native soil." But he refused to admit into Yoknapatawpha the kind of subservience to other artists as may be found in *The Marble Faun* and *Soldiers' Pay,* as well as in *Mosquitoes.* Yoknapatawpha was his, and everything that was in it, including its Negroes. Accordingly, in Faulkner there are two fictive Negroes, the Negro before Yoknapatawpha and the Negro as he developed, a reliable transcript and model of Faulkner's sincerest inner impressions and convictions, after Yoknapatawpha preempted Faulkner's art.

Yoknapatawpha does have its ample quota of Negroes. They are not all identical. They differ in color, size, age, disposition, mental ability, and moral character. In so doing they resemble the whites of Yoknapatawpha and they suggest that, like the whites with whom they mingle, they are, at least, not stereotypes. Some of them are obviously meant to be, and to be perceived, as superior human beings. What, for instance, as has often been remarked, would the Compsons of *The Sound and the Fury* be without Dilsey Gibson? Yet none of them is a member of that most beleaguered and maligned (by both blacks and whites) class in all America, the black bourgeoisie—which, incidentally, was not void, in Faulkner's time, of black Mississippians. Justice to Faulkner at this point, however, certainly requires an admission that, when Faulkner did, rarely, encounter directly members of the black bourgeoisie he seemed to take them easily in stride. He treated them, that is to say, no better and no worse than whites of comparable social status with whom he was not personally intimate. Drunk or sober, moreover, Faulkner did not always curb his propensity to comment with an acid tongue upon the foibles of human kind. Nor was he, for all of his compatibility and involvement with the small-town world of Oxford, a yokel. He lived in New England, New York, Montreal, New Orleans, Paris, and Virginia. He visited as far afield as Japan and Scandinavia. He called himself a sixth-grade scholar, yet read voraciously, intently and extensively, and not always in nursery rhymes. Cosmopolis was not alien to him. Strangers, apparently, did not bother him. But Yoknapatawpha clearly to him was not the place where he chose to exercise his art upon that about which he could believe he should, at his best, be only tentative. He adhered in Yoknapatawpha to his own Negroes, his own whites, his own South, and to all of those almost solely only according to his own assessment of their relation to his own America and to his own sense of the whole of human kind. Thus, he derived, for Yoknapatawpha, a Negro who was not an ideogram but a multifaceted human individual, living and acting, in his consistencies and inconsistencies, much as actual people do, somehow, really live and act. Not every Negro in Yoknapatawpha, therefore, is an ideal citizen, even though Faulkner did seem to like to say (and not too sardonically) that Negroes were better than whites. Some Yoknapatawpha Negroes, like some Yoknapatawpha whites, inspire, as a reaction to their personalities, in judicious observers, more loathing than love. Others, like some other Yoknapatawpha whites, possess a greater share of virtue in themselves than of vice. But none of Yoknapatawpha's Negroes, especially after *Sartoris*, are non-Faulknerian. The history of the Negro in Faulkner's fiction is the history of an import superseded by a product native to the self-generated judgments of its creator.

In freeing himself from the dominance of other authors and from a total subjection to the attitudes toward Negroes expected of him, Faulkner found himself engaged in, among several enterprises, the construction of a parable about man's inhumanity to man. In its fullest detail this parable involved Indians as well as Negroes and whites. Meditations by Faulkner about the Southern past affected it deeply, as did his concept, famous to Faulknerians, of the big woods. Faulkner was, of course, of more than one mind about the Southern past. He did not ignore the good in it. But he brooded most, perhaps, upon the elements in it, none more obviously operative than slavery, which had, as he perceived it, left the South accursed. His romanticism asserted itself in his concept of the big woods, although it must always be remembered of Faulkner, who was, at times, almost Hobbesian in his strictures on the damned human race, how antiromantic he could be. Even so, he had hunted in a surviving forest near Oxford with male elders of his under conditions which enhanced for him his abhorrence of a plutocratic, vulgarized, xenophobic, insensitively urbanized America. How much better than all of America's grosser indulgences seemed to him a simple life respectful of nature and of all nature's creatures, including man, his concept of the big woods articulated superbly and allegorically, as well as factually, for him. It is, then, in no vacuum exempt from contact with philosophic musings of great import to him, that his Yoknapatawphan Negroes hold their sway. Rather, it is their connection with their creator's thought about the region of his birth and his at least partially symbolic big woods that confer upon them the final proof of their authenticity as indications of what Faulkner, in the deepest recesses of his being, really was. There he was a humanist in the finest meaning of this fine term. It was as a humanist that he added what may well be the most significant dimension to his Yoknapatawphan Negroes.

For Faulkner took seriously his role as artist. He did believe that he should, if he could, instruct as well as delight. Therefore, he felt himself obligated not only to picture Negroes as he believed they actually were, but also to speak honestly and constructively of how they became that which, as he saw it, until "things" changed, would be forever their inevitable state. Whatever their African background, about which he never pretended to be an authority, it seemed to him their condition in America resulted crucially from their American experience, an experience in which they were much more the victims than the victimizers. He could not, like Vardaman, for instance, consider them hopeless degenerates. He anguished over the effect upon them of over two hundred years of bondage. Not too incidentally, he also anguished over what that same two hundred years had done to whites. His problem with America's whites and blacks— neither of whom, he once wryly remarked, liked each other— was more their present and their future than their common past.

Slavery was over. Yet whites and Negroes in America continued to live in two separate hostile worlds of which the black world was by far the most disadvantaged. Freedom for American Negroes had done little, if anything, to improve their status among their fellow Americans. If slavery had not been the institution that accounted most for the ostracism of Negroes from American democracy, what institution had, and still did? Faulkner's search for an answer to that, unmistakably, for him, urgent conundrum and the result of his search provide, it may well be, the most insightful and, as it were, greatest moral triumph of all of his improvements over an earlier Faulkner Negro in the Negro of his Yoknapatawphan fiction. It also well may be that nowhere in his Yoknapatawphan fiction does his search, with its result, appear more clearly, and more trenchantly, than in "The Bear" and "Delta Autumn" of his *Go Down, Moses.*

Traditionally "The Bear" has been categorized as a short story, which certainly does not necessarily constitute an error in describing it. But "The Bear" is a very long short story. There must be, somewhere, works of prose fiction called novels not so long as it is. Moreover, "The Bear" possesses some of the qualities of a novel that it is very difficult, if not impossible, for the short-story form to permit. Most particularly does "The Bear" deal with its characters and its theme and subthemes at such a level of cumulative, complex explication as a narrative less capacious than it could hardly attain. "The Bear" is structured simply, but effectively, like a three-act play. Act 1 is the big woods act. In act 2 Ike McCaslin, whose consciousness above all other agents unites "The Bear," finds a matter of great interest in the ledgers kept jointly as a record of their business transactions and some of whatever else enters their minds by his father and his father's twin. Act 3 in the present context may safely be ignored.

Ike McCaslin is, as it happens, in the somewhat startling genealogy of the Yoknapatawphan McCaslins, the grandson of the Lucius Quintus Carothers McCaslin, born in 1772 and dying in 1837, to whom the McCaslins owe their eminence in Yoknapatawphan affairs. In the Yoknapatawphan saga Lucius migrates to Mississippi and becomes a plantation magnate. He marries a white wife by whom he has three children, a daughter who marries an Edmonds, and two sons, Theophilus, or Uncle Buck, Ike McCaslin's sire at a late age, and Theophilus' brother, Amodeus, or Uncle Buddy. It is important to note here of Lucius that he was a man of strong appetites and a tyrannical will, a freebooter well-suited to enjoy his affluence, his accretions of arbitrary power, and all the other perquisites he could acquire in a frontier society such as the Mississippi of his life and times. It is, also, perhaps equally important to note that neither of his sons was like him. Both were men of great compassion and, indeed, of something additional to their compassion possibly well designated as tenderness. If anything, Ike is more compassionate and more tender than either his father or his uncle and certainly more given, apparently, than either of these two, to the pursuit of epistemological profundities. Without being a mollycoddle, moreover, he is possessed by a certain saintliness, a purity of character that will not let him, whatever the cost, abandon righteousness once he thinks he knows what righteousness is. He is a seeker, therefore, who can be trusted with the outcome of what he seeks, and it is principally because of him and this seeker's propensity of his that acts 1 and 2 of "The Bear" function as coherently, and as magnificently, as they do.

Act 1 recounts the eventual confrontation with, and killing of, the legendary bear after whom the story takes its title. This portion of the story presents Faulkner at his best. He has a boy, young Ike, to induct into manhood. He has the big woods to describe and to fit into the homily about good and evil in which the big woods serve him much as Keats's great odes of 1819 served Keats. It is for Ike here to learn from the big woods, to accept their message and, in a sense, to follow that message as Sir Galahad followed the Holy Grail. The human tutor of most significance in act 1 of "The Bear" is no white man, but the part-Indian, part-Negro Sam Fathers, and in act 1 of "The Bear" its titular bear and Sam Fathers essentially accompany each other into the oblivion of death at a most propitious time for their contributions to Ike's education to remain with him forever. A hunt, then, dominates "The Bear's" act 1. But the motif of a hunt, changed though it is in form, persists into "The Bear's" act 2. In this act an Ike still young traces through the ledgers hitherto cited here the story, which he must partially ferret out, of his grandfather's dalliance with a young black slave girl his grandfather owns named Eunice. Eunice has a daughter, Tomasina, by Ike's grandfather. Then, some twenty-two years later Eunice discovers that Ike's grandfather has impregnated Tomasina, whereupon Eunice, horrified beyond all measure, commits suicide by drowning. So, Tomasina bears a child, a daughter, by her own father, who continues to live, nevertheless, apparently as blithely as ever throughout his days, until his peaceful death, a man well past his prime, five years after Eunice has taken her own life.

Ike has already lived longer than his grandfather when the action of "Delta Autumn" begins. All of his life, since his initiation into the big woods at the age of ten, he has gone hunting with comrades in the month of November. In "Delta Autumn" again he joins fellows of his in his oft-repeated annual delight of another November hunt. The associates of his in this hunt now have changed mightily from much of what once they were. So has the scene of the hunt. It has moved far south of the big woods into the Mississippi Delta. But still, here, a moment comes when the tragic, sorrowful past intrudes upon Ike and his annual delight. Ike no longer goes every morning into the open with the other hunters, one of whom is a younger kinsman of his, Carothers Edmonds, known as "Roth," the great-great-grandson of Ike's father's sister. So, Ike is alone in his hunter's bivouac, not out in the great outdoors on the trail of game, when the incident occurs which takes him back to other incidents long gone and, specifically, to the ledgers in "The Bear." This incident is precipitated by the great-great-granddaughter of Tomasina, who braves a visit to the hunters' quarters seeking "Roth," since "Roth" has fathered a child by her, his blood relative and Ike's.

The specter of old Lucius Quintus Carothers McCaslin has, in effect, risen from its ashes to confront Ike and his saintly vision of the world as it should be. Moreover, Ike receives from Tomasina's great-great-granddaughter a projection of possibilities that hardly, Ike is all too ready to believe, were ever asserted by either of her ancestors whom Lucius Quintus had bedded. This woman claims to be in love with "Roth" and wants to marry "Roth," inspiring thus in the unspoken thought of even the saintly Ike the almost automatic reaction, "Maybe in a thousand or two thousand years in America. . . . But not now! Not now!"

In combination "The Bear" and "Delta Autumn" deliver the most meaningful statement ever made by Faulkner in his fiction about the Negro in America. He at least refused in either of these stories to stoop to the indignity of the subterfuges about race employed in a *So Red the Rose* or a *Gone with the Wind* and, so, to pretend that blacks in America differ from whites because of a divine decree or a biological fault. He recognized, and would not hide what he recognized, why the end of slavery had signified so little to Negroes, why Lucius Quintus McCaslin could, with impunity, father a child by his own daughter and why Lucius's descendant, "Roth," could repeat, so many years later, the same enormous crime, with the same impunity, upon another of Lucius's descendants. It was because of color caste, the central commandment of which was, and is, a ban on marriage between whites and blacks. Discrimination against America's Negroes and its concomitant of black segregation have been commandments, too, of color caste, as have been other sanctions, such as a prescribed etiquette of social behavior between America's whites and America's blacks, the false premises and deliberately erroneous assumptions about Negroes so brilliantly and tersely outlined by Melville Herskovits in his *Myth of the Negro Past*, the sometimes cunning and always devilish legal and extralegal harassments of Negroes simply because of their race, many intimidations of Negroes that exceed mere harassment, and even terrorism against Negroes, of which race riots and lynchings are only the most conspicuous of a multitude of sickening examples. Whatever Negroes were when they were brought to America, Faulkner would not have them judged without a due admission of the external circumstances that have surrounded and degraded them in a land where they have been, except for a brief period of indecision at the beginning of their American experience, always an oppressed minority. Nor would Faulkner, in "The Bear" and "Delta Autumn," blink his eyes either at the utter nastiness of color caste itself or at the casuistries resulting from it in the work of artists who supported it. By color caste America has hoped for generations to have its cake and eat it too, actually to try to temporize with its own iniquity and to proclaim itself as the haven for all humanity which it never yet has been. In Yoknapatawpha Faulkner did try increasingly, it would seem, to play well the roles of both artist and enlightened critic of man's struggles not merely to endure, but to prevail. To the best of his abilities, in spite of the weather of his youth and the closed society around him of his prime, he did try, that is, in Yoknapatawpha to speak the truth, the whole truth, and nothing but the truth. He died in the early 1960s. He was right about color caste then. He may not, thankfully, because of something very decent elementally in the souls of many Americans, black and white—and other colors, too—have been right in regard to Ike McCaslin's thousand or two thousand years. He had seen an autumn in the Delta. He failed to foresee there the imminence of spring.

From Jazz Syncopation to Blues Elegy: Faulkner's Development of Black Characterization

Thadious M. Davis

Listening to W. C. Handy's 1916 blues song "Ole Miss," re-corded by jazz pianist James P. Johnson in 1922, I am reminded of the way in which blues and jazz intermingled in the music of that period. Southern-born Handy, called "the father of the blues," and Northern-born Johnson, father of the hot piano, did not single-handedly invent the music that they composed and performed; instead, for creative inspiration, each drew upon traditional black music, secular and sacred, during a time when, following Scott Joplin's successful ragtime compositions at the turn of the century, black American musicians laid claim to all the possibilities of their multicultured heritage. I am reminded, too, that "Ole Miss" is Handy's tribute to the University of Mississippi where, as a Memphis bandleader and cornetist, he frequently played for campus dances and balls.

One of the Oxford youngsters attending those dances was William Faulkner. In describing Faulkner's social activities dur-ing the fall of 1915, Joseph Blotner points to dances in the ballroom of Gordon Hall: "There were no tangos yet; instead there were fox trots and one-steps of the day interspersed among the jazz numbers. A year before [1914], Handy had composed a popular piece . . . called 'The St. Louis Blues.' Late in the evening he might launch into its melancholy, syncopated strains or those of another one he had called 'The Memphis Blues.'"[1] There were also dances given by Sallie Murry at The Big Place, where Chess Carothers would "pump the player piano" for the dancers on the porch, and there were other dance parties at Myrtle Ramey's house, or Estelle and Dorothy Oldham's, where Lucius Pegues's three-piece band would sometimes play.[2] Faulkner and his hometown friends were already enjoying the kind of social dancing that would become a national phenomenon a few years later when jazz rhythms would inspire the Shimmy, Charleston, and Black Bottom, all dances invented by blacks but popularized by whites such as Irene and Vernon Castle whose arranger was the black musician Fletcher Henderson.

As a budding writer in the decades during and after World War I, William Faulkner of Oxford was not isolated from the changes in popular tastes or from the spread of the "new music." Like others of his generation, he witnessed the rapid dissemination of hit tunes that, thanks to Thomas Edison's phonograph, Emile Berliner's disc records, and the radio receiver, could arrive in small Southern towns almost as quickly as they appeared in major cities. Radio and records combined with sheet music from Tin Pan Alley and small bands or orchestras to send popular music into every part of the country and into every segment of the population. It was, Philip Eberly observes, "the first time in our history that we developed a national consciousness about a popular music."[3]

It was also a period of reverse acculturation, in which aspects of the minority culture moved into the dominant one with an accumulative effect of transforming the majority. Specifically, the new music, rooted in the ragtime of black pianists and in the blues of black folk derivation, progressed into American culture by means of direct contact with black musicians and indirect contact with black music adapted by white composers and musicians. It positioned blacks as referential structures for whites, so that within the dominant cultural constructs blacks became more visible as operatives, even if limited, as opposed to their being seen primarily as respondents. Though it was associated with whites as much as with blacks by the mid-1920s, the new music remained in the public arena very much a product of blacks, and as such it fostered a fusion of black and white cultural references. Cultural diffusion, then, was not simply a one-way street with blacks as the beneficiaries, despite the fact that their increased opportunity and mobility also revitalized black culture.[4] That revitalization may be witnessed perhaps most vividly in the New Negro or Harlem Renaissance. The emergent, racially derived music marked a cultural formation that gave expression to new practices, values, and ideologies. As Neil Leonard concludes:

> Jazz fulfilled various esthetic needs for those who rejected traditional values. For the jazz men and their close followers it provided a voice of rebellion and a source of positive morality. For its less ardent young supporters, jazz furnished accompaniment to their growing pains and adolescent enthusiasms. Intellectuals found it an exciting new form of art. And in one way or another it titillated the sensibilities of well-to-do members of slumming parties. However differently people responded to jazz, it provided all of them with emotional symbols for the relative values that were replacing the standards of traditional idealism.[5]

The infusion of the new music into white American culture helped in part to bring about changes in artistic images of blacks, at the very least to help drag some ingrained, negative images of inarticulate servers and bearers out of the nineteenth century, and to encourage a marketplace for art produced by blacks themselves. Unfortunately, though servitude was no longer the only viable image of blacks, new sets of conventions for portraying blacks emerged, especially that of their music as an unstudied, instinctive art form conveying primitive passions. Racial stereotyping with a few new twists remained, and it affected conceptions of the music. "Traditionalist concepts of race bore strongly on the opposition to jazz"; however, proponents were not immune to racist beliefs.[6] Even while influencing European and American orchestrations, harmonic lines, rhythms, and forms, jazz "developed a reputation for being loud, bawdy, untamed and low-class," simply because it emanated from blacks.[7] And blues was largely rejected by respectable people, black as well as white, not only because of its early acceptance by the world of brothels and saloons, but also because of its association with lower-class, rural origins.

Despite the fact that acute racial prejudice did not deter cultural borrowing,[8] the movement of jazz and blues into the larger society did not alleviate cultural chauvinism or racism. Private and public statements by emergent young writers who placed themselves in the artistic vanguard, such as Faulkner himself or F. Scott Fitzgerald, indicate as much. Fitzgerald, who reputedly gave the Jazz Age its name and whose works evidence clear signs of the cultural flow between blacks and whites (see especially his use of jazz, saxophones, and Handy's "Beale Street Blues" in *The Great Gatsby*), would write to Edmund Wilson in 1921: "The negroid streak creeps northward to defile the Nordic race. . . . My reactions [to Europe] were all philistine, antisocialistic, provincial, and racially snobbish. I believe at last in the white man's burden. We [Americans] are as far above the modern Frenchman as he is above the Negro."[9] Such statements notwithstanding and despite the new music's inability to democratize ethnocentricism, neutralize racism, or otherwise perform miracles in American society, the expansion of black music up from the supposedly "lower rungs" of race and class hierarchies did begin an exchange of norms and beliefs that at least contributed to modifying and blurring the rigid lines or stratifications between the majority and minority cultures. And if nothing else, the presumed cultural inadequacy of blacks in America had to be questioned—even if only on a subliminal, rather than conscious, level.

The dominant sound of the new music, generally referred to as "jazz" by the mid-1920s, emerged from Faulkner's own region, the American South, and from Southern blacks, whose unique contribution to the national music had already included spirituals before Emancipation and ragtime at the turn of the century. After 1917 commercial blues had thoroughly saturated the popular music that Faulkner and his Mississippi cohorts listened and danced to. In the late teens and early twenties, instrumental jazz incorporated diverse musical elements from black culture, especially the declining ragtime and the ascending blues form, to become the most prominent music not just in the South, but on the American scene. Its mass dissemination was observed on numerous fronts, such as that of folk music collectors Howard Odum and Guy Johnson who, in 1926, remarked what they termed a "disappearing process" of the black folk songs they had heard twenty years before, a process they attributed directly to "the multitude of blues, jazz songs, and others being distributed throughout the land in millions of phonographic records."[10] By examining 1,320 titles from the catalogs of three leading record companies, Odum and Johnson concluded that over forty per cent of the secular songs had the word "blues" in the titles, but that "upwards of seventy-five per cent" of all the popular songs listed could be classified as blues simply because "the term is now freely applied to instrumental pieces, especially to dance music of the jazz type, and to every vocal piece which, by any stretch of the imagination, can be thought of as having a bluish cast."[11]

Faulkner and his university community were in an especially fortuitous position: within W. C. Handy's range for travel with his Memphis-based band. From 1905 when Handy arrived in Memphis to take over the Knights of Pythias Band until 1919 when he moved permanently to New York to set up his music shop in Tin Pan Alley, Handy was one of the leading band directors, musicians, and composers living in the South. He was the first to write, though not the first to publish, a blues composition—the 1909 "Mr. Crump," a mayoral campaign song for E. H. Crump, published in 1912 as "Memphis Blues" (Artie Matthews's "Seals Blues," August 1912, and Hart Wand's "Dallas Blues," September 1912, preceded it in print). And Handy was the first to popularize the blues with songs such as "Yellow Dog Blues" (1914, originally entitled "Yellow Dog Rag") and "St. Louis Blues" (1914), the classic song that made him the undisputed master of blues compositions, just as Scott Joplin's "Maple Leaf Rag" had made him the master of ragtime. The

Handy Band was actually a chain of bands involving up to sixty-seven musicians sent out to various parts of Memphis and the surrounding states; their repertoire included seventeen different kinds of music (from minstrel shows, circuses, concert companies, vaudeville, and so on).[12] They performed not only for dances and parties at clubs, schools, or homes, but also for picnics, rallies, and meetings. Their most innovative performances were instrumental serenades outside the homes of the sweethearts of young white men who hired them; the serenading was something Handy had begun in his native Florence, Alabama, where he sang as a tenor in a quartet known for its serenades.

Whatever the Handy Band played, however, was marked not only by syncopation, antiphony, and polyrhythms, but also by the use of "blue notes" (slurred thirds or sometimes sevenths) and of "breaks" (filled-in pauses). The syncopation followed the lead of ragtime in which the left hand beat out a percussive rhythm while the right hand played a syncopated melody, and which was made popular after 1896 in works such as William Krell's four-part *Mississippi Rag* (1897, "Cake Walk," "Plantation Song," "Trio," and "Buck-and-Wing Dance") and Joplin's *Original Rags* (1899).[13] But Handy's blue note and break were new to written composition; they helped to lay the groundwork for the commercial blues and jazz fusion in the 1920s.

Faulkner may well have had Handy's band in mind as a model when he drew a sketch of a seven-piece black jazz band for the 1921 annual *Ole Miss*. (Only six musicians are visible; the piano player is hidden behind a dancing white couple.) Although the drawing depicts the musicians, as Erskine Peters points out in *William Faulkner: The Yoknapatawpha World and Black Being*, in a "minstrelsy-like hilarity of . . . gestures and facial contortions,"[14] it is an early indication of an associative link between blacks and the new music in his art. The association was at that time so widely recognized that by 1925 James Weldon Johnson in his preface to *The Book of American Negro Spirituals* had to resist "discussing the origin of Negro secular music and its development until it was finally taken over and made 'American popular music.'"[15]

During Faulkner's literary apprenticeship in the 1920s, he absorbed many influences from literature and life, as H. Edward Richardson, Max Putzel, Judith Sensibar, and others have shown. His movement from Mississippi to New York, New Orleans, Paris, and back to Oxford was not without stopovers in the Memphis Tenderloin which, like the New Orleans fabled Storyville and French Quarter where he listened to jazz clarinetist George "Georgia Boy" Boyd,[16] was an area where barrel house music, alongside rags, jazz, and blues, could be heard either in phonographic or live versions. In New York there were not only the prolific song writers of Tin Pan Alley (Irving Berlin, Jerome Kearn, George Gershwin, and lesser known songsters) turning out white versions of black music, but there were also musicians, such as Vincent Lopez, Ted Lewis, and Fred Waring, performing in clubs, cabarets, stage shows, concert halls, and for radio. And there was Axel Christensen's "system" of teaching rag and jazz, a system which graduated a total of 350,000 mainly white students between 1903 and 1930.[17] All cashed in on the popularity of blues and jazz in the aftermath of two successful black syncopated bands: Jim Europe's 369th Army band and postwar orchestra of sixty-five musicians, who played at the New York Opera House and toured the United States and France in 1919; and Will Marion Cook's New York Syncopated Orchestra of forty-one pieces and nine singers, which in 1919 performed both in the United States and, as the American Syncopated Band, in Paris and London, where part of the orchestra with Sidney Bechet on clarinet played a command performance at Buckingham Palace.[18] Europe's and Cook's successes resulted in more white musicians adapting and stylizing black music; perhaps the most famous of them was Paul Whiteman, who was billed somewhat presumptuously as "the king of jazz." He fronted a twenty-eight piece dance orchestra that, at different times, featured Bix Beiderbeck, Red Nichols, Jimmy and Tommy Dorsey, and that imitated black models. His 1922 hit "It's Three O'Clock in the

Morning" made its way into Fitzgerald's *Great Gatsby* (1925).
However, his greatest fame stemmed from his 12 February 1924
"All American Symphonic Jazz" concert at New York's Aeolian
Hall; the program premiered George Gershwin's "Rhaposody in
Blue," which Whiteman had commissioned.[19] Faulkner claims
to have worn out three recordings of "Rhapsody in Blue" while
writing *Sanctuary* (1931), because he used the music to help "set
the rhythm and jazzy tone."[20]

Before the composition of *Sanctuary*, Faulkner had already
admitted to having a few favorites among the new songs: "Yes,
Sir, That's My Baby," "I Can't Give You Anything But Love,
Baby," "Ain't She Sweet," and "My Blue Heaven."[21] And he had
already begun to use titles or lines from distinctly black songs in
his fiction: "Frankie and Johnny" (*The Double Dealer*, January
1925) with its title from one of the more famous blues-ballads;
"The Longshoreman" (*The Double Dealer*, January 1925) with its
phrases from black work songs, from the spiritual "Swing Low,
Sweet Chariot," and from the gospel "All God's Chillen Got
Wings"; "Damon and Pythias Unlimited" (*The Times-Picayune*,
15 February 1925) with its title echoing the name of Handy's first
Memphis band; "Father Abraham," an unfinished work with its
title from a spiritual of the same name; "That Evening Sun"
(1930, earlier entitled "That Evening Sun Go Down" and "Never
Done No Weeping When You Wanted to Laugh") with its title
taken from the opening line of Handy's "St. Louis Blues." He
had, as well, tentatively explored music as referential theme
affecting characterization ("The Longshoreman," which mixes
black secular and sacred songs in a rhythmic sung monologue,
and "The Rosary," *The Times-Picayune*, 3 May 1925, which ends
with the "excruciating, succulent bray of a saxophone blown by a
rank amateur").[22] This early use is largely a typographical assimilation of popular forms which had an expressive base in black
music.

In Faulkner's first novel, *Soldiers' Pay* (1926), two different
styles of black characterization stem directly from the new music. Both are paradigmatic constructions reflecting Faulkner's

mediation between art forms and life forms; both have, as a main
constitutive element, modern black music. In one, dominated
by a sophisticated, modern jazz band, not unlike Handy's, black
figures are emblematic of postwar changes and disruptions in
manners, morals, and conventions. Faulkner's governing impulse in this style of black characterization is modernistic. An
animated band plays for a white dance in the post–World War I
South, and its stylized position in the piece depends upon an
understood racial differentiation. In a sense, there is an implicit
syncopation in which the two races, black musicians and white
dancers, play off each other in a dialogical scheme in which
music, rather than words, forms the basis for discourse:

> Along the balustrade of the veranda red eyes of cigarettes glowed; a
> girl stooping ostrich-like drew up her stocking and light from a
> window found her young shapeless leg. The negro cornetist, having
> learned in his thirty years a century of the white man's lust, blinked
> his dispassionate eye, leading his crew in fresh assault. Couples
> erupted in, clasped and danced; vague blurs locked together on the
> lawn beyond the light.
> "... Uncle Joe, Sister Kate, all shimmy like jelly on a
> plate. . . ."[23]

In terms of the musicians, Faulkner is a minimalist, constructing
them largely by inference from the imagined sound of their
music. He sketches only a few brief descriptions that lack linear
development, but in each he presents the blacks in exaggerated,
collective motion that functions within a structure of cultural
fluidity and racial interaction. "The negro cornetist unleashed
his indefatigable pack anew and the veranda broke again into
clasped couples" (210). The exchange of cultural messages is
dynamic and repetitious, yet the actual interaction between the
musicians and the dancers is limited.

The music, of course, is the common ground of rhythmic
response that shapes and orders the chapter through dislocations
in time and disruptions of action. "The negro cornetist spurred
his men to fiercer endeavor, the brass died and a plaintive minor
of hushed voices carried the rhythm until the brass, suspiring

again, took it" (204). Faulkner's description of flowing melody and steady rhythm, suggestive of a blues scale and of playing between what Handy called the "breaks," is part of his dramatization of new sexual mores throughout the dance scene. Dancers "drowned by the music . . . took the syncopation"; others "locked together . . . poised and slid and poised, feeling the beat of the music, toying with it, eluding it, seeking it again, drifting like a broken dream" (195). In spite of Scott Joplin's insistence in his 1908 *School of Ragtime: Six Exercises for Piano* that "syncopations are no indication of light or trashy music,"[24] syncopated rhythm insinuates loose sexual behavior, even to the worldly-wise character Joe Gilligan, who quips: "This is what they call polite dancing, is it? I never learned it: I would have been throwed out of any place I ever danced doing that. But I had an unfortunate youth: I never danced with nice people" (196).

Faulkner de-emphasizes the individual musicians, who remain collectively "the pack" or "the crew" outside the spatial configuration of the dance floor yet simultaneously creating it. He emphasizes the procreative, libidinal connotations of their music ("the rhythmic troubling obscenities of saxophones" [195]) and by implication links blacks in general to an overt sexuality heard in the music. He stresses as well the sexual connotations in the motion of the white dancers: "The dancers moved, locked two and two" (197); "The couple slid and poised, losing the syncopation deliberately, seeking it and finding it, losing it again" (197). While dancing, one girl, the flapper Cecily Saunders, is "conscious of physical freedom, of her young, uncorseted body . . . pleasuring in freedom and motion, as though freedom and motion were water, pleasuring her flesh to the intermittent teasing of silk" (199). Freedom, motion, and their relation to popular images of sexual attraction are her concerns, the same concerns that generally accompanied contemporary views of jazz as freeing whites of repressions. This same girl wonders whether her partner is comparing her to Ella Wilcox or Irene Castle, popular dancers of that time (200), and she is subsequently shown "striking her body sharply against [a dance partner], taking the broken suggestion of saxophones" (209).

The white dancers perform in the foreground of a jazz scene replete with "light, motion, sound: no solidity. A turgid compulsion, passionate and evanescent" (200). The blacks are rhythmic echoes in the background; their music "a troubling rumor," their interspersed lyrics a suggestive undertone: "throw it on the wall. Oh, oh, oh, oh . . ."; "shake it and break it, shake it . . ."; "I wonder where my easy, easy rider's . . ." (200). Even though the refrain, "I wonder where my easy rider's gone," is from Handy's "Yellow Dog Blues," little of the private, personal vocality of blues infiltrates the dance sequence, which is rendered here as a jazzy, public, and collective form of moans and riffs interpolated across racial lines, but with the stresses continuously external to blacks and internal to whites.

This style of black characterization is not confined to the jazz musicians in the central chapter, though it is most visible there. Other blacks less prominently positioned in the text are similarly developed. The several undifferentiated porters in the opening chapters function as a backdrop to the rowdy, returning white veterans. Indiscriminately called "Othello," they fit into a fast-paced, modern arena of cultural exchanges and interaction. And their appearances are also occasions marked by racial differentiation based on stereotypes; one porter's description, for instance, consists entirely of one sentence: "White teeth were like a suddenly opened piano" (16). The same style applies to Loosh, the black grandson of Donald Mahon's mammy, Cal'line; he happens to be one of the returned soldiers, and is suggestively placed in a different relationship to whites than his grandmother. In addition, a black gardener mowing a lawn throughout most of the narrative is as well a development of black character based upon the syncopated rhythms of jazz music (104, 115, 155, 182, 281). At several points, he is referred to as a "languid conductor" (115, 281), and the sound of his mower provides an incessant melodic base for the rhythms of life in Charlestown, Georgia, the fictional town.

One fleeting glimpse of this style is seen in the description of black school children whose teacher, "a fattish negro in a lawn tie and an alpaca coat . . . could take a given line from any book from the telephone directory down and soon have the entire present personnel chanting it after him, like Vachel Lindsay" (116). The implication is one of rhythm devoid of sense, linked to the poet Lindsay whose poems such as "That Daniel Jazz," and "The Congo" were chanted and sung to the imagined rhythms of jazz.

In these examples, there is a projection of intimacy with blacks, but it is a projection external to the blacks themselves and propelled by the observable rhythm or motion of their activities. All of the examples suggest a primarily nameless collectivity, or a lack of individuation, and an implicitly comic portraiture, both of which, I believe, recur in varying degrees throughout Faulkner's canon in very different black characters; for example, Caspey, the young rebellious veteran in *Sartoris* (1929): "I don't take nothin' fum no white folks no mo'. . . . War done changed all dat." (65); T. P., Versh, and Luster in *The Sound and the Fury* (1929); Tomey's Turl and George Wilkins in *Go Down, Moses* (1942); Ned McCaslin in *The Reivers* (1962). (Some characters, such as Lucas Beauchamp in *Go Down, Moses*, are developed in two different styles of characterization.)

I am suggesting that instrumental jazz, as adopted and disseminated into the majority culture, becomes one basis for Faulkner's developing a style of black characterization that is a configuration of collectivity and syncopation, reverberating with meanings of group cohesiveness (particularly in relation to presumed "racial" traits), with meanings of race differentiation dependent upon encounter between blacks and whites, and with meanings of amassed motion and rhythm that, though distinctive, discourage individuation, and forward comic portraiture. This style of characterization is evidenced in what I term a structure of rhythm.

In the second style of black characterization from *Soldiers'*

Pay, dominated by a processional of singing churchgoers, black figures are rooted in a traditional folk culture that defies time while accepting mortality.

> Under the moon, quavering with the passion of spring and flesh, among whitewashed walls papered inwardly with old newspapers, something pagan using the white man's conventions as it used his clothing, hushed and powerful, not knowing its own power:
> "Sweet chariot . . . comin' fer to ca'y me home. . . ." (312–13)

The blacks, isolated in a personal experience symbolized by the sound of their singing the spiritual "Swing Low, Sweet Chariot," remain on an observable periphery of the cultural processes central to the narrative, yet are situated in an active core of their own making. Theirs is an amalgamated culture, yet it retains a basic integrity that renders it uniquely theirs. While Faulkner places some emphasis on the "pagan," and by extension "un-civilized," aspect of their voices "filled with all the old despairs of time and breath" (312), he does not forward the notion of pulsating rhythm or primitive abandon. His emphasis throughout is on an elegiac tone in the sound of the voices.

Though there is a validity in reading the processional scene as contrapuntal antidote, it functions more strictly as a self-contained private, but voiced expression. Rector Mahon and Joe Gilligan observe the processional from a distance that is simultaneously spatial and racial: "'They are holding services. Negroes,' the rector explained. . . . An occasional group of negroes passed them, bearing lighted lanterns that jetted vain little flames futilely into the moonlight. 'No one knows why they do that'" (318). Ritual and its meanings are bounded by privacy and racial hegemony. Reciprocity is not between the two races (as in the case of jazz moving into the modern white American consciousness in the twenties and in the dance scene), but among the blacks whose autonomous knowing is resolution to the frenetic pace and structures in the dominant world shaped in the text.

Specific cultural formations within the black community be-

come the focus of attention, for the spatial and temporal config-
urations of whites are no longer central. These formations may
once have been partially borrowings, but when subsumed into
the specific music, they become new forms of expression.
"Within it [the church] was a soft glow of kerosene serving only
to make the darkness and the heat thicker, making thicker the
imminence of sex after harsh labor along the mooned land; and
from it welled the crooning submerged passion of the dark race.
It was nothing, it was everything; then it swelled to an ecstasy,
taking the white man's words as readily as it took his remote God
and made a personal Father of Him" (319). Passion, unlike in the
jazz dance scene, is synonymous with emotion, not sexual excitement. The depiction of song emanating from the "submerged
passion of the dark race" suggests a racial music not unlike that
in Handy's description of blues: "In its origin, modern blues
music is the expression of the emotional life of a race."[25]

Cultural transactions are relegated to the past, though there is
a residual emotionalism that remains. The present is the vocal
music itself as a form larger than the singer, yet capable of individualizing and humanizing them:

> Feed Thy Sheep, O Jesus. The voices rose full and soft. There was
> no organ; no organ was needed as above the harmonic passion of bass
> and baritone soared a clear soprano of women's voices like a flight of
> gold and heavenly birds. . . . The shabby church became beautiful
> with mellow longing, passionate and sad. Then the singing died,
> fading away along the mooned land inevitable with to-morrow and
> sweat, with sex and death and damnation. (319)

Without the accompaniment of instruments, the singing blends
melody and harmony in the chorus of the spiritual "You Hear the
Lambs A-Crying."[26] Sound in the human voice evokes a particular
cluster of emotions communally felt and centered in the material
rather than spiritual configuration of a secular world. At the same
time, there is a distinct individuality to the sound. The soaring
voices of the women may resemble "a flight of gold and heavenly
birds," but the singing is grounded in the shared considerations

of earth-bound beings—work ("sweat"), sex, and death—and most especially those black human beings who have experienced lives stripped to bare essentials.

These common considerations echo in content and attitude a major subtext in *Soldiers' Pay*. More importantly here, they are personalized by the signature of black music, and they draw a tonality from the music that encompasses not simply the spirituals heard on the surface, but also the blues reverberating below. Just as musicologist Eileen Southern maintains, "The dividing line between blues and some kinds of spirituals cannot be sharply drawn"; in fact, "some songs have such vague implications that they are classified as 'blues-spirituals.'"[27] Though neither "Swing Low, Sweet Chariot" nor "You Hear the Lambs A-Crying" is necessarily in this category, both were standard inclusions in general concert programs of popular black music and both were sung in the call and response pattern that filtered into classic blues during the twenties.[28] And the two evidence what Handy calls "the racial traits" shared by blues and spirituals, in particular the one he emphasizes: "groping blues tonality."[29] Further, "You Hear the Lambs A-Crying," entitled "Listen to the Lambs" by Nathaniel Detts, was one of the main selections of Will Marion Cook's Syncopated Orchestra, an orchestra which was comparable to a modern day Fisk Jubilee Singers in publicizing traditional, though frequently updated black vocal music. But perhaps more importantly, as cultural historian Lawrence Levine concludes, "Given their sacred mentality, [for blacks] the line between purely religious and purely secular songs was not clear," and moreover, "the musical style of the blues indicates a holding on to the old roots at the very time when the rise of radio and the phonograph could have spelled the demise of a distinctive Afro-American musical style."[30]

I am suggesting that in the second style of black characterization in *Soldiers' Pay*, there is an impulse toward blues as a mode of development. The style is marked by what I term a structure of emotion, a structure grounded in the folk existence of blacks. It magnifies an internal life that is substantially unaffected by the immediacy of the white world, yet simultaneously reflective of that world's past enslavement and present oppression of blacks. And it is primarily elegiac in tone. Functioning in autonomy and relative independence, the blacks exercise some control over their lives, retain their cultural practices and racial values, and withstand the erosion of value or meaning in the white world. Their traditions, though not static, are not subject to the whims or fads of the dominant society. And their aesthetics are not so easily absorbed, or understood, by the white majority, who remain external to the essential quality and substance of black life. Nevertheless, the characters developed within this structure are no less free of the burden of inadequate racial assumptions in the portraiture than those developed according to a structure of rhythm.

Examples of characters developed in this second, but parallel, style are not confined to the final pages of the novel. There is the cook who raises her voice "in comforting, crooning song," but breaks "off her mellow, passionless song" in order to console a grieving child (298–99). There are the lumber mill workers who sing "snatches of song in a sorrowful minor" under the watchful eye of a white supervisor (157). And there are the three young men shadowboxing on a road and saying "You may be fas', but you can't las'; cause yo' mommer go' slow you down" (313). These examples suggest a style of characterization marked by folk survivals and expressions, rooted in both the material experience of blacks and their expression of it in song—song that bears the imprint of the blues.

In Faulkner's subsequent fiction, there are also numerous examples among minor and major characters, from Elnora and several musicians in *Sartoris*, to Dilsey and Reverend Shegog in *The Sound and the Fury*, to Joe Christmas in *Light in August* (1932), and Charles Etienne Bon in *Absalom, Absalom!* (1936), to Molly Beauchamp, Rider, and Samuel Worsham Beauchamp ("Butch") in *Go Down, Moses*. (Nancy Mannigoe in "That Evening Sun" and *Requiem for a Nun* [1951] is, like Lucas Beauchamp, developed in both styles.) The characters from *Sartoris* deserve some attention here because in a novel that might on the whole be termed transitional, they suggest a transition as well to a proportionately larger emphasis on emotion rather than rhythm, on a blues style of characterization, though both styles continue throughout the fiction, sometimes contiguously so. And Rider from "Pantaloon in Black" also deserves attention because his characterization illustrates the substantial development of the blues style, or structure of emotion, and suggests why I have included characters such as Joe Christmas, Butch Beauchamp, and Charles Etienne Bon in that style.

Gene Bluestein in *The Voice of the Folk* contends that *Sartoris* "contains some prime examples of the quality, style, and range of black music";[31] I would agree, but add that the examples are primarily of a specific black music, blues. Elnora's voice, "rich and mellow," punctuates much of the early sections of the novel with song:

> Sinner riz from de moaner's bench,
> Sinner jump to de penance bench;
> When de preacher ax 'im whut de reason why,
> Say, "Preacher got de woman jes' de same ez I."
>   Oh, Lawd, oh Lawd!
> Dat's whut de matter wid de church today.[32]

She sings secular songs while she works in the Sartorises' kitchen, and her voice either floats "in meaningless minor suspense" or wells "in mellow falling suspense." The emphasis on minor suggests a blues scale, in which the minor third and seventh degrees are drawn from the minor mode.[33] Though the lyrics might be mistaken for a spiritual, as Bluestein does,[34] they are more of a personal expression of her dissatisfaction, masked as a religious righteousness, and, importantly, the song is of her own making. The story she tells is brief, her imagery plain, and her humor plaintive; these are characteristics of the blues.[35] After her father's death, her voice is "chastened a little by her recent bereavement but still rich and mellow"; "she sang sadly and endlessly and without words" (296). Here it seems that the emotions associated with blues are dominant; nevertheless, the actual sound of her voice has not changed; it remains a sound conveying the private feelings of an individual singer and a sound marking Elnora's separateness from the white household in which she labors. Houston Baker's apt description of the blues in Afro-American literature might well be applicable to Elnora's singing: "One way of describing the blues is to claim their amalgam as a code radically conditioning Afro-Americans' cultural signifying."[36]

The brief depiction of three serenading musicians is comparable to that of Elnora:

> The Negroes descended and lifted the bass viol out, and a guitar. The third one held a slender tube frosted over with keys . . . and they stood with their heads together, murmuring among themselves and touching plaintive muted chords from the strings. Then the one with the clarinet raised it to his lips.
>
> The tunes were old tunes. Some . . . were sophisticated tunes and formally intricate, but in the rendition this was lost, and all of them were imbued instead with a plaintive similarity, a slurred and rhythmic simplicity; and they drifted in rich, plaintive chords upon the silver air, fading, dying in minor reiterations. (129)

The description identifies the music as "plaintive," "slurred" and the chords as minor; it places the music within the formal context of blues music, and establishes the musicians as bluesmen who sign all of their tunes, old or new, with blues chords.

There is one folk or country blues musician who also appears briefly in a scene dominated by a community of blacks on the streets: "Against the wall, squatting, a blind Negro beggar, with a guitar and a wire frame holding a mouth-organ to his lips, patterned on the background of smells and sounds with a plaintive rendition of rich, monotonous chords, rhythmic as a mathematical formula, but without music" (108). What is described is the blues, which becomes more pronounced when Bayard Sartoris places a coin in the begger's cup: "his tune became a single repeated chord, but without a break in the rhythm, until the coin rang into the cup . . . then once more guitar and mouth-organ resumed their monotonous pattern" (109). This blind street musician, with his traditional folk instruments, is like those bluesmen who wandered through the South, spreading blues music and their own life stories, which were often stories of hard luck, racial oppression, and lost love. The beggar's worn-out Army uniform, "with a corporal's stripes on one sleeve" and "a small metal brooch bearing two gold stars, obviously intended for female adornment" (108–9), has emblems of the stories that he might tell in his song. When Faulkner describes the sound as "meaningless strains" (109), "monotonous chords" (108), and "without music," he is at once suggesting the presence of a blues tonality, and missing it. "Primitive blues," LeRoi Jones (Amiri Baraka) reminds us in *Blues People*, was almost always "a conscious expression of the Negro's *individuality* and, equally important, his *separateness*"; its meanings, Baraka insists, "existed only for Negroes."[37]

With the character Rider in *Go Down, Moses*, Faulkner does not miss the blues tonality of his life. In fact, Rider is his most complex (and, I believe, conscious) extended treatment of a black protagonist developed by means of a structure of emotion, in which audible music is absent. The chapter, "Pantaloon in Black," in which he appears, however, occupies the crucial space of a blue note, the interpolated flattened third or slurred third characteristic of blues compositions. The note denotes "sad or mournful qualities" and is a kind of "semi-tone wavering between major and minor third, or simply the lowering of the third and seventh of a scale."[38] "Pantaloon" is not only the third chapter in the text, but it is also distinctly different from the others. Perhaps the positioning of Rider's story is coincidental, just as perhaps is the placement of the seventh chapter, "Go Down, Moses," which may function as a secondary blue note, the flattened seventh linked to the stress of the third and often ending blues compositions. And "Go Down, Moses" is not only the title of one of the best known and most performed spirituals, it is also the title that James Weldon Johnson plays off in "Go Down Death—A Funeral Sermon" in *God's Trombones: Seven*

Negro Sermons in Verse, published in 1927,[39] two years after his *Book of American Negro Spirituals* appeared with "Go Down, Moses" as the first inclusion. (Faulkner's private library did not include any creative works by blacks from this period, but he may well have read Johnson's books.)

Nevertheless, Rider, whose name is a common one in blues songs, is related to the "easy rider" in Handy's "Yellow Dog Blues" and in the refrain from that song in *Soldiers' Pay* ("I wonder where my easy rider's gone"). "Yellow Dog Blues" is the lament of Susan Johnson who lost her man and moans "Wonder where my Easy Riders gone?"[40] Her rider has caught a train, where the Yellow Dog (the Yazoo Delta line) crosses the Southern (at Moorhead, Mississippi), and much of the song chronicles his travels through the South of "Buck shot land," "cotton stalks," "boll wevil," and tough times. "The Memphis Blues" also contains a reference to an "easy rider": "Crump don't 'low no easy riders here/ We don't care what Mr. Crump don't 'low we gonna bar'l house any how."[41]

In "Pantaloon," Rider's life has the contours of a blues song: he has been a man of the world—a drinker, a gambler, a womanizer, generally a "bad" man type such as Dupree or Staggolee in blues ballads; he has found a true love, his wife Mannie; and he has lost her. ("Memphis Blues" ends with the lines: "the Mississippi river's so deep and wide/ Gal I love she on the other side.")[42] His work environment, a saw mill, is typical of those figuring in the blues of laboring men, and it emphasizes his masculinity. Once his wife dies, he wanders through a night scene, lonely, despairing, grieving, but trapped in a material world. His emotional response to his situation becomes the subject that cannot be shared by anyone who has not heard his personal story, moved with him through the "shadows flitting broken and intermittent among trees or slanted long . . . across . . . old abandoned fields upon the hills."[43] The elongated measures in the night-bound world reiterate the submerged themes in Rider's consciousness: suffering, longing, deprivation, and injustice (specifically in re-

gard to his own loss with Mannie's death, but generally in regard to the treatment of blacks by whites, as symbolized by the cheating white gambler).

"The depth and intensity of Rider's feelings," Lee Jenkins points out in *Faulkner and Black-White Relations*, are "so paradoxically and ironically expressed," that "his true attitude is misrepresented."[44] But if Rider is related to a blues ethos and embodied in a blues tradition, rather than seen as "the personification of Fallen Man" that Jenkins forwards,[45] then the irony of the expression is not troublesome, but appropriate, necessary, and expected. The blues is, Richard Wright reminds us, "fantastically paradoxical."[46] Rider's solitary position becomes an extremely personal message of one man's meaning, of his life and death, a message impossible to convey in a situational context exterior to his experience, as is the case both with the white mob that kills Rider and with the white sheriff's deputy who fails to understand Rider's individual humanity. However, for the privileged audience placed in an empathetic relationship of knowing, feeling, and understanding Rider's interior reality, the message of his private life is powerful with meaning that is both personal and communal. Rider is a blues figure extrapolated from notes and images in music; he is representative of a sustained style and genuine "type" in Faulkner's canon.

In "The Heart of the Blues," Handy writes, "If my songs have value, it is not that of dance numbers alone. I have tried to write history, to crystallize a form for the colored workman's personal music. . . . I have the feeling that real blues can be written only by a Negro, who keeps his roots in the life of the race."[47] Though he may well be right about the writing of "real blues," he could not have imagined the impact that his own and black people's "real blues" would have on William Faulkner's syncretic form. Although Faulkner initiates two styles of black characterization in tangent and gives them parallel development throughout his fiction, he inclines toward the one with its paradigm in blues; it becomes the more prominent as he moved farther away from the cultural excitement of the "Jazz Age," or perhaps as he grew more comfortable with his creative impulses, more confident of his own vision. Or, it may well have been the more compatible with his own felt emotional proclivities and psychological experiences, such as those projected in his early poetry. Although neither of his two styles of developing black characters obviates racially biased views in his texts, both may perhaps contribute to understanding how in an ethnocentric, culture-specific, but elastic and reversely acculturated milieu, he gave more attention to developing black characters than anyone listening to Handy's music in Gordon Hall would have imagined.

NOTES

1. Joseph Blotner, *Faulkner: A Biography*, 2 vols. (New York: Random House, 1974), 1:175. Ben Wasson recalled Faulkner's excitement over the Handy Band and his insistence that Wasson listen to it (*Count No 'Count: Flashbacks to Faulkner* [Jackson: University Press of Mississippi, 1983], 36–37).

2. Blotner, *Faulkner,* 1:174.

3. Philip K. Eberly, *Music in the Air: America's Changing Tastes in Popular Music, 1920–1980* (New York: Hastings House, 1982), 4.

4. Lawrence Levine, *Black Culture and Black Consciousness: Afro-American Folk Thought from Slavery to Freedom* (New York: Oxford University Press, 1977), 444–45.

5. Neil Leonard, *Jazz and the White Americans: The Acceptance of a New Art Form* (Chicago: University of Chicago Press, 1962), 72.

6. Ibid., 38, 29–46.

7. Hildred Roach, *Black American Music: Past and Present* (Boston: Crescendo Publishing, 1973), 65.

8. Bill C. Malone, *Southern Music/American Music* (Lexington: University of Kentucky, 1979), 4–5.

9. F. Scott Fitzgerald, *The Letters of F. Scott Fitzgerald*, ed. Andrew Turnbull (New York: Charles Scribner's Sons, 1963), 326–27.

10. Howard Odum and Guy B. Johnson, *Negro Workaday Songs* (Chapel Hill: University of North Carolina Press, 1926), 16.

11. Ibid., 29.

12. Abbe Niles, "Critical Text," in *A Treasury of the Blues*, ed. W. C. Handy (New York: Charles Boni, 1926), 18, 25. Reprinted as *Blues: An Anthology* (New York: Collier-Macmillan, 1972).

13. Malone, 40; Eileen Southern, *The Music of Black Americans: A History* (New York: W. W. Norton, 1971), 317.

14. Erskine Peters, *William Faulkner: The Yoknapatawpha World and Black Being* (Darby, Penn.: Norwood Editions, 1983), 30.

15. James Weldon Johnson, ed., *The Book of American Negro Spirituals* (New York: Viking Press, 1925), 31–32.

16. Carvel Collins, ed., *William Faulkner: New Orleans Sketches* (New York: Random House, 1958), xxvi.

17. Rudi Blesh and Harriet Janis, *They All Played Ragtime* (1950; rpt. New York: Grove Press, 1959), 140.

18. Southern, *The Music of Black Americans,* 367–69.

19. Eberly, *Music in the Air,* 5.

20. Blotner, *Faulkner,* 1:754.

21. Ibid., 1:536, 558, 598.

22. *William Faulkner: New Orleans Sketches,* 65.

23. William Faulkner, *Soldiers' Pay* (New York: Boni and Liveright, 1926), 192. Hereafter cited parenthetically in the text.

24. Blesh and Janis, *They All Played Ragtime,* 141.

25. W. C. Handy, "The Heart of the Blues" (1940), in *Readings in Black American Music,* ed. Eileen Southern (New York: W. W. Norton, 1971), 203.

26. Music and lyrics in John W. Work, *American Negro Songs and Spirituals: A Comprehensive Collection of 230 Folk Songs, Religious and Secular* (New York: Bonanza Books, 1940), 114.

27. Southern, *The Music of Black Americans,* 336.

28. Johnson, *The Book of Negro Spirituals,* 25–27.

29. Handy, "The Heart of the Blues," 206.

30. Levine, *Black Culture and Black Consciousness,* 170, 223.

31. Gene Bluestein, *The Voice of the Folk: Folklore and American Literary Theory* (Amherst: University of Massachusetts Press, 1972), 122.

32. William Faulkner, *Sartoris* (1929; rpt. New York: New American Library, 1964), 36. Hereafter cited parenthetically in the text.

33. Leroy Ostransky, *The Anatomy of Jazz* (1960; rpt. Westport, Conn.: Greenwood Press, 1973), 120.

34. Bluestein, *The Voice of the Folk,* 122.

35. Odom and Johnson, *Negro Workaday Songs,* 22.

36. Houston Baker, *Blues, Ideology, and Afro-American Literature: A Vernacular Theory* (Chicago: University of Chicago Press, 1984), 5.

37. LeRoi Jones, *Blues People: Negro Music in White America* (New York: William Morrow, 1963), 86, 87.

38. Roach, *Black American Music,* 71.

39. James Weldon Johnson, *God's Trombones: Seven Negro Sermons in Verse* (New York: Viking Press, 1927).

40. Handy, *A Treasury of the Blues,* 75–78.

41. Ibid., 60–63.

42. Ibid.

43. William Faulkner, "Pantaloon in Black," in *Go Down, Moses* (1940; New York: Random House, Vintage Books, 1973), 142.

44. Lee Jenkins, *Faulkner and Black-White Relations: A Psychoanalytic Approach* (New York: Columbia University Press, 1981), 252.

45. Ibid., 248.

46. Richard Wright, "Foreword," in *Blues Fell This Morning: The Meaning of the Blues,* ed. Paul Oliver (New York: Horizon Press, 1961), vii.

47. Handy, "The Heart of the Blues," 206.

Who Killed Simon Strother, and Why?
Race and Counterplot in *Flags in the Dust*

Pamela E. Rhodes

"Now comes Flags in the Dust and we're frankly very much disappointed by it. It is diffuse and non-integral with neither very much
plot development nor character development. We think it lacks plot,
dimension and projection. The story really doesn't get anywhere and
has a thousand loose ends."[1]

Horace Liveright's criticism was not encouraging, especially as
Faulkner had been confident that this would be "the damdest
best book you'll look at this year."[2] Later readers have, on the
whole, been more generous and, while granting the weaknesses,
have enjoyed the thousand loose ends as evidence of the abun-
dance to come, the eye finding the missing projections and dimensions in the topography of Yoknapatawpha. Even so, Liveright's
strictures are, I think, worth more consideration; for if, as
Jean-Paul Sartre suggested, that, in terms of craft, the novel is a
place where Faulkner betrays himself, where "we catch him red-
handed all the way through,"[3] much of the life and interest of
Flags in the Dust lies in the very features the publisher enumer-
ates: the inchoate narratives and the arrested characters. In this
paper, I take up only one of these loose ends, a slight, but
niggling, unanswered question which might well have annoyed
Horace Liveright: who killed Simon Strother, and why?

No one in the novel even asks the question, or seems particularly to care; the "blunt instrument anonymously wielded,"[4]
which crushes his grizzled head, remains firmly anonymous.
The episode is written so casually almost as to escape attention.
Certainly, those who have seen Simon as a caricatured, less than

saintly "Uncle Tom" figure (the majority of recent commentators) have scarcely remarked on it, thus inadvertently, perhaps, supporting their own arguments: Faulkner disposes of the
character with a lightness of touch that prevents sympathy for
him as an individual, allowing the reader to concentrate instead
upon the general eclipse of the Sartoris line. And if this is
oversimple, we could still credit Faulkner with more concern for
Simon, without significantly altering the critical perspective. It
is possible, for instance, to develop a view of Simon which leaves
him essentially as the benign black stereotype, while allowing
him rather more substance: as a white man's old-timey darkie he
is last heard celebrating the birth of "de young marster" (360)
whose arrival announces that "de olden times comin' back again,
sho'" (358), so voicing the millenial hopes of all the unreconstructed Bourbons who expect the return of a "Marse John"
(358). His reward is to die like an honorary Sartoris (only with
"some shadow of a reason" [361]), in a comic/gallant killing, as an
"old gray-headed reprobate" (361) in a January/May affair. Taken
in this way, his end is perhaps not so very "loose" after all: it
supplies answers to some rudimentary questions of the plot (the
destiny of the church funds, the nature of the "collateral"), and
parodically mirrors and reinforces the glamorous fatality of the
white Sartoris escapades. But I cannot help feeling that this is
not quite all there is to say about the matter, for there are other
problems with Simon elsewhere in the narrative that suggest a
greater pressure behind the blow.

   In Simon's case, many readers have shared (though possibly
for different reasons) Liveright's regret at the paucity of character
development:5 whether drawn from plantation literature or from
the features of one of the Faulkner family retainers, Simon's
portrait has the reassuring face of a black happy with paternalism. I have no real quarrel with this conclusion; it is the
occasional detail in the presentation that is perhaps rather more
interesting than some liberal critics have been prepared to allow.
To suggest that we "appreciate" Simon as a character might seem
to be a request that readers enjoy, and endorse the power

relations inscribed in, all kinds of timeworn racial "jokes," shored up by various racist assumptions. And in many ways, it is true, Simon flatters a sense of white superiority. We might instance the conventional physical denigration in, among other moments, Faulkner's passing reference to the man's "normal odors" (277), or the vision of him as the "grandfather of all apes" (233)—unless we are sharing Narcissa's viewpoint here, the image is unmediated and authoritative; or we might point at Faulkner's suggestion that the black soul is of simpler substance, in Simon's marvelous affinity with horses (7) or, in the draft, with flowers.[6] But above all, of course, there is Simon's role as a link with the Old South and as custodian of memory. Warding off technology with a rabbit's foot, conserving and animating the Sartoris livery (in Simon's presence, Faulkner makes even a carriage tongue or mute top hat speak loudly on the past's behalf [101–2]), he resists change even more strongly than the Colonel does; and in the only passage where Faulkner shows the inner man, he talks directly to the ghost of Marse John himself (102). In this form, Simon is little different from the comforting black stereotypes of *Soldiers' Pay*. However, there are also passages where Faulkner tries to do more with the character, allowing him some intelligence and autonomy as an actor.

Walter Taylor has noted this advance: "In *Soldiers' Pay* the porter's nostalgia for the South of his youth suggested a one-sided commitment to the Old Order; Simon, who was also sentimental, was self-serving in his loyalty as well. Under the mask of the comic darky, Faulkner now saw a series of other masks, all hiding an agreeable but casually corrupt old man."[7] It is helpful to be reminded that Faulkner's interest in masks did not just go away between Pierrot and Joe Christmas, Lucas Beauchamp, or Ned McCaslin, but it is a pity to let the observation rest here. Although the final effect of the portraiture may still be to leave Simon as a harmlessly loveable old rogue, Faulkner's manner of representation provided him with a potential means of entry into social worlds he had hitherto acknowledged only from outside. In exploring Simon's use of the system in which he finds himself, Faulkner takes significant steps towards uncovering the social bases of stereotype, and of character. While it was still lamentably common to find uncritical images of the loyal black servant in novels of the twenties and thirties, Faulkner, like contemporary sociologists, was himself becoming more interested in the processes of constructing and sustaining the role. I have mentioned Joe Christmas and Lucas Beauchamp, and recognize that of course Simon nowhere becomes as disruptive as the one or as independent as the other; he does, however, enable Faulkner to set up a rudimentary critique of the black picturesque of *Soldiers' Pay*.

Much of Simon's theatricality is a self-composed and, as Taylor says, self-serving manipulation of spectacle. When Simon arranges the "drama of the departure" (8), "communicating by some means the histrionic moment to the horses" (7), no doubt there *is* rapport with the animals, but Faulkner also shows Simon as only too well aware of the exact calibrations of status and prestige in the community aroused by each piece of the "equipage" (22), and through his conspicuous association with his white "fambly" (261). Even though Simon's rewards may seem insignificant—a parking-space (22), greens and ice cream in one of the best kitchens in Jefferson (24), the trust of his church committee, or the payment of his debts—through the accumulation of detail, Faulkner conveys what social historians have elaborated since, the notion of a working space, within the constraining stereotype, first for slaves in the plantation system, and later for black people in the circumscribed world of the South;[8] and as a precarious independence, it is easily set in jeopardy. Caspey's short-lived revolt is settled by the Colonel's decisive blow with the stick of stove wood which knocks him "through the door and down the steps at his father's feet" (73). Although he helps his son up from the ground, Simon's reprimand is equally pointed: he rebukes his "new-fangled war notions," asks why "us niggers want ter be free . . . anyhow," and reminds him that they have "ez many white folks now ez [they] kin suppo't" (74). Simon's anger is couched in terms of a syco-

phantic joke about mutual dependency, but it is a serious warning against disturbing the limited freedoms of one system with
no thought for what may follow (why, otherwise, should sentiments so apparently pleasing to a master be spoken, as Faulkner
specifies, "out of earshot"?).

Faulkner's characterization of Caspey deserves its own paper,
but on this occasion I want to turn to Simon's career, to the more
extended sequence of events which culminates in Simon's death,
for the banking story as a whole exemplifies some fairly new-
fangled notions on Simon's own part; and, in larger terms, it
demonstrates both Faulkner's interest in finding alternative directions for his stock characters, and his hesitancy in following
them through.

When a recent critic dismissed the embezzlement scheme as
"outrageous" and the adventures with Meloney as the token of
Simon's "archaism,"[9] what was overlooked, I think, is that the
banking plot belongs to two distinct novelistic modes. At the
more obvious level, it is a piece of embroidery, to individualize a
Southern fabliau, a "John and Old Master" scrape that provides a
comic frieze and reinforces the prevalent white notions of the
black as a child (anecdotes about the servant who apes his
master's civilization are the stuff of many a colonial memoir; with
Faulkner, the type lingers on, perhaps, in the cook, Ash, in "The
Bear");[10] but it is also a more protracted attempt at realism,
whereby Faulkner places the individual within the system that
forms him and shows him maneuvering it in his turn. And in the
context of the novel as a whole, it is this latter movement that
exerts a strong pressure against the conservative force of the
humorous local coloring, offering an alternative narrative of
change and initiative; to say, too, that it calls into question the
static categories of caste and class would be excessive, but it
nudges them toward the forefront of the attention and, in *Flags
in the Dust*, that makes them sufficiently prominent to be unsettling—they become part of the novel's larger debate.

What makes Simon more than just another Isom prancing
around in somebody else's uniform is that for his prank Faulkner

gives him what might have been a reasonable and serious means of black advancement; at the same time, the particular choice of activity—banking and investment—inserts the episode into a wider set of related stories that would otherwise appear to be completely unconnected. For a more immediate context for Simon, then, I want to move outside the novel, to look for a while at nonliterary territory, at the kind of social field in which he operates. If we follow the transmission of the church funds from the hands of the black Baptists through Simon's "bank" to Meloney's beauty parlor, at each stage, from source to investment, Faulkner keeps the transaction in touch with social possibility. With the comic chicanery stripped away, Simon might not have seemed out of place as a case study in, for example, Abram L. Harris's *The Negro as Capitalist* (1936). In converting himself from treasurer to banker, Deacon Strother mimics the way the early black banks emerged from the finances of the church and ministry and their fraternal insurance and burial societies. (It is Simon's own burying society that later takes care of his funeral [363].) Harris stresses that churches of any size could have such an organization attached to them, that for the preacher-founder and the black manager the venture could be a means to power and prestige in the black community, and that, as Simon's does in its unorthodox way, the foundation could furnish employment for others.[11] In addition to their more practical functions, these groups also played a significant symbolic role in supporting and establishing a racial philosophy of self-help and solidarity, sharing the stated aim of the Alabama Penny Savings and Loan Company of Birmingham: "to encourage the saving and accumulation of money in order to demonstrate the capacity of the race by the successful maintenance of banking institutions."[12] In the thirty years following the Civil War, the growth of such institutions constituted the basis of a "petit-bourgeois class in Negro life"; and in the years 1888–1934, "no fewer than one hundred and thirty-four banks" were organized by black people, the majority in the South, with a steady increase in resources in the years 1918–1929, in particular. But as

Harris makes plain, this mushrooming success was matched by the numerous failures: of the dozen banks organized in Mississippi, for example, between 1902–11, ten failed to outlast the war, and the remaining two had collapsed by 1926.[13]

Harris repeatedly emphasizes that the fly-by-night nature of many black businesses derived from their complete interdependence with the frail structures of the black banks.[14] "Those things never do last, here" (169), Belle Mitchell says of Meloney's beauty shop; but whether it does or not (who owns the beauty parlor that Eula visits in *The Town*?), Meloney herself represents a part of the growing spirit of black enterprise at the start of the decade. Her chosen occupation typifies the expression of this spirit that had best chance of material success, namely the field of personal service:[15] as a servant so perfect as to unnerve Horace Benbow and earn the testimonial of being able to give guest or client an "incalculable amount of uncomfortable superiority" (169), she clearly has a good background. In allowing her the transition from private servant to the owner of her own skills, Faulkner also shifts gear between literary worlds, taking her from a decadent milieu, as the handmaiden of the Beardsley-esque Belle, into a contemporarily naturalistic one, as part of Jefferson's new commercial life. Having said this, I recognize that I am being overschematic and simplifying Belle, whose posturing Faulkner makes equally a product of her cultural moment, but the quibble need not make the diagram entirely useless. There are, surely, aesthetic gulfs between Meloney's business or the "negro cabin in town" (361) where Simon's head is crushed in, and the nineties set piece which exists for the reader at the time of reading as purely as it does for Horace's imagination:

> And presently Meloney would bring tea out and lay it on the table at Belle's side. Between the two of them, Belle with her semblance of a peahen suave and preening and petulant upon clipped sward, before marble urns and formal balustrades, and Meloney in her starched cap and apron and her lean shining legs, they made a rite of the most casual gathering; lending a sort of stiffness to it which Meloney

seemed to bring in on her tray and beneath which the calling ladies grew more and more reserved and coldly watchful and against which Belle flowered like a hothouse bloom, brilliant and petulant and perverse. (167)

From this evocation of *The Marionettes*, then, Faulkner advances Meloney to the sort of part outlined for blacks by their spokespeople in the twenties. Elise Johnson McDougald's essay in *The New Negro* (1925) defines the task of Negro Womanhood, even in the South, as the seizing of opportunity, the pursuit of capital, and the development of the "creative instinct" in appropriate trades.[16] Faulkner gives Meloney an undertaking that responds to such encouragement. From this angle, the character becomes part of the world of postwar consumption that keeps on showing its edges throughout the novel: Faulkner introduces the girl as she clears away fancy party food "copied from pictures in ladies' magazines" (24), and implicitly composes her activities against the background of—for example—Jefferson's recently opened department store (291–92), young girls in "stiff mail-order finery" (108), novel kinds of labor (assistant to the local distributor for an oil company [66]), or entertainment (the picture show "with its lobby plastered with life in colored lithographic mutations" [149]), and most conspicuously perhaps the rash of the "gasoline-propelled paupers" (8) in their new automobiles.

As Faulkner moves Meloney aesthetically from the nineties to the twenties and turns her into a would-be beautician, so, sociologically, the perfect servant who produces the hothouse bloom of the perfect lady becomes overtly commercial, helping to turn other women into "ladies," to assist their "commodification" in the marketplace. There seems to be only one bobbed head in Jefferson, the girl, Frankie, whom Horace is intent on turning back into a nymph (171–72), but the conversation around the tennis court is full of calculated sexual competition and studied appearances. And while I have no evidence that Faulkner subscribed to the *Ladies' Home Journal*, his treatment of Cecily and Mrs. Powers in *Soldiers' Pay* alone indicates his interest and awareness of the so-called feminine arts; even Joan Heppleton appraising Horace is positioned in the drug store by a showcase of cosmetics (293). If Faulkner did not know that the magazine had announced that the twenties were to be the advent of the "Cosmetic Age" (recommending that cosmetology be taught in the nation's high schools),[17] he certainly felt it in the air. Where advertisements for beauty aids were encouraging women to take seriously the "self-maintenance" of the body, and to regard self-enhancement as a "job" (in purchasing the goods, they would be improving their own economic prospects), Faulkner offers Meloney a role in the opening of the market. Whether Meloney hoped to have white clients (as Belle seems to imply [169]), or black ones, she is poised at the beginning of a class rise within her caste: as the proprietor of a business catering to white women, or, as a "light" good-looking "mulatto" woman herself (24, 361), performing the hair-straightening and skin-whitening such shops promised their black clientele, she could hope to improve her own status while selling the dream of mobility to others: for women of either race, "beauty" offered the best chance of marriage upwards (even Belle, with Harry secure, is looking for a richer husband); while, to take an extreme, the actual inventor of the first successful hair-straightening formula, Madame C. J. Walker, a St. Louis laundress, had recently and conspicuously made herself into a millionaire on the proceeds.[18]

However, as Elise McDougald warned her readers, no matter how sharp or well-trained the new woman, she could still be held back by all the doubts surrounding black credit.[19] In the face of white reluctance to extend a loan, black businesses persistently demanded black banks. Belle Mitchell's remarks make clear (169) what her own attitude would have been to any request from her servant and, in town, the Sartoris bank, at least, is described as notorious for its intransigent dislike of modernity, so, in Faulkner's plot, Meloney is compelled to use her acumen to gain credit in other ways. Horace's question—whether she has "got married some more" (168)—hints at the solution, as Meloney offers her body as her only collateral, to turn Simon into the black bank of Jefferson.

Playing this part, Simon may, as readers have said, be cynically exploited by Meloney,[20] but he, too, embodies an individualistic ethic, seeking rewards at others' expense. The triviality of the sums in *Flags in the Dust* does not necessarily belittle the status of the transactions: Faulkner makes clear that, for the Baptist group, even the last forty cents of the fund are important (265). Harris's study emphasizes that both the black businessman and the black banker operated at the margin of gain, in the realm of small finance: "Like the Negro businessman, the Negro banker is a marginal man whose opportunities for profit are few. His success must depend in a large degree upon skilful exploitation of the Negro masses."[21] When Simon first introduces the topic, Faulkner shows Old Bayard treated to a theatrical performance where Simon plays the nigger-as-clown (through Bayard's eyes, we see an "apelike head," "the swaggering tilt of the top-hat," the acted acted-laughter, "heartily, from the teeth out" [221]). The show works: for all the Colonel's bluster, the final appeal to paternalistic pride has its force when the deputation eventually arrives at the Sartoris door. As Simon speaks in the carriage, which is, as he knows, the place where his master is most the "gen'lum" (221), Faulkner sets them against a scene that is quintessentially that of the plantation: beyond them there are even the "blue shining hills" (221), *the* Faulknerian A. E. Housman trademark of nostalgia,[22] and there are "the field niggers laboring among the cotton rows" (223). Simon's "tolerant and easy scorn" (223) towards these workers arises, certainly, from the caricature of the house servant, "a member of de bes' fambly 'round here" (222), but also from the less atavistic complacency of a man financing new bourgeois ventures, who despises those whose good faith, and cash money, enables him to do it.

Faulkner could have used the Baptist Church board to exemplify the solid respectability of the black middle class,[23] but their self-reliance and social interest are not what the reader remembers, as Faulkner prefers to emphasize their status as Simon's victims. Brother Strother's brotherhood extends no further than extracting the money first, and winning back their trust and his position afterwards. As the group shuffles round the corner, Faulkner shows Simon promptly judging the kinesics of the moment, putting by any caste solidarity, and mounting the steps to face the deputation, "leaving no doubt in the beholder's eye as to which side he was aligned with" (261). The men themselves are drawn as a chorus of buffoons and pedantic simpletons (descendants of Shakespeare's Mouldy and Wart, or Dogberry and his squad), with the contents of the secretary's pockets enumerated in the stock manner of novels about grubby little boys. This is a patronizing treatment, as marked a displacement in its own way as the dark laughter in *Soldiers' Pay*, and it has an unfortunate consequence, which takes me to the uncertainties that trouble Faulkner throughout the novel. It might have seemed that he was using a broad brush to discriminate his wily entrepreneur from those he tries to fleece, by depicting them as self-important children just waiting to be duped, except that a reader's anxieties may stray beyond questions about technique and literary tact to the more pressing ones entangled in them, of the issues preoccupying Faulkner and of his own difficulties with regard to them.

Here, having taken up the notion of social change, Faulkner wavers. First, it seems to be a significant half-measure that he chooses to show individualistic enterprise—Meloney and Simon both look forward to purely private gratification. By making Simon the "brother" who betrays the rest (he is stripped of his title until the community fund is restored), Faulkner not only indicates that there will be no general beautification of the group's experience as a whole, but he defuses what threat might reside in any suggestion that suppressed masses might be advancing. I realize that my tone might seem somewhat strident for a story which is itself so lightly sketched, but its themes gather weight by association, in their reiteration in other strands of the novel, and in the larger context of Faulkner's time of writing. Such best sellers as Lothrop Stoddard's *The Revolt Against Civilization* (subtitled *The Menace of the Under-Man*) (1922) and *The Rising Tide of Color Against White World Supremacy* (1920) set out to alarm, propagating a world view which showed the white flower of civilizations almost defenseless against the vigorous and multiplying numbers of its "inferiors." Stoddard is particularly keen that we should believe that "[e]very society engenders within itself hordes of savages and barbarians, ripe for revolt and ever ready to pour forth and destroy";[24] and frequent reversion to the figure of the ape-man of course plays a good part in his rhetoric. For Fitzgerald's Tom Buchanan, "The Rise of the Colored Empires by this man Goddard" is "a fine book and everybody ought to read it. . . . It's all scientific stuff; it's been proved."[25] Presumably, he, like Stoddard, takes as axiomatic that "the congenital caveman, placed in civilization, is always in trouble and usually in jail."[26] *Flags in the Dust*—read with no sense of its complexities—would have supplied little to disappoint them.

Although Stoddard might, it is true, have liked more focus on the rising tide of color, he would have found corroboration of the menace, hovering in the parallel advance of a second group of undermen, the redneck Snopes clan seeping into town, "seemingly inexhaustible" (154); where Faulkner writes that they were perceived by the genteel older residents with a growing sense of "something like consternation" (154), Stoddard would no doubt have understood. But although Faulkner leaves Flem ensconced in the vice-president's seat of the Sartoris bank, Byron Snopes's dealings with the institution bear out the Stoddard thesis; he flees from the novel in decided trouble, only just avoiding jail. And, to put the Snopeses aside, it is only the paternalistic joke (whether contrived by Simon or not) that reprieves the Sartoris servant who tries to emulate white practices: "Ef somebody dont pay 'um dey'll put me in jail. And den whut'll y'all do, widout nobody to keep dem hosses fed en clean, and to clean de house en wait on de table?" (262).

Stoddard's sentiments take me to what appears to be a second manifestation of Faulkner's own nervousness. If we can rely at all upon a reconstructed edition of *Flags in the Dust*, there are several places where the curiously random blocks of narrative begin to have some suggestive import. The section I have already remarked on, where Simon introduces his problems to old Bayard, is one of these. It is followed immediately by Will Falls's tale of John Sartoris's exploits at the ballot box (223–25), which provides a further instance of potential take-over by the underman, this time in a historical parallel. Going back to "the day them two cyarpet-baggers brung them niggers in to vote that day in '72" (224), Will Falls celebrates the more direct methods of preventing access to civilization; the "dern'ger" breaks and scatters the group who are about to penetrate the political system, at risk of all sorts of unknown societal changes, those who assist them are wiped out as "vermin" (225), and the exterminator praised for allowing them such a privilege. John Sartoris's own death recounted earlier in the novel (6) similarly renounces the prospects of change; having finished his railroad and won his fight to the legislature, he again stands at a threshold, preferring to block it, or turn his back to it, as guardian of the past. His monument observes a moral suicide meant as atonement for betraying the principles of a life lived for others:

Soldier, Statesman, Citizen of the World

For man's enlightenment he lived
By man's ingratitude he died (365)

It is, however, an exclusive clientele who profit by the enlightenment. There is no sharing of the plantation goods throughout other groups, and "the World" of which Sartoris was citizen endures Reconstruction, to survive in recognizable form until the later disruptions of the novel's present.

Intimidation of "presumptuous" blacks continued, of course, long past either this moment at the ballot box or the writing of *Flags in the Dust*. From 1876, the year of John Sartoris's death, the number of blacks in the legislature had remained stable for a while (rather than revealing any swelling tide), and by the turn of the century the black vote had been all but eliminated, for to exercise the franchise had become, in the words of one of the leaders quoted by Vernon L. Wharton, "a mighty discouraging proposition."[27] The herded group of Baptist churchmen are rendered ineffectual from the start, the butt of Faulkner's humor as well as Simon's. Their leader is even turned into a joke Sartoris monument himself, wearing a Prince Albert coat like Colonel John's, and being teased by a simile into the likeness of "a congressional candidate being photographed" (261), neither being roles he could ever be allowed to assume.

With Simon, Faulkner is more subtle. In the jarring of the two modes in which he presents the man—the comic stereotype and the more complexly independent figure who pursues opportunities for self-definition—Faulkner is engaged with a problem of characterization and style that derives directly from his problems in confronting social change. The question seems to arise from within the blur between the use of character as type and as typification. It is an issue that Faulkner does not fully articulate perhaps until *Light in August*, with the supreme expression in *Absalom, Absalom!*; but in *Flags in the Dust* it may account for some of the reader's difficulties. For as Faulkner shows Simon using the given personae to implement his departure for an independent theatre, what seems to have set out as a stereotype begins to quicken into typicality. Simon takes up the role, never allowed to the men at the ballot box, of a representative figure at the nodal point of change, offering a reflection of one particular possibility of social movement at that particular time: the "grandfather of all apes" (233), then, is seen at the point of evolving into a different line. That it never quite happens, that (as Liveright protested) the character fails to develop, is a disappointment. The category of the typical, as Frederic Jameson has warned, is liable to mishandling, by author or critic, tending itself to revert to vulgar ahistorical allegory of fixed social types.[28] In *Flags in the Dust* the failure is not exactly of this order, although, certainly, it is close to it. Simon does "revert to type," in that where the distance closes between mask and man his behavior confirms the predicated terms of the cultural stereotype.

Behind this retardation lies the recapture of Simon by the essential forms of one of Faulkner's old "poetic" plots. Since we never enter Meloney's cabin in town, I can only speculate as to its social reality. Had Faulkner sustained the impulse towards realism, a reader might perhaps have left the novel imagining it in a place with a history, grown up between the square and the grist mill (150), an area of small businesses, shady dealings, and sudden death in sordid circumstances. (It is the quarter, too, presumably, to which Byron Snopes goes to negotiate with the black car-hire man [251].) As such, there would have been a clear change from the mystique of the black town in *Soldiers' Pay*, paralleled in a way by the humble domestication of the church from mysterious lanterns and golden singing in the night to the concern with building funds, committees, and church finances. In this setting, we might attempt a plausible reconstruction of the crime: Simon is killed by a sexual rival, perhaps, or even Meloney herself, who having been compelled to invest her "femininity" in her business now exercises her boldness and resourcefulness to take it back again. As a creditor, Simon could have been an embarrassment socially and sexually; he might even have been trying to further his advantages by asking for the return of the money; the blow on the head might have been Meloney's desperate answer to all the obstructions in the way of a woman seeking self-determination in the South. Since the novelist here offers or confirms none of these explicitly—at this period, sharing, in effect, his white culture's lack of interest in investigating black crime—he leaves Simon as another victim who dies poetically, through implication with a *femme fatale*. Because there is no follow-through, Meloney, then, is returned, stylistically and sociologically, to static categories—old Bayard's "nigger wench" (223), or a nineties vampire—incapable of change over time.

Faulkner treats Simon similarly. The individualizing financial venture, which would lead to social and economic argument, to typicality, is suddenly reprivatized: Simon's innuendo about "putting it out" (see 222, 361) takes on only the cruder sense of the pun, for where sexual exchange is all that is going on, a sexually motivated murder is a noncatching form of violence. And although the independent black burial society takes care of Simon, he is repossessed by the antebellum paternalistic form of social solicitude, when Miss Jenny says that she reckons he, like the rest of the Sartorises, will have to have a headstone (363). Dressed in the garlands of the family doom, Simon's death, then, falls back into a personal line of plot, as Faulkner covers over again the traces of the economic alternatives that are compressed in the Sartoris iconography; and caught finally by literary conventions (whether they be those of Faulkner's verse, or those of plantation fiction), his image monumentalizes and perpetuates the more rigid cultural perceptions.

Flags in the Dust, then, sees Faulkner exploding an incipient model of social understanding into melodrama, a murky crime of passion. Historically perceptive, culturally sensitive, in his fiction at this stage, Faulkner begins to develop Simon as a "realistic" character, but drops him abruptly back into a racist literary stereotype; and we do, indeed, catch him "red-handed," as, whoever the culprit may be in the plot, the unseen blunt instrument is, undisguised, perhaps the pen, or even the typewriter, and the anonymous hand behind it Faulkner's. If it is Faulkner, then, who steps in as the authoritarian author, with his own stick of stove wood, to hit an awkward character over the head and murder him, the gesture is only the most overt of a number of homologous movements in the novel as a whole. Had he allowed the historical momentum of characterization to continue, with Meloney and Simon, Faulkner would have charted the class rise of individuals who, duplicating white institutions, would not significantly disturb the sanctions of caste. But if even this, essentially reformist, interest in the possibilities of new forms of labor and of self-definition for blacks is redirected and abruptly terminated, then we should expect more violent dislocations to produce equally violent symptoms of disruption at the novel's surface. If Faulkner nowhere else hides his intervention behind the passive voice and the anonymous weapon, in subsequent novels he brings the issues into the open, and in pursuing his critique, begins to dramatize and interrogate his own uncertainties in characters, who, like Henry Sutpen, will block off lines of narrative that threaten to develop too dynamically, and who will do the murder for him.

NOTES

1. The publisher's letter of rejection is cited by Joseph Blotner, *Faulkner: A Biography* (London: Chatto and Windus, 1974), 560.

2. "To Horace Liveright," [16 October 1927], *Selected Letters of William Faulkner,* ed. Joseph Blotner (London: The Scolar Press, 1977), 38.

3. Jean-Paul Sartre, *Situations I* (Paris: Librairie Gallimard, 1947), 7. English version, "William Faulkner's *Sartoris,*" in Jean-Paul Sartre, *Literary and Philosophical Essays*, trans. Annette Michelson (1955; rpt., London: Hutchinson, 1968), 73–78. I have also found helpful the essay's remarks on the secrecy and the peculiar evasiveness of *Sartoris*, and suggest that Sartre might have found his suspicions only confirmed had he been able to read the fuller text.

4. William Faulkner, *Flags in the Dust*, ed. Douglas Day (New York: Random House, 1973), 361. All page references in the text are to this edition.

5. See especially, Thadious M. Davis, *Faulkner's "Negro": Art and the Southern Context* (Baton Rouge: Louisiana State University Press, 1983), 66, 101n.; Walter Taylor, *Faulkner's Search for a South* (Urbana: University of Illinois Press, 1983); Lyall H. Powers, *Faulkner's Yoknapatawpha Comedy* (Ann Arbor: The University of Michigan Press, 1980), 15, 19–20; John R. Cooley, *Savages and Naturals. Black Portraits by White Writers in Modern American Literature* (Newark: University of Delaware Press, 1982), 103–4; and Blotner, *Faulkner: A Biography*, 538.

6. *Flags in the Dust*, Autograph MS, William Faulkner Collection, Alderman Library, University of Virginia (6074).

7. Taylor, *Faulkner's Search for a South*, 32. In *Faulkner's "Negro"* Thadious Davis elaborates similar strategies with regard to characters in Faulkner's subsequent fiction: see, for instance, her analysis of Deacon in *The Sound and the Fury* (94–98).

8. See particularly, Eugene Genovese, *Roll, Jordan Roll* (New York: Pantheon Books, 1974); Stanley M. Elkins, *Slavery*, 3rd ed., rev. (Chicago: University of Chicago Press, 1976), especially 130–33; Lawrence Levine, *Black Culture and Black Consciousness: Afro-American Folk Thought from Slavery to Freedom* (New York: Oxford University Press, 1977); John Dollard, *Caste and Class in a Southern Town*, 2nd ed. (New York: Harper and Brothers, 1949), 250–66; Allison Davis, Burleigh B. Gardner, and Mary R. Gardner, *Deep South* (1941; rpt. Chicago: University of Chicago Press, 1965); and Joel Williamson, *The Crucible of Race: Black-White Relations in the American South Since Emancipation* (New York: Oxford University Press, 1984), 23–24, 35–38, 44–78.

9. Taylor, *Faulkner's Search for a South*, 32.

10. Lee Jenkins, *Faulkner and Black-White Relations* (New York: Columbia University Press, 1981), 223–24.

11. Abram L. Harris, *The Negro as Capitalist: A Study of Banking and Business Among American Negroes* (Philadelphia: American Academy of Political and Social

Science, 1936), 47–48. See also, August Meier, *Negro Thought in America, 1880–1915* (Ann Arbor: University of Michigan Press, 1969), 127, 139–57; Arnold H. Taylor, *Travail and Triumph: Black Life and Culture in the South Since the Civil War* (Westport, Conn.: Greenwood Press, 1976), 106–8; and William P. McMullan, Jr., "History of Banking in Mississippi" (Ph.D. diss., University of Pennsylvania, 1949), 34.

12. Meier, *Negro Thought in America*, 130–33, 143.

13. Harris, *The Negro as Capitalist*, Appendix II, 191–92.

14. Ibid., 53–61.

15. Ibid., 53.

16. Elise Johnson McDougald, "The Task of Negro Womanhood," in *The New Negro: An Interpretation*, ed. Alain Locke (New York: Albert and Charles Boni, 1925), 369–82.

17. Mary P. Ryan, *Womanhood in America* (New York: New Viewpoint, 1975), 295.

18. Madame C. J. Walker (Sarah Breedlove) died in 1919. The "Walker System," distributed through franchise, was widely advertised, and both her lavish consumption and her philanthropy made her life and work well known. See *Dictionary of American Negro Biography*, ed. Rayford W. Logan and Michael R. Winston (New York: W. W. Norton and Company, 1982), 621, and Roi Ottley, *"New World A-Coming": Inside Black America* (Boston: Houghton Mifflin Co., 1943), 170–73.

19. McDougald, *The New Negro*, 378.

20. Walter Taylor's phrasing, *Faulkner's Search for a South*, 32.

21. Harris, *The Negro as Capitalist*, 175.

22. A. E. Housman's lyric "XL" in *A Shropshire Lad* (1896) was echoed variously by Faulkner. See, for example, "Mississippi Hills: My Epitaph," in *"Helen: A Courtship" and "Mississippi Poems,"* ed. Carvel Collins and Joseph Blotner (Oxford, Miss., and New Orleans: Yoknapatawpha Press and Tulane University Press, 1981), 156, or "David"'s remark: "'So you are a writer? . . . Do you write like this book?' From his sorry jacket he drew a battered 'Shropshire Lad' and as he handed it to me he quoted the one beginning, 'Into my heart an air that kills—' telling us he kind of thought it was the best he had seen" ("Out of Nazareth," in *New Orleans Sketches*, ed. Carvel Collins [New York: Random House, 1968], 48). For a convenient overview of the Housman borrowings, see Cleanth Brooks, *William Faulkner: Toward Yoknapatawpha and Beyond* (New Haven: Yale University Press, 1978), 346–47.

23. Davis, Gardner, and Gardner, *Deep South*, and Vernon L. Wharton, *The Negro in Mississippi, 1865–1890* (1947; rpt. New York: Harper and Row, 1965), 258–59.

24. Lothrop Stoddard, *The Revolt Against Civilization* (London: Chapman and Hall, Ltd., 1925), 23. For a fuller context of contemporary racist historical writing, see I. A. Newby, *Jim Crow's Defence. Anti-Negro Thought in America, 1900–1930* (Baton Rouge: Louisiana State University Press, 1965), 52–82; and, for an account of the nineteenth-century legacy to this debate, George M. Fredrickson, *The Black Image in the White Mind* (New York: Harper and Row, 1971), 228–55. Eric J. Sundquist, in particular, has discussed some of Faulkner's later novels in terms of similar rhetoric, *Faulkner: The House Divided* (Baltimore: Johns Hopkins University Press, 1983), 80–84, 108–11, 139–40.

25. F. Scott Fitzgerald, *The Great Gatsby* (1925; rpt. New York: Scribner's, 1953), 13.

26. Stoddard, 22.

27. Wharton, *The Negro in Mississippi*, 215 (in Chapter 14, "The Elimination of the Negro as an Active Factor in Politics," 199–215); and see also, Joel Williamson, *The Crucible of Race*, 224–49.

28. Frederic Jameson, *Marxism and Form* (Princeton: Princeton University Press, 1974), 193.

Faulkner's *Reivers:*
How to Change the Joke
without Slipping the Yoke

WALTER TAYLOR

Americans, Ralph Ellison commented in 1958, create their self-image in terms of "a joke at the center of the American identity." That joke was a masking joke: a ritual of disguise whose central figure was "a smart man playing dumb." Ellison saw the principle operating in our great men. Franklin had "allowed the French to mistake him for Rousseau's Natural Man"; "Lincoln allowed himself to be mistaken for a simple country lawyer." It had descended to his contemporaries. "Hemingway poses as a non-literary sportsman, Faulkner as a farmer." It was so deeply embedded in the American grain, Ellison concluded, that "America is a land of masking jokers."[1]

For Ellison that fact explained a great deal about black and white Americans. Since colonial times, the joke that mask concealed was frequently an ethnic joke: "Americans began their revolt from the English fatherland," he pointed out, "when they dumped tea into the Boston harbor, masked as Indians." Codified, these white rituals eventuated in the minstrel show. Despite "its ringing of banjos and rattling of bones, [and] its voices cackling jokes in pseudo-Negro dialect," the "role" of the minstrel show did not "grow out of the Negro American sense of the comic"; it grew "out of the white American's Manichaean fascination with the symbolism of blackness and whiteness." In such performances blacks were "caught up associatively in the negative side of this basic dualism of the white folk mind, and . . . shackled to almost everything it would repress from conscience or consciousness." The minstrel show thus "constituted a ritual of exorcism." In it "the specific rhetorical situation . . . [involved] the self-humiliation of . . . [a] 'sacrificial' figure," and "one of the powerful motives at work in the audience" was "a psychological dissociation from this symbolic self-maiming."[2] For Ellison, the dynamics of the minstrel show were like the dynamics of a lynching: by projecting its own darker motives onto this black figure, the minstrel's audience purged itself— through laughter at his "self-maiming" rather than by executing him.

This was "the joke at the center of the American identity": but for Ellison there were alternative versions of that joke. Black Americans could "slip the yoke" of bondage if they could find ways to "change the joke" that supported it, and Ellison had a tale about a "very dark Southern friend" of his to illustrate his point. His friend had been bargaining with a white businessman who complained of his "recalcitrance" in finalizing the deal. The complaint prompted this dark Southerner to what Ellison pointedly called a "laughing reply." The reply was "I know, you thought I was colored, didn't you?"[3]

Let us pause here to belabor the obvious. In this anecdote the white businessman starts with the notion that the joke is on Ellison's friend: that because he is black this man will have to act out the "self-maiming" clown role, which means he will settle for less in the deal. But when Ellison's friend remains laughingly recalcitrant, the joke turns around. The white businessman realizes the clown mask has obscured his vision: that the joke is on him for assuming this "very dark" man was also "colored." Change the joke and slip the yoke. But there were other ways of doing that, and Ellison had suggested one in 1952 in *Invisible Man* through the deathbed speech of his protagonist's grandfather, a "quiet old man who never caused any trouble":

> "Son, after I'm gone I want you to keep up the good fight. I never told you, but our life is a war and I have been a traitor all my born days, a spy in the enemy's country ever since I give up my gun back in the Reconstruction. Live with your head in the lion's mouth. I want you to overcome 'em with yeses, undermine 'em with grins, agree 'em to death and destruction, let 'em swoller you till they vomit or bust wide open."[4]

Ellison's old man advises his son to accept the "joke at the center of the American identity" as a condition of black American life;

but he also shows him one way to use that joke. The old man's "mask of meekness," he commented, "conceals the wisdom of one who has learned the secret of saying the 'yes' which accomplished the expressive 'no.'" A dangerous game, but a "spy in the enemy's country" must obviously wear a disguise. And this is no passive response. The old man puts on his mask to "overcome"; he plans the "death and destruction" of his enemies. This too was "the joke at the center of the American identity," and Ellison thought its significance for relations between the races was profound: "It is across this joke," he concluded, "that Negro and white Americans regard one another."[5]

I know of no evidence that, when some three years later Faulkner sat down to write *The Reivers*,[6] he had read Ellison's essay. I rather think he had not.[7] But through a long career, Faulkner had been fascinated by "the joke at the center of the American identity." In Simon Strother of *Flags in the Dust* (1927), Ringo Strother of *The Unvanquished* (1938), and Lucas Beauchamp of *Go Down, Moses* (1942), this figure had provided Faulkner with memorable characterizations. Now he was ready to make the masking joker a focal point of his new novel, and the result was a work that, I believe, ranks rather high in his canon artistically. It was also a paradigm of the paternalistic ethic of Faulkner's youth.

Raised in a family that styled itself aristocratic, Faulkner inherited the world of noblesse oblige, the neofeudal code effected by Southern aristocrats. Their paternalist lifestyle was predicated on a trifurcated population with two underclasses, one white and one black, presided over by a minority of affluent aristocrats. In this world noblesse oblige was not merely the aristocrat's code of honor, it was also his rationale. It was important to the aristocrat's conscience to preside over the welfare of his black and white dependents, who were, he insisted, irresponsible and in need of his protection; but it was just as important to have irresponsible dependents to protect, in order to justify his lifestyle—in order, that is, to rationalize his monopoly of the land and, in the case of the blacks, the fact that he had enslaved them and extended their bondage as sharecroppers.

During Faulkner's youth, that world was under siege by poor-white voters led by James Kimble Vardaman, whose racism signalled the hardening of a stone age of Jim Crow; the force of that threat is revealed in the fact that Faulkner's aristocratic grandfather, former state senator John Wesley Thompson Falkner, found it necessary to ally himself politically with the "White Chief," as Vardaman was called. I believe that the tensions of those years played a significant role in Faulkner's career.[8] During the major phase of that career Faulkner set out, in Robert Penn Warren's happy phrase, to do "a more difficult thing" than Joyce's Dedalus: "To forge the conscience of his race, he stayed in his native spot and, in his soul, in images of vice and virtue, reenacted the history of that race."[9] No modern writer has engaged himself in a more deeply motivated, or a more agonized, struggle to come to grips with the realities of his homeland; and in 1954, when *Brown* v. *the Board of Education* made the question of the "real" South once more a national issue, Faulkner responded as his code of noblesse oblige demanded: in a series of interviews and lectures he took on himself the task of spelling out what he saw as the "moderate" position on integration. This position was not always so moderate; often it consisted of firing off invective at those he considered extremists of both persuasions. But there was no denying Faulkner's sincerity, or the price his stand cost him in pain. And a great deal of that pain was personal. A long-standing criticism from many Southerners was that, by emphasizing the South's failures in his novels, he had helped deliver it into the hands of outsiders who did not understand; now he was receiving the same criticism from Southerners about his statements on the "moderate" position, some of it from his own family.[10] As Faulkner began *The Reivers*, there were thus pressures on him to write something affirmative about the South. And as he composed the novel, daily headlines made it plain that the time for that was running out, that an era was coming to an end. Not long after his final novel was published, the new era exploded in a bloody riot less than a block from where we are now gathered.

In the midst of such confusion Faulkner seemed surprisingly serene. His tone was nostalgic as he composed *The Reivers*, his mode comic. "This book gets funnier and funnier all the time," he told Joseph Blotner, and he had composed a facetious dust jacket blurb that revealed his mood: "A very important statement," the blurb said, "this book will become the Western world's Bible of free will and private enterprise." But there were other things on Faulkner's mind those days as well. He had been thinking about Shakespeare. With *The Tempest*, he asserted, Shakespeare had "said at last, 'I don't know the answer, so I will break my pencil and stop,'" and Faulkner added teasingly, "At my age I know how he felt. You never will have the answers to the human condition so you might as well give up."[11] In a land of masking jokers, one should think twice about such statements. Faulkner's *Tempest*, at any rate, was more than just another novel about the human condition; it was also one of Faulkner's most overtly personal novels, and stands with *The Unvanquished* (1938) and *Intruder in the Dust* (1948) as his most blatantly political.

Faulkner took care in the early going to separate Lucius Priest, his narrator, from certain political attitudes. Lucius identifies the imperious whorehouse landlord Mr. Binford as a "Republican" and a "Conservative," and proceeds to offer an economic-determinist assessment of the entire political spectrum: "A Republican is a man who made his money; a Liberal is a man who inherited his; a Democrat is a barefooted Liberal in a cross-country race; a Conservative is a Republican who has learned to read and write."[12] But *The Reivers*, from the beginning, articulates a more conservative politics than Republicanism, and in this it is also personal. The Priest family, a branch of the McCaslin family of *Go Down, Moses*, resembles the Falkner family pointedly. Old Carothers McCaslin is a family patriarch on the order of Colonel W. C. Falkner. "Boss Priest," Jefferson banker and grandfather of the novel's narrator, recalls Faulkner's banker grandfather, J. W. T. Falkner. Mr. Maury Priest, Lucius's father, runs a livery stable, as did Faulkner's

father, Murry C. Falkner. Like the Falkner children, the young
Priests are presided over by a servant known as "Mammy
Callie"; and the Priests, like the Falkners, are served by a black
retainer known as "Uncle Ned." As the novel opens, aging
Lucius explains to his own grandson about his 1905 introduction
to what he calls "Non-virtue" (54). While Boss, Mr. Maury, and
his mother are out of town, Lucius and Boon Hogganbeck, a
hand at the livery stable, steal Boss's Winton Flyer auto for a trip
to Memphis; on the way they discover a stowaway in the person of
"Uncle Ned" McCaslin, who as old Carothers's black grandson is
also Lucius's kinsman. In Memphis, while Boon takes Lucius to
visit Everbe Corinthia, his girlfriend who is also an employee of
Miss Reba's whorehouse, Ned swaps the Winton Flyer for a
racehorse named Coppermine—the first stroke in an involved
scheme through which he hopes to win the Winton back by
betting on the horse and, in the process, buy back his cousin
Bobo Beauchamp from a Memphis loan shark. This bizarre
scheme climaxes with Lucius racing the stolen horse in Parsham, Tennessee, when Boss unexpectedly appears to end the
charade. By that time a chastened Lucius has had his fill of
"Non-virtue" and is ready for punishment. "Do something about
it," he tells Boss of his guilt. "Do anything, just so it's something" (301). He receives, instead, an initiation into the adult
world of the paternalistic gentleman.

Punishment, Boss knows, is the one reward no paternalist can
receive. One of Mr. Maury's stable hands might be punished for
unauthorized use of the stable's teams by being "fired": which
means, in Lucius's words, "docked a week's pay (with vacation)"
(14). But there is no one above the paternalist, who is the sole
judge of his own actions. "Live with it," Boss counsels Lucius. "A
gentleman always does. A gentleman can live through anything.
He faces anything. A gentleman accepts the responsibility of his
actions and bears the burden of their consequences" (302). The
joke, Lucius thus learns, is on him. As an innocent, he had
thought he could be purged of his guilt by punishment; now,
knowledgeable in the nature of "Non-virtue," he must "live with

it"—that is, he realizes he cannot be purged, and hence must assume total responsibility for his actions. Lucius is thus initiated into the cult of noblesse oblige, a godlike responsibility beyond which there is no appeal. And at the heart of the situation, for William Faulkner as for Ralph Ellison, lies "the joke at the center of the American identity." As Lucius bursts into tears over this discovery Boss offers his eleven-year-old grandson the paternalist's only consolation for his predicament: a toddy.

But the central comic image in *The Reivers* is not that of the bland paternalist embarrassed by the absoluteness of his power. It is that of the underclass whose dependent status validates the paternalist's protective role. The "joke at the center of the American identity" surfaces rather early in *The Reivers*. As Lucius begins to explain his confrontation with "Non-virtue," what comes to his mind is the story of an old black man: "I was in the position," he laments, "of the old Negro who said——" (62).

Before dealing with *what* this old Negro said, let us once more pause to belabor the obvious. Why must Lucius invoke an "old Negro" to make his point? Why not, for example, a young Negro? Why not a young white man? For that matter, what sex is Lucius's "old Negro"? Is this an "old Negro" woman? For Lucius to make his point he must invoke an "old Negro" man, and that signals the presence of the masking ritual exemplified by the minstrel show: a ritual that according to Ralph Ellison is a white invention. We would, then, expect this "old Negro" to play the "self-maiming" clown, which he proceeds in a rather mild fashion to do, talking Faulkner's version of black idiom as he converses with his God about the joke God has played on him: his own Non-virtue. "Here I is, Lord," he says. "If You wants me saved, You got the best chance You ever seen standing right here looking at You" (62).

That, of course, is funny, but it may not be quite as funny as it sounds. In Ellison's terms, such a joke would invoke a "ritual of exorcism." Those things that "the white folk mind . . . would repress from conscience or consciousness" would be projected onto this black figure, then purged through laughter. In the

comic world of *The Reivers* those things come under the heading
of Non-virtue, which is here revealed as a permanent condition
of the old man's character. But Lucius's "old Negro" has managed
to alter the terms of the joke. Without denying his non-virtuous
nature, he has shifted the responsibility for it: he is open minded
on the subject, willing to change if his Lord is willing to intervene and bring the change about. The joke is thus not merely on
the "old Negro"; it is also on the Lord, who, having created this
old man's non-virtuous nature, must now take responsibility for
it. In Ellison's terms, he has "overcome" his Lord "with yeses,"
and is undermining Him "with grins." Lucius's "old Negro" has
thus maneuvered his Lord into a position very much like that of
the paternalist who, faced with the dependency of a working
class he is responsible for, must bear the burden of protecting it.
This of course is something less than agreeing his Lord "to death
and destruction." The "old Negro" has his Lord exactly where he
wants Him: if his Lord assumes responsibility for his Non-virtue,
He thus absolves the "old Negro" of his own responsibility, and
he is free to behave as he pleases. It is the Lord, in short, who
now seems to need a toddy.

Lucius's "old Negro" story foreshadows the emergence of the
novel's central comic figure. Ned McCaslin is the epitome of the
masking joker; like Ellison's B. P. Rinehart he glides, chame-
leonlike, through a repertoire of roles, the most important of
which is identified by Lucius as "Uncle Remus" (182). Lucius
identifies two more: "the spoiled immune privileged-retainer
impudence of . . . [Ned's] relations with Boon" and "the avuncular bossiness of those [relations] with me" (128). To this list
should be added, among many, the roles of the con man and the
sweet-talking lover.

If Ellison's "ritual of exorcism" is operating here we should
experience Ned as "self-maiming"—that is, as playing the clown
when the laughter is at his expense. He is, in fact, one of the
funniest characters in Faulkner, and as often as not the joke is on
him. Ned is not the only source in *The Reivers* of malapropisms,
a disease that is epidemic in the poor white as well as in the

black community. But Ned is their fountainhead in the novel, the author of the richest and best. For Ned a sardine is a "sour dean" and unattached women are arrested for "fragrancy." In a snobbish mood about his McCaslin-Priest family, Ned insists that Boss needed "to put Colonel Sartoris back in his place he had done upstarted from." When someone tells him Memphis "is where the jack's at"—meaning, of course, where the money is, Ned replies, "In course they has jacks here. Dont Memphis need mules the same as anybody else?" When Lucius asks what blue laws are, Ned responds that he doesn't know either, "Lessen it means they blewed in all the money Saturday night" (286, 257, 117, 141–42, 140).

Here, of course, we laugh at Ned's ignorance, although the humor is rather bland; when he glides into his role as lover the humor descends to burlesque. Ned has had four marriages, Lucius reports, and his relation to his wife Delphine in 1905 is less than successful. Ned "was . . . often nowhere in range of any voice" around Boss's household, Lucius relates, "since one of them was his wife's" (30). His marriage does not deter him from other amorous endeavors; he is a hard man to get out of any kitchen with a woman in it, and he is never satisfied merely to let nature take its course. "When I sugars up a woman," he tells a fat cook at the Parsham hotel, "it aint just empty talk. They can buy something with it too" (219). If it is "money you talking about, Good-looking," he tells Miss Reba's maid Minnie, "I got it or I can get it." Ned has nothing against flattery either. Impressed with Minnie's gold tooth, he is ready to "let that tooth do its shining amongst something good enough to match it." To Ned, that would be "like a dish of catfish or maybe hog meat if it likes hog meat better" (118). But Ned plays the lover's role with more persistence than success. "Maybe," the cook advises Minnie, "that Mississippi sugar will spend where it came from, but it wont buy nothing up here in Tennessee. Not in this kitchen, nohow" (220). The cook could have spared this advice to Minnie, who has already survived one encounter with Ned. "If all you got to depend on for appetite is me," Lucius hears her say when she

carries Ned's food to the porch, "you gonter starve twice between here and morning." Soon Lucius and the others hear "a
quick sharp flat sound" and Minnie reappears—"breathing a
little quick," Lucius reports. "He like most of them," Minnie
tells Miss Reba. "He got plenty of appetite but he cant seem to
locate where it is" (134).

Ned's misadventures as a lover veer toward low humor of
which his Non-virtue is the butt; the same can be said of another
side of Ned, his prejudices. Ned can be a snob about his own
white family. Boss "had to buy that automobile," he tells Lucius,
"to put Colonel Sartoris [who had recently purchased one] back
in his place" (117). He can sound like a racist on the subject of
other blacks. "With a horse anything can happen," he tells
Lucius of the upcoming race. "And with a nigger boy on him, it's
twice as likely to" (263–64). Perhaps his failures with Minnie and
the cook result from the fact that these women sense what Ned's
wife Delphine already knows: Ned has a formidable streak of
chauvinism. When Boon beats up Everbe for sleeping with the
poor-white sheriff Butch Lovemaiden, Ned lectures Lucius,
"Hitting a woman dont hurt her because a woman dont shove
back at a lick like a man do; she just gives to it and then when
your back is turned, reaches for the flatiron or the butcher
knife." For Ned, this is useful knowledge. "That's why hitting
them dont break nothing," he tells the boy; "all it does is just
black her eye or cut her mouf a little" (263).

Again, all this is meant to be funny, and again the laughter is at
Ned's expense. Ned, in short, frequently does not know when
the joke is on him, and his unconscious "self-maiming" is in the
tradition of the minstrel burlesque. Still, Ned is aware of "the
joke at the center of the American identity," and more than any
other character in Faulkner he thrives on its nuances. Ned's
conscious use of the interracial joke surfaces early in the
Memphis trip when Lucius and Boon discover him beneath a
tarpaulin in the rear of the Winton Flyer. "I wants a trip too," he
tells them, and adds a half-jovial, half-challenging, "Hee hee
hee" (70).

That "Hee hee hee" is worth pondering. It is Ned's equivalent of the "laughing" statement of Ellison's dark friend: "I know, you thought I was colored, didn't you?" That is, it is Ned's signal that the interracial joke is in operation. The joke here is on Boon and Lucius: noblesse oblige demands that they cannot summarily dump a black McCaslin dependent this far from home, much less Ned, who is Lucius's blood kin. The incident suggests the second and third roles Lucius mentions ("spoiled immune priv-ileged-retainer" and "avuncular bossiness") and foreshadows the "Uncle Remus" role that Ned glides into when it pleases him. The term "Uncle Remus," which is used by both Lucius and Sheriff Butch (177), is somewhat misleading. In most ways Ned has little in common with Joel Chandler Harris's kindly, white-locked old man. Lucius's mother is alone in wanting to call Ned "Uncle." At age forty-five he "hadn't earned" the title, Lucius asserts, "even by just living long enough for the fringe of hair embracing his bald skull to turn gray, let alone white." Ned, in fact, "may not have wanted to be called Uncle," he points out (30). And his "Uncle Remus" role is more like a composite of Uncle Remus and Brer Rabbit; the role Lucius is describing is the role of the masking joker.

This role is illustrated as Lucius, Boon, and Ned confront a poor-white "mud farmer," a man who charges two dollars a passenger to pull the Winton Flyer through a bog he himself has created in the road. When this man flippantly remarks that "mud's one of our best crops," Ned plays the "old Negro" to express his irritation. "At two dollars a mudhole," he tells the man, "it ought to be your best" crop. The mud farmer, interested only in profit, wants no confrontation; but this is an interracial joke he cannot ignore, an impertinent response that implies extortion. "I don't know but what you're right," he replies, but then, as he orders Ned to hold the mule team's doubletree, he seems to be trying to put Ned in his place. "You look like a boy that knows which end of a mule to hook to," he says (88).

Once more to belabor the obvious, the two men at this point appear to be even. Ned has used the interracial joke to call the mud farmer an extortionist and the mud farmer has used it to call Ned a boy, and by implication, a field hand—an insult to any "spoiled immune privileged retainer." But now Lucius, Boon, and Ned are faced with yet another mud hole, a "reserve patch" the mud farmer calls it, and that elicits a more complex response from Ned. "You means the Christmas middle," he says, and launches into a rather obtuse explanation of what that means. "It's how we done at McCaslin [plantation] back before the Surrender when old L. Q. C. was alive. . . . Every spring a middle is streaked off in the best ground on the place, and every stalk of cotton betwixt that middle and the edge of the field belongs to the Christmas fund, not for the boss but for every McCaslin nigger to have a Christmas share of it. That's what a Christmas middle is. Likely you mud-farming folks up here never heard of it" (89–90).

The joke is again on the mud farmer. He is not only being castigated for his extortion, but also for greed and for his poor-white ignorance of plantation ways—in particular for what is represented here as plantation charity toward blacks. Yet how can the mud farmer be sure that this is more than the garrulous rambling of a black eccentric—the "old Negro" figure whom Lucius invoked earlier? The mud farmer is forced to take notice. His response is appropriate and shows that he, too, is aware of the "joke at the center of the American identity." The man looks at Ned, and "after a while," Lucius reports, "Ned said, 'Hee hee hee'"—to which the mud farmer replies, "That's better. . . . I thought for a minute me and you was about to misunderstand one another" (90). The fact is, they do understand one another perfectly. Ned can make his feelings known through the indirect route of the "old Negro" role and they are heard; but the mud farmer reclaims his own status by making Ned acknowledge that the role is a joke.

Ned uses this Uncle Remus mask in his first encounter with belligerent sheriff Butch Lovemaiden at black Uncle Parsham Hood's home, where the horse Coppermine is stabled. Here the stakes are higher. Ned is in alien territory where blacks without local connections are powerless. Butch, who claims to be investigating the horse race, has taken a fancy to Everbe, and is trying to provoke Boon into attacking him—a move which will allow Butch to jail Everbe's only adult white male defender. Ned, in his Uncle Remus role, appears blandly unaware of any problems as he comes on the scene. "Morning, Mr. Boon," he says. "You and Mr. Shurf want Lucius to bring the horse out?" By giving the title of "Mister" to both men—in other situations he gives it only grudgingly to either—Ned elevates both to a status above him; he then proceeds to manipulate them, asking about the horse to get both men's minds off Everbe. Butch is not so easily placated, launching into a tirade about "strange niggers" designed to intimidate Ned and ending with a compliment that contains an implied threat: "at least you got sense enough to recognize the Law when you see it." Ned's bland response invokes the interracial joke. "Yes sir," he says. "I'm acquainted with the Law," and he adds ambiguously, "We got it back in Jefferson too" (173). But before the ambiguities of that remark have time to sink in on Butch, Ned has changed the subject, asking Boon about the horse again. As the puzzled sheriff hesitates, Everbe has time to head for the stable, where Butch quickly follows her with Ned a few steps behind. Ned has thus managed to separate Butch from Boon, and to keep the two men apart he now allows the conflict between him and Butch to intensify. Lucius recounts the story:

> "We just sent for . . . [the horse's] jockey," Ned said, "then you can see him work." Then he said, "Unlessen you in a hurry to get back to yourn."
> "My what?" Butch said.
> "Your law work," Ned said, "Back in Possum or wherever it is."
> "After coming all the way out here to see a race horse?" Butch said. "All I see so far is a plug standing half asleep in a lot."
> "I'm sho glad you tole me that," Ned said. "I thought maybe you wasn't interested." (176–77)

By gliding in and out of his Uncle Remus role, Ned thus manages to hover on the borderline of disrespect without suffer-

ing the consequences; and Butch, trying to decide whether he
has been insulted, has no time to worry about Boon. As a calmer
Boon approaches the stable, Ned's next move identifies Butch's
real motives. Since Butch's reason for coming to Uncle Parsham's
house is the horse, Ned tells Boon, "maybe what you and Miss
. . . [Everbe] better do is go on back to town now." Butch now
has no choice but to order them to stay with him, a de facto
admission of his designs on Everbe. Ned has thus used the
interracial joke to strip Butch publicly, and Butch's response
proves he knows it. "Ha ha ha," he says. He says it "without
mirth," Lucius reports, "without anything." And it is at this
point that Butch labels Ned "Uncle Remus" (177).

Ned's Uncle Remus mask is only a partial success with Butch,
a stall to keep Boon out of jail; but it anticipates his final and
most impressive effort at playing the "old Negro," when he is
summoned by Boss Priest for a climactic confrontation with
Boss, the aristocratic patriarch of Parsham Colonel Linscomb,
and the Chicagoan-turned-Memphian Mr. van Tosch, owner of
Coppermine and former employer of Bobo Beauchamp. The
atmosphere of this smug scene is heavy with moonlight and
magnolias. The setting is old Parsham Place, Colonel Linscomb's
home. It is "big," Lucius reports, "with columns and porticoes
and formal gardens." Colonel Linscomb's office has a "special
table" for his stud book, another for toddy mixings. Lucius
remembers "a French window that opened onto a gallery above
the rose garden . . . and honeysuckle too and a mockingbird
somewhere outside" (281, 284). The Colonel is dressed in white
linen, Boss in his Confederate gray.

For Ned, this confrontation is crucial; at stake is not merely his
position with Boss but also the fate of his cousin Bobo. His
response is a triumph of "old Negro" role playing. Ned's ploy
here is to emphasize the distance between him and these formidable white men. His first opportunity surfaces when Colonel
Linscomb offers him a drink. Ned respectfully accepts the drink,
then sets it on the mantel untouched; when Boss insists, he kills

the drink at one swallow. Refusing to drink with his "betters" allows Ned to deal with Mr. van Tosch—"an alien, a foreigner," as Lucius points out (287)—in the role of a dependent, a context in which his charade with the white man's horse seems almost reasonable. He begins by planting an idea in van Tosch's head. "Bobo," he says, "got mixed up with a white man." This Northerner, Lucius relates, "hadn't lived in our country long enough yet to know the kind of white blackguard a young country-bred Negro . . . would get involved with." He is appalled to learn, and the impact of this new knowledge is registered by an unconscious, "Ah!" That "Ah" marks a pivotal moment for Ned. From that point van Tosch, facing the guilt of noblesse oblige for the first time, is his. When the Northerner asks, "Why didn't . . . [Bobo] come to me?" Ned reminds him that Bobo did. "You told him No," he says, and proceeds to hammer home the Southern facts of life. "You're a white man," he says. "Bobo was a nigger boy" (287, 288).

No wonder Ned declines to drink with these aristocrats. The greater the distance between him and them, the greater his advantage. When Boss tries to close this gap he only widens it. "Then why didn't he come to me?" Boss asks Ned. But the battle is already lost. "What would you a done?" Ned scolds. "If he had come . . . and told you, Dont ask me no questions: just hand me a hundred and a few extra dollars and I'll go back to Memphis and start paying you back the first Saturday I gets around to it?" The point hits home, and Boss, sensing defeat, can only plead his own kinship to Bobo: "I'm a McCaslin too." But this allows Ned to widen the gap further. "You're a white man too"—and as Ned continues, telling how his outrageous scheme was hatched in a Beale Street bar, an idea takes shape in Boss's mind which explains everything. "Now I'm beginning to understand," he announces. "A nigger Saturday night. Bobo already drunk, and your tongue hanging out" (288, 289, 290–91). This is exactly what Ned has been looking for, and as he admits that "with my people Saturday night runs over into Sunday," he has these white aristo-

crats exactly where he wants them. Colonel Linscomb now joins
the dialog. That "nigger Saturday night," he tells Ned, runs over

> "into Monday morning too. . . . You wake up Monday morning sick,
> with a hangover, filthy in a filthy jail, and lie there until some white
> man comes and pays your fine and takes you straight back to the
> cotton field or whatever it is and puts you back to work without even
> giving you time to eat breakfast. And you sweat it out there, and
> maybe by sundown you feel you are not really going to die; and the
> next day, and the day after that, and after that, until it's Saturday
> again and you can put down the plow or the hoe and go back as fast
> as you can to that stinking jail cell on Monday morning. Why do you
> do it? I don't know." (291)

Ned does know, and because he knows, Colonel Linscomb's
tirade signals the triumph of Ned's "old Negro" act. In Ellison's
terms Ned's "self-maiming" ("with my people Saturday night
runs over into Sunday") has afforded the Colonel an "exorcism"
by means of which he projects his own guilt onto all blacks and
purges it—this time not through laughter but through scorn.
Ned now comes up with the one response that will cement the
idea in Linscomb's mind. "You cant know," he tells the Colonel.
"You're the wrong color. If you could just be a nigger one
Saturday night, you wouldn't never want to be a white man
again" (291). That, of course, is precisely what Boss, the Colonel,
and the initiate van Tosch want to hear, and one is tempted to
add, in Ned's behalf, a raucous "Hee hee hee." More than any
other character in Faulkner, Ned knows how to "overcome 'em
with yeses, undermine 'em with grins." His role as "old Negro"
reinforces these aristocrats' self-esteem in their own roles. He is,
in fact, a godsend: a black oracle who articulates the theories of
paternalism at the same time that he illustrates them. There are
two worlds, Ned has shown these aristocrats, and there is something in them for everybody. For blacks, there is the jubilee of a
"nigger Saturday night." For paternalists, there is the responsibility of caring for their black dependents, a duty that absolves
not only their aristocratic lifestyle but also their responsibility of

having enslaved those dependents in the first place. Ned has these white men exactly where he wants them, and by the time he has finished his tale a defeated Colonel Linscomb is ready to acknowledge that the joke, finally, is on them. "Let's all have a toddy," he says. He says this "briskly," Lucius reports (293). Predictably, Ned allows this drink also to remain untouched.

But this, again, is something less than a commitment to "agree 'em to death and destruction." Ned may have changed the joke, but the last thing he wants to do is slip the yoke. The color line is his piece of cake, and he intends to have that cake and eat it too. Faulkner's facetious jacket blurb for *The Reivers* contains a kernel of truth. There is a sense in which his novel is a "Bible of free will and private enterprise" for the Western world. But Ned's characterization, created at the end of one era and on the threshold of another, raises questions of a different sort. It is most suggestive that Faulkner decided to set his *Tempest* in 1905. If a vigorous and intelligent black like Ned could thrive in that era—so Lucius's narrative implies—others could thrive as well. Faulkner is careful, moreover, to surround Ned with successful blacks like hard-working John Powell and dignified Uncle Parsham Hood. And in this stone age of Jim Crow, the only truly prejudiced white in the novel is Butch Lovemaiden, the sheriff who is more interested in making love than war.

Faulkner, three years younger than Lucius in 1905, had other memories of that era. The grandson of aristocratic J. W. T. Falkner could hardly have been unaware of the opinions of the family's political ally, White Chief James Kimble Vardaman, who thought that "the Negro" was a "lazy, lying, lustful animal" whose nature "resembles the hog's."[13] And with the rest of Oxford he had learned about Jim Crow the hard way when a mob took black Nelse Patton from the town jail, dragged his mutilated body to the square and left it hanging from a tree.[14] But one could learn rather little of all that from *The Reivers*, set two years after Vardaman's inauguration as Governor and three years before the lynching of Patton.

It is one thing to write comedy; it is another to ask readers to accept a mind-bending version of history orchestrated to sanctify the social outlook of an archaic class. A novel, for better or worse, affirms a world. By the way its vision is structured, by the way it praises virtue and blames evil, it sets up systems of values. In these ways, great books liberate us from our narrowness of vision; but lesser books, sometimes by their very persuasiveness, enforce that narrowness. For Ralph Ellison, there was another way to "slip the yoke" of the "joke at the center of the American identity." That was by stripping away all masks, black and white, until the human being behind them was visible. The "mode" of his protagonist was "confession, not concealment," he wrote, and his development was "a process of *rising* to an understanding of his human condition."[15] Faulkner, in works like *Light in August* and *Absalom, Absalom!*, had made the confessional the mode of his own protagonists, as he set out, Dedalus-like, to "forge the conscience of his race." Now, admitting that he did not "know the answer to the human condition," he had written one of his funniest books; and in doing so he had enlisted our humor in praise of a regressive society. Written at the end of one South, published on the threshold of another, Faulkner's mellow reminiscence beams the very loud political message that Jim Crow was not so bad. And the speaker of that message, the final face through which Faulkner regards us, is that of Ned McCaslin. Based on a white man's perception of "the joke at the center of the American identity," Ned does not represent black Americans in any significant way; he represents, rather, the distilled essence of the tradition that enslaved them.

From behind Ned's black face Faulkner's eyes look out at us. He stares at us a moment, then smiles and laughs a mellow "Hee hee hee." To which we can only respond by changing our own jokes. We can, perhaps, with Butch Lovemaiden, mumble "Ha ha ha"—"without mirth," as Lucius tells us, "without anything." Or perhaps, with the mud farmer, we can stare at him a moment and say, "That's better. . . . I thought for a minute me and you was about to misunderstand one another."

NOTES

1. Ralph Ellison, "Change the Joke and Slip the Yoke," in *Shadow and Act* (New York: Random, House, 1964), 54, 55. The phrase "a smart man playing dumb" is Stanley Edgar Hyman's; Ellison's essay was written as a response to statements by Hyman about *Invisible Man* (1952).

2. "Change the Joke and Slip the Yoke," 54, 47–48, 49.

3. Ibid, 54.

4. Ellison, *Invisible Man* (New York: Random House, 1952), 13–14.

5. "Change the Joke and Slip the Yoke," 56, 54. Faulkner consciously patterned *The Reivers* in some degree on *Huckleberry Finn*. See Joseph Blotner, *Faulkner: A Biography*, 1-vol. ed. (New York: Random House, 1984), 418. Ellison wrote of his more early experiences with Clemens's novel: "I could imagine myself as Huck Finn . . . but not, though I racially identified with him, as Nigger Jim, who struck me as a white man's inadequate portrait of a slave." The characterization, he thought, made blacks "uncomfortable." That was because, "writing at a time when the blackfaced minstrel was still popular, . . . Twain fitted Jim into the outlines of the minstrel tradition." It was "from behind this stereotype mask that we see Jim's dignity and human capacity—and Twain's complexity—emerge." He added this suggestive comment: "A glance at a more recent fictional encounter . . . , that of Chick Mallison and Lucas Beauchamp in Faulkner's *Intruder in the Dust,* will reinforce my point. For all the racial and caste differences between them, Lucas holds the ascendency in his mature dignity over the youthful Mallison and refuses to lower himself. . . . Faulkner was free to reject the [white Southern] confusion between manhood and the Negro's caste status." See "Change the Joke and Slip the Yoke," 58, 50. Lucas Beauchamp is, of course, a far more dignified and serious figure in *Intruder in the Dust* than he is in *Go Down, Moses,* or than Ned McCaslin is in *The Reivers*. Ellison voiced a more complex statement of his opinions on Faulkner in "Twentieth-Century Fiction and the Black Mask of Humanity." See *Shadow and Act*, 41–43.

6. See Blotner, 691. Faulkner had conceived the germ of the plot as early as 1941 (Blotner, 418).

7. Faulkner's biographers and interviewers reveal rather little record of contact with, or comment on, black writers. In a rare statement on the subject in Japan in 1955 he claimed knowledge of Ellison, Richard Wright, and "others that don't have the talent of those two." Faulkner thought Wright had "a great deal of talent." But Wright had written "one good book and then went astray, he got too concerned in the difference between the Negro man and the white man and he stopped being a writer and became a Negro." Faulkner thought Ellison "has talent and so far has managed to stay away from being first a Negro, he is still first a writer." For that reason, apparently, Faulkner thought Ellison "will go far." See James B. Meriwether and Michael Millgate, eds. *Lion in the Garden: Interviews with William Faulkner, 1926–1962* (New York: Random House, 1968), 185.

8. I have discussed these questions at length in *Faulkner's Search for a South* (Urbana: University of Illinois Press, 1983), 4–17.

9. Warren, "Faulkner: The South and the Negro," *The Southern Review,* 1 (Summer 1965), 529.

10. See *Faulkner's Search*, 166–83. Also, Blotner, 615, 616–18, and David Minter, *William Faulkner: His Life and Work* (Baltimore: Johns Hopkins University Press, 1980), 235, 237.

11. Blotner, 689, 691.

12. Faulkner, *The Reivers* (New York: Random House, 1962), 109. Subsequent references to this work are cited in the text.

13. Albert D. Kirwan, *Revolt of the Rednecks* (Lexington: University of Kentucky Press, 1951), 146.

14. See *Faulkner's Search*, 14–15; Blotner, 31–32.

15. "Change the Joke and Slip the Yoke," 57.

Man in the Middle:
Faulkner and the Southern White Moderate

NOEL POLK

For Evans Harrington

William Faulkner wrote *Intruder in the Dust* in the winter and early spring of 1948, seasons during which the Mississippi Democratic party geared itself for a vital confrontation with the national Democratic party at the summer convention in Philadelphia, over the report of President Truman's Commission on Civil Rights. Truman was urging Congress "to adopt his civil rights program embodying voting rights, employment opportunities, and other provisions destined to draw fire from Southern Democrats."[1] Governor Fielding Wright called a meeting of Mississippi Democrats for February 12, Lincoln's birthday, in Jackson. All members of the legislature attended, hoping to find some way to counter in advance the proposed civil rights planks in the national party's platform. On February 22, Washington's birthday, Mississippi Democrats met with representatives from the Democratic parties of nine other Southern states to plan strategies to force upon the Democratic platform planks favoring states', rather than civil, rights. Failing to sway the national body at the August convention, the entire Mississippi delegation and part of Alabama's walked out. In a subsequent convention in Birmingham Southern delegates founded the so-called Dixiecrat party, which nominated the fiery states' righter Governor Strom Thurmond of South Carolina for president and Mississippi's own Governor Wright for vice-president. Mississippi voted 87 per-

Portions of this essay appeared in slightly different form in "Faulkner and Race," *Review*, vol. 6, ed. James O. Hoge and James L. W. West III (Charlottesville: University Press of Virginia, 1984), 1–19.

cent for the Dixiecrat ticket, and was joined in the colossal losing battle by South Carolina, Louisiana, and Alabama.[2] The political and emotional issues at stake in this Dixiecrat year—states' rights, antilynching laws, mongrelization, the future of the white race, and other associated issues—were surely not lost on William Faulkner as he wrote *Intruder* in the spring and then saw it through the press during the summer.

Intruder was published on September 27. On October 23 Edmund Wilson wrote in the *New Yorker* that *Intruder* seemed to have been, at least "partly . . . stimulated by the crisis at the time of the war in the relations between Negroes and whites and by the recently proposed legislation for guaranteeing Negro rights. The book contains," Wilson went on, "a kind of counterblast to the anti-lynching bill and to the civil-rights plank in the Democratic platform." This was a line that many reviewers would take, and most commentators since have agreed with Wilson's assessment that "the author's ideas on this subject are apparently conveyed, in their explicit form, by the intellectual uncle, who, more and more as the story goes on, gives vent to long disquisitions that seem to become so 'editorial' in character that . . . the series may be pieced together as something in the nature of a public message delivered by the author himself."[3] About the time Wilson's review appeared, Faulkner paid his first visit to the New England home of Malcolm Cowley, a friend since their collaboration on *The Portable Faulkner* of 1946. Cowley had reviewed *Intruder* for *The New Republic* along the same lines as Wilson, although he had been a bit more generous than Wilson about the novel. In writing about Faulkner's visit, Cowley reports that Faulkner discussed *Intruder* in terms that might have been an "indirect answer" to his review: "[Gavin] Stevens, he [Faulkner] explained, was not speaking for the author, but for the best type of liberal Southerners; that is how they feel about the Negroes."[4]

In this comment to Cowley, Faulkner seems to be distancing himself from Stevens and his views on the South's racial problems in a way that should make the average New Critic very proud, although to be sure, it is not a distance many new or old critics either have been successful at finding. Yet barely three months later, in January 1949, he sent to Robert Haas, at Random House, a two-page addition to *Intruder* that he wanted inserted if there were ever a second printing: it was something, he wrote, that he had "remembered . . . last year only after the book was in press."5 What he sent Haas, on February 7, was a two-page addition to Stevens's long speech on Southern blacks and whites as the only homogeneous groups left in the United States. In the addition Faulkner has Stevens conclude this speech with the prediction that social and political assimilation of whites and blacks will eventually result in the extinction of the black race. In the closing lines of the speech, Faulkner makes Stevens actually refer to and quote from *Absalom, Absalom!*, a book, Stevens says, by "a mild retiring little man over yonder at Oxford"; he quotes what he calls the book's "tag line," from a conversation, he says, between a "Canadian [and a] self-lacerated Southerner in a dormitory room in a not too authentic Harvard." He identifies the "tag line" as Shreve's parting shot to Quentin on the subject of the amalgamation of the races—"I who regard you will have also sprung from the loins of African kings."6

In identifying Stevens as "the best type of liberal Southerner," Faulkner was placing him in pretty good company—the company of such people as Hodding Carter, P. D. East, James Silver, Frank Smith, Duncan Gray, and many others, all of whom risked lives and fortunes in numerous ways in the fight for racial justice in the South. If Faulkner, in responding to Cowley, was distancing himself from Stevens, was he simultaneously taking himself out of the company of what he called "the best type of liberal Southerners"? If so, why did he go out of his way to inject himself, by way of Stevens's reference, into what Stevens has to say? If he were trying to distance himself, did he have in mind another category for such Southerners as himself? Was he trying to make some sort of statement about the "best type of liberal Southerner"? Was he, in speaking to Cowley, being serious, then, or was he simply putting on his novelist's mask of anonymity? Did he have a different opinion of this "type" of "liberal Southerner" in 1948 than he was to develop during his association and public identification with them during the fifties?

Granted, it is difficult to escape a considerable sense of urgency, of "message" in Stevens's diatribe against the North, and equally difficult to resist assuming that Stevens is mouthing Faulkner's own sentiments, especially given the similarity of Faulkner's rhetoric to Stevens's as his own public involvement in civil rights issues grew over the next few years. Nevertheless, we need to take seriously Faulkner's effort to distance himself from Stevens. The novel itself insists that we be careful about Stevens's opinions about race. Stevens is, in *Intruder*, as in the other works in which he appears, more interested in talking than doing. The essence of Stevens in *Intruder* is not the political relevance to 1948 of his diatribe against the North, but rather, I would argue, his inability to see past the persiflage of his own words. Three times in the closing pages Faulkner describes Stevens as talking while he smokes his cob pipe:

> his uncle even struck the match to the cob pipe still talking not just through the smoke but into it with it;

> his uncle struck the match again and puffed the pipe still talking, talking through the pipe stem with the smoke as though you were watching the words themselves;

> again his uncle was striking the match, holding it to the pipe and speaking through with into the smoke.[7]

It could hardly be clearer that in *Intruder* Gavin Stevens is largely blowing smoke—not altogether because of what he says, however, but because of the relationship between what he says and what he actually does. Stevens says to the North: let the South free the black man; we owe it to him and we will pay him and we don't need anybody to interfere. Yet *Intruder* is precisely about the wrongful imprisonment of an innocent black man; given the opportunity to defend Lucas in court, or even to listen to his side of the story, Stevens—the "type" of the best of liberal Southerners—hastens to an assumption of Lucas's guilt that is

worthy of even the reddest of Beat Four necks. Proven wrong by
his nephew's impetuous trust of Lucas, Stevens takes some pains
to elbow, and mouth, his way into Lucas's salvation. Much of
what he has to say, then, should be taken as a vain attempt to fill
up the gap between what Chick has done and what he has failed,
with all the best intentions, to do: to act.

Stevens talks about everything but his own failure: he is
defensive about the hypocritical North, fearful of government
interference, worried about amalgamation of the races; he is
concerned whether blacks are ready for full equality; he is
bothered that they imitate the ways of the lowest class of whites
(instead of, apparently, the more acceptable manners of the
Gavin Stevenses of the world); he condescendingly concedes that
the reason rednecks fear blacks is that blacks can work harder
and do more with less than whites can. What he has to say is in
fact very much in line with what other moderates of the forties
and fifties in Mississippi had to say and not at all unlike the sorts
of things Faulkner himself said publicly during the same period;
but as they come from Stevens in the dramatic context of the
novel, all of these topics are merely his devices to avoid having to
confront his own particular guilt in regard to a very particular
Lucas, his failure to operate according to the rhetoric, at least, of
his own highest moral and social standards. He is, as I say,
blowing smoke to hide behind: he throws up Sambo, the conde-
scending abstraction, to avoid Lucas, the concrete human being.
This is the same Stevens, we should remember, who in *Light in
August* pontificates so superfluously on Joe Christmas's ambiguous blood, and the same Stevens whose good intentions in the
concluding chapter of *Go Down, Moses* are seriously undercut
by his consternation upon confronting Molly Beauchamp's real,
impenetrable grief and by the reader's simultaneous discovery
of how arrogantly Stevens has presumed to know what Molly—
The Negro—wanted, and of how terribly little he understood of
her life: how much he talked, how little he said: how much less
he did. Among the other important things Chick comes to
recognize is the "significantless speciosity of his uncle's voice"

(80), and his "uncle's abnegant and rhetorical self-lacerating, *which was . . . phony"* (133, my emphasis).

What is novelistically at stake in *Intruder*, then, is Chick Mallison and his efforts to find his own way through the tangle of Southern race relations. In this, Lucas and Aleck Sander and even the Gowries themselves represent the quality of his concrete experience of that tangle; Stevens represents its abstraction, the looming and ponderous weight of history, of the tradition of black-white relations as seen from the secure financial and social position of the educated aristocrat who can afford their easy platitudes, can afford to be "concerned" about Sambo precisely because, unlike the rednecks in Beat Four, they do not have to compete with Sambo for what living they can muster with their own sweat.

Faulkner's attitude toward Stevens in *Intruder*, then, seems reasonably clear from the context that the novel creates: that is, the novel provides sufficient evidence of Stevens's shortcomings to make us wary of accepting his words at their face value. The extent to which Faulkner endorsed Stevens's opinions, if not Stevens himself, may be discerned in the series of speeches, public letters, and more formal essays of the next few years, which got him more and more embroiled publicly in the problem and more and more formally associated with the moderate point of view. As with other moderates in the South, Faulkner's moderation earned him the contumely and spite of both sides— whites, including family and friends, who were outraged at his break with traditions; and blacks, who felt that such moderates were more a part of the problem than of the solution. The middle was not an easy position to hold. Faulkner gave his white neighbors and friends plenty to scream at him about and, on one occasion, at least, gave black accusers a real reason to question his racial sensibilities.

In February of 1956 Faulkner submitted to an interview by Russell Howe. Among numerous thoughtful responses to questions in which he articulated both his abhorrence of the injustices of racial segregation and his fear that the current crisis

would precipitate bloodshed, he also, according to the interviewer, said this amazing thing:

> If I have to choose between the United States government and
> Mississippi, then I'll choose Mississippi. What I'm trying to do now
> is not have to make that decision. As long as there's a middle road, all
> right, I'll be on it. But if it came to fighting I'd fight for Mississippi
> against the United States even if it meant going out into the street
> and shooting Negroes. . . . I will go on saying that the Southerners
> are wrong and that their position is untenable, but if I have to make
> the same choice Robert E. Lee made then I'll make it.[8]

When published, the remark created such controversy that
Faulkner wrote a public letter in which he contended that the
statement, as reported, was "more a misconstruction than a mis-
quotation." Without explaining how the statement could have
been misconstructed and still be accurately quoted, he went on
to say that such statements were both "foolish and dangerous";
they were "statements which no sober man would make and, it
seems to me, no sane man believe."[9]

There seems to be no question that Faulkner was accurately
quoted in the interview, that he actually said he would shoot
Negroes in the street to defend Mississippi. He himself did not
directly deny having said it and his editor, Saxe Commins, who
was present at the interview, never denied it—and one has to
assume that he would have been quick to defend his author from
the effects of such an admission if he could have.[10] Faulkner
apologists in the matter take some comfort in his implicit admission that he was drinking during the interview, and indeed,
according to Blotner's account, he had been drinking heavily
during the period of the interview, responding to pressures of
the mounting racial crisis in his native state and particularly to
that developing at the University of Alabama. His critics suspect
that, liquor or not, the statement reveals William Faulkner for he
really was, at heart, a white Mississippian, with all the moral and
cultural and even intellectual limitations that soubriquet implies.

The episode is a significant one in Faulkner studies because in it are crystallized and intertwined all of the biographical and historical and political considerations and, radiating outward from it are a number of artistic and aesthetic considerations, which make "Faulkner and Race" a hellishly complex topic. One can hardly call "moderate" his purely outrageous confession that he would shoot Negroes in the street to defend Mississippi—a statement that seems to be such a dramatic departure from the very straightforward moderate positions he had been taking during the decade of the fifties, a far cry, indeed, from a more personal, intimate, view he had offered to Else Jonsson not quite a year earlier, in a letter of 12 June 1955:

> We have much tragic trouble in Mississippi now about Negroes. The Supreme Court has said that there shall be no segregation, difference in schools, voting, etc. between the two races, and there are many people in Mississippi who will go to any length, even violence, to prevent that, I am afraid. I am doing what I can. I can see the possible time when I shall have to leave my native state, something as the Jew had to flee from Germany during Hitler. I hope that wont happen of course. But at times I think that nothing but a disaster, a military defeat even perhaps, will wake America up and enable us to save ourselves, or what is left. This is a depressing letter, I know. But human beings are terrible. One must believe well in man to endure him, wait out his folly and savagery and inhumanity.[11]

There is a very long distance between on the one hand abandoning in despair a homeland one loves and, on the other, being willing to go to armed battle against overwhelming odds in defense of the very land, people, who have caused the despair that makes him consider leaving. He made his comment to Russell Howe in the context of a discussion of Autherine Lucy's attempts to enroll at the University of Alabama; he expressed a fear that she would be killed, and worried over the consequences of that eventuality. Just three months after Faulkner died, James Meredith enrolled at the University of Mississippi. I doubt very much that Faulkner, had he lived, would have taken up arms, along with other Mississippians, against the Federal Marshals who were posted here to keep the peace and to insure Meredith's right to an education.

I said that Faulkner's statement to Howe that he would shoot Negroes in the street *seemed* to be a departure from his more moderate statements; for if the part of his statement about shooting Negroes is an appalling contradiction of his previous positions on racial justice, his willingness to "defend Mississippi against the United States" is at the same time perfectly consistent with his often reiterated desire to hold at bay any sort of outside intervention into Mississippi's affairs. While racial matters clearly dominate Faulkner's nonfictional pronouncements of the fifties, they are not his only concerns; there are others whose relationship to the Negro question, in Faulkner's mind, or at least in his rhetoric, has not, I think, been sufficiently noted.

Part of his anxiety about the modern world was caused by the degree to which social, economic, and political phenomena seemed to be conspiring to rob individual man of his capacity to act and even think as an individual. The very idea of collective man, which he found abhorrent, expressed itself politically in the post–World War II world as a product of communism and of the American government's various welfare and support programs that, in Faulkner's view, were depriving individual man of his capacity and of his right to depend upon himself; socially and economically it expressed itself in Madison Avenue's enforcement of a consumer conformity through the brand new power of television advertising; psychologically, it expressed itself as an increasing dependence upon technological gadgetry to do not just our work but our thinking for us. All of these forces were causing, in Faulkner's view, a standardization of life all across the world and, particularly in America, an intolerable conformism that threatened to swallow up the individual, to render the individual human being invalid.

To be sure, many of the views on the modern world that Faulkner expresses in his nonfiction emerge from a deeply rooted political and personal conservatism. At one level, for example, he never seemed quite able to reconcile himself to

many of the New Deal's welfare and assistance programs, especially those programs of farm subsidies designed to bring
some sort of order and stability to farm produce markets that
were increasingly involved in very complicated national and
international economies that made his own implicit ideal, the
Jeffersonian self-consumer, not only obsolete, but virtually impossible even to imagine, except as a historical oddity. His world
vision also seems to be marked by a kind of xenophobia, which
can be seen in a variety of his reactions both to the international
problems connected with the Cold War and, especially, to the
local and national problems connected with the racial antagonisms in his home state and region. That is, while he supported
unequivocally equality of opportunity for all races as the morally
right thing to do, he made his arguments along the very prag-
matic lines that for the South not to solve its own problems
would be to invite the federal government to intervene in its
affairs. Southern whites and blacks, he argued, had more in
common with each other than any Southerner had with any
Northerner; therefore, Southerners, black and white, had better
stick together to stave off any outsider's challenge to their way of
life. By the same token, he felt, all Americans, black, white,
Southern, Northern, needed to stick together in order to present a united front to combat the menace of Communism.[12]

It was therefore in the best interests of the white majority to
abolish the system that kept Negroes in economic and educa-
tional slavery; not to solve our own problems was to invite the
federal government to solve them for us, probably in ways not to
our liking. It was also in the best interests of Negroes, who had
made enormous gains and who now had the political and economic power to continue the initiative, to "go slow," not to
precipitate crises which would weld the white majority, including moderates like himself, into a unit in backlash resistance,
precipitate violence and bloodshed, and so create the conditions
for yet another kind of federal involvement. Indeed, the violence
and federal intervention he feared did occur. But it may also be
true—how will we ever know?—that the positions Faulkner was

advocating would have delayed those necessary social and political changes for many years, perhaps generations; certainly we
look back now on the words and good wishes made by such
moderates as Faulkner with an overwhelming sense of how
empty the words advocating caution, patience, and good will
must have seemed to blacks, who had practiced these virtues for
generations. The violence that Faulkner feared had a bloody but
immediate impact, and we seem now, on the other side of the
chaos and misery of those awful years, to be at least some the
better for it, though I, a male Mississippi WASP, may not be
qualified to say how much better. It seems clear, in retrospect,
that Faulkner simply underestimated the impatience of Negroes
and their willingness to suffer and die for their rights as American citizens. He also may have overestimated the capacity of
Southern whites to act in their own best interests. This, of
course, is a mistake he *never* made in his fiction.

We should be very careful, however, not to read backwards
from the public statements into the fiction, as the Faulkner field
has done so readily, for his attitude toward the modern world, as
writer and citizen, was neither simplistic nor simple, and he was
not, as he has sometimes been thought, simply a reactionary
retrenched against the modern world and longing sentimentally
for the lost innocence of the Big Woods that he described so
gorgeously and movingly in *Go Down, Moses*. Quite simply put,
Faulkner was no mid-century Miniver Cheevy, born out of his
time and resenting it. In fact no writer I know of places more
value than he on the ability to cope with change—change of
environment, of relationship, of historical and social circumstance. This was, from one way of looking at it, the point of his
entire argument—certainly it was the point of the rhetoric he
employed in all of his pronouncements on the race issue. That is,
he did not waste his or anybody else's time trying to change the
hearts of Southern whites, but only their behavior: he did not
hope to bring about brotherly love and understanding overnight
or any time in the future. What he did was argue very prag-
matically that change was inevitable and that it was in every-

body's best interest, blacks and whites, North and South, for Southern whites themselves both to effect that change and to learn to live with new social and political conditions. A large part of Gavin Stevens's problem in *Intruder* is that, unlike Faulkner, he is so completely wedded, even if he does not know it, to the status quo.

An even larger part of Stevens's problem is that he, like other Faulkner heroes, is so completely wedded to the abstraction of justice that he does not see the concrete; he is so completely concerned with what he would call the larger and very complex picture that he cannot see the details which make up that larger picture. We may indeed see many similarities between Stevens's and Faulkner's rhetoric; but Stevens's abstractions, his preference for talking instead of doing, his overriding interest in Sambo rather than in Lucas, point directly to the differences between Stevens and the public Faulkner. So far as there is any record, Faulkner's concern was consistently with the *individual* Negro. Even while making public and private generalizations about race that could be construed as racist, he never lost sight of the needs of the individual, black or white, or of the need to make concrete contributions to the solution of the problem, rather than just blow smoke. His chief concern during the crisis at the University of Alabama was for the life of Autherine Lucy, whom he feared would be killed if she tried to enroll there.[13] Rather than simply declare that blacks needed more education to be worthy of equality, he took a good part of his Nobel Prize money to establish a scholarship fund for needy and worthy black students who otherwise would not have a chance at an education.[14] Malcolm Cowley reported that Faulkner's farm was run by "three Negro tenant families. . . . He lets them have the profits, if any, because—he said, speaking very softly—'The Negroes don't always get a square deal in Mississippi.' He figures that his beef costs him $5 a pound."[15] His actions in these and doubtless other cases did not, of course, speak louder than his words, but they certainly did help alleviate racial misery in these individual cases.

Faulkner, too, was a complex combination of historical, economic, psychological, and social forces; he was, like the rest of us, a product of his own time and place, and it would be surprising indeed if this were not reflected in his work. It would be astonishing if, writing fifty years ago and more, he had been able to please an audience of the 1980s, who are much more sensitized to the subtleties of racial prejudice than any white person in 1920s Mississippi, or in the entire United States either, for that matter, could possibly have been. Can we argue that Caspey and Simon Strother never existed? Can we argue that individual Negroes have never been irresponsible, have never looked like the stereotype even if they were deliberately puttin' on ol' massa? Have no Negroes ever played to their white bosses' prejudices either to save their skins or to keep their jobs? If we can allow Faulkner to describe the dark and violent and unsavory underside of the average Mississippi redneck as he saw and tried to understand him, why can we not also allow him the same privilege to describe the dark and violent and unsavory underside of the blacks he saw? Is there no coin for verisimilitude, much less historical accuracy? Should we then revise Faulkner to make him more up-to-date? Can we impose a 1970s and '80s social mentality upon folks of a bygone era who were simply trying to cope, the best of them, in the best way they knew how? I believe that we have tried too hard to discover the number and kinds of things that Faulkner *did not* or *could not* write about, and not nearly hard enough to find the profound and perplexing human drama that within his lights—illuminating ones they were indeed—he did draw so convincingly.

The closing scene of *Intruder* is significant in a number of ways. A proud, independent man, Lucas comes to Stevens's office to pay Stevens his lawyer's fee. Early in the novel, Lucas had had the dignity to refuse Chick's attempts to pay him for his hospitality after pulling him from the creek: he knows that there are some things you can't buy, some things you can't pay for. Stevens doesn't have that kind of knowledge, or that kind of dignity, and he takes Lucas's proffered coins, even though he in fact has done *nothing* to save Lucas's skin. It's a trivial, symbolic amount ($2), of course, and he does refuse to let Lucas pay him a "fee"; but Stevens, having by now effectively taken the initiative away from Chick, now safely on the other side of his guilt, does allow Lucas to pay his "expenses." This is a patently paternalistic ruse that can hardly be interpreted otherwise than as his allowing Lucas Beauchamp, an innocent black man, to pay him for something he, Stevens, did not do, allowing Lucas to pay for the very freedom that Stevens has throughout the novel said the South, if left alone, would eventually give him. In this way, Stevens, the "best type of liberal Southerner"—and with what irony that phrase now rings in our ears—tries to keep Lucas obliged to him, to keep him, in effect, in the bondage of gratitude. The shrewd Lucas understands what Stevens is doing, however, and in the novel's final line demands a receipt. Michael Millgate perceptively reads this scene as "Lucas's insistence on . . . keeping affairs between himself and his white 'benefactors' on a strictly business footing, makes it clear that he does not intend his recent experience to affect his behaviour in the slightest degree and that he will not even release Charles from that indebtedness, that sense of being always at a disadvantage, which prompted the boy to his original intervention on Lucas's behalf."[16] Lucas's demand for a receipt here is also a very direct way of saying that he does not trust Stevens, a symbolic way of protecting himself from any future demand Gavin Stevens and the best type of liberal Southerner might make on him. He wants proof that he is fully paid up.

Thus there is plenty of distance between Gavin Stevens and William Faulkner. I do not know certainly why Faulkner wrote that curious addition to *Intruder* four months after its publication, why he would want to associate himself with what Stevens was saying. I can only propose a partial answer that may be more ingenious than useful: even as other critics and reviewers like Edmund Wilson and Malcolm Cowley had quoted *Intruder* and others of Faulkner's novels to their own social and political purposes, making of *Intruder,* for example, a polemic where no polemic was intended, so does Faulkner have Stevens quote Faulkner out of context and for his own self-justifying purposes. Like others who have quoted Faulkner on the race issue, Stevens condescends to the author—Stevens's Faulkner is "a mild retiring little man over yonder at Oxford"—and to *Absalom, Absalom!* itself—Stevens, an old Harvard man, notes, just a little too archly, that Quentin and Shreve live in "a dormitory room in a not too authentic Harvard"—and he calls Shreve's flip and callous parting shot—"I who regard you will have also sprung from the loins of African kings"—the novel's "tag line,"[17] thereby glibly reducing the entire novel to that one line, a line that is hardly representative of the complexities or myriad meanings of *Absalom, Absalom!* And we cannot forget that Stevens quotes not the tortured and ambiguous testament—"*I dont hate it. I dont. I dont hate it.*"—of Quentin Compson, but rather Shreve McCannon's nonsense. Shreve is, of course, a Canadian, an outsider who has no experience of the South but what he has learned from Quentin, but who nevertheless can reduce the South's problems to a clever rhetorical flourish. Faulkner, then, here makes Stevens a Faulkner critic. Like other critics, Stevens takes the words of one character more or less as Faulkner's own and, like many critics, he homes straight in on the easy, the simple, the clever, and avoids the hard and even dangerous complexities of a tragic situation. More critics than Stevens have done this: more critics than Stevens have misunderstood *Absalom, Absalom!,* and more critics than should have have taken Stevens in *Intruder* as Faulkner's voice.

Faulkner apparently did not pursue the insertion of the new material into new printings of *Intruder in the Dust,* and I suspect that he simply forgot about it, having written it on an impulse, perhaps even a whimsy, in response to being subjected yet again, by Wilson and even his friend Cowley, to the sort of manipulation and misunderstanding he had already had to put up with, and would increasingly have to endure during the coming decade.

Was Faulkner a racist? If by "racism" one means a hatred or fear of Negroes, one can say, I think, clearly No: Faulkner seems never to have been any more intolerant of blacks than of whites, or any more fearful of their capacity for mischief; he seems, in fact, to have been equally intolerant of just about everybody. If, however, by "racism" one means a belief in the inferiority of Negroes, one could probably answer that question with a Yes, but only by citing his numerous invocations of historical, rather than biological and genetic, circumstances as being responsible for the Negro's social and economic and cultural disadvantages. In this, too, he was fairly consonant with other moderate Southerners of his day. Even Hodding Carter did not generally argue for immediate social equality, perhaps not believing blacks capable of immediate social amalgamation; what he, and Faulkner, *did* confront was the issue of political and economic justice.[18]

But suppose it could be proven that in his very heart of hearts Faulkner was in fact a raging racist, that like his Southern and Mississippi brothers and sisters of the stereotype he imbibed from his mother's milk an absolute hatred of all people with black skins. Even if this were the case, shouldn't we still give him credit for the love and compassion and understanding with which he treated his black characters, his white ones too, and for the courage with which he spoke out, publicly, to try to correct a situation which his intellect, even if not his passions, found intolerable? One of his Negro characters opines that "Quality aint *is*, it's *does*." The same is true, I submit, of racism, since by certain psychological and social definitions we are *all* racists of one sort or another: however ingrained they are, whatever their sources, whatever their objects, our prejudices and their capacity to do mischief can only be measured by what they force us to *do*.

The fact is that even though a grandchild of slaveholders and a very defensive Southerner, Faulkner acted quite responsibly toward the Negro, both in his fiction and in the public forum. So even if in his early work some of his generalizations about Negro intelligence and physical characteristics offend, can't we still see in the works, from beginning to end, a powerful sympathy with both the individual and the race? And doesn't his concern with the problem of Negro humanity express itself more eloquently and more profoundly in *Light in August, Absalom, Absalom!*, and *Go Down, Moses* than in any other book by any other author, written any where, at any time, ever? What more could be expected of an artist?

If in his public declarations during the fifties he expressed moderation, we must remember that he hardly seemed "moderate" to white Southerners of the day. Even if black leaders were right in perceiving the white moderates of the day as part of the problem rather than as part of the solution, we must also remember that Faulkner made his public statements at a time when it was very dangerous to do so, and did so even though it cost him the contumely of his family and of his community and of the entire state. What more could be expected of a citizen?

As a novelist, Faulkner knew that nearly all significant problems are too large and complex to be contained by any single opinion or point of view; as a novelist, he could and regularly did dramatize those problems without being obliged to solve them. As a citizen he undertook the perhaps quixotic task of solving those problems precisely by talking about how complex they were. Thus he was man in the middle indeed, a sitting duck for the extremist activists on both sides.

In his life, then, as in his fiction, Faulkner focused on the individual human being, and we do his Negro characters an injustice if we do not at least try to see them as human first, and black only second. Part of the power of his depiction of black characters comes directly from his refusal to sentimentalize or simplify the humanity out of them. What makes "That Evening Sun" remarkable is not just its depiction of Mr. Compson's abandonment of his responsibility to Nancy, or of the children's inability to understand what is happening. What strikes one is rather the intensity and the complexity of the relationship between Jesus and Nancy. They do, in fact, seem to love one another very much; but their relationship is thwarted by a variety of forces, some of which they have no control over, others which perhaps they do. How victimized are Nancy and Jesus? Nancy is pregnant—by a white man? Apparently so, though there is no proof; Jesus certainly appears to think so. Has Nancy been raped, forced? Apparently not, since she has at least one "customer," a Mr. Stovall. One critic tells us bluntly that Stovall had "made her his whore and got her pregnant,"[19] though there is no direct evidence in the story to support such a conclusion. Is Nancy perhaps here, as in *Requiem for a Nun*, a "casual prostitute"? Does she entertain Mr. Stovall, and others, for enough money just to stay alive? for her own sexual pleasure? to get back at a husband who is apparently something of a philanderer? When Mr. Compson patronizingly thinks to comfort her by telling her that Jesus won't hurt her because he has probably gone away and "got another wife by now and forgot all about you," Nancy is outraged: "If he has," she says, venomously, "I better not find out about it. . . . I'd stand right there over them, and every time he wropped her, I'd cut that arm off. I'd cut his head off and I'd slit her belly and I'd shove—."[20] Jesus' love and sexual fidelity are clearly important to Nancy. Her response indicates that neither she nor her creator subscribe, as Mr. Compson obviously does, to the myths of sexual casualness among all Negroes.

Is Jesus, by the same token, more outraged at a social structure that allows a white man to come into his house, for sexual and other purposes, but refuses him the opposite privilege, or only at Nancy, for cuckolding him in the first place and then for compounding the cuckolding by publicly humiliating him when she attacked Mr. Stovall in front of the bank? Clearly his outrage and his frustration spring from very complex combinations of both these things, and clearly there are significant ways in which he and Nancy are helpless victims of circumstance. Jesus is injured, yet impotent to strike back at the white world he blames, rightly or wrongly, for his troubles. Yet why should he take all of his frustrations out on Nancy if he blames the white man, particularly since Nancy is no less a victim of those same forces? The answers are, I'd suggest, more psychological than sociological; he strikes out at the only thing he feels he possibly *can* strike out at, the woman he loves—but is that his only recourse? Nancy, for her part, strikes rather at herself—out of what combination of guilt or self-reproach or simple despair it is impossible to say—when she attempts suicide in the jail, and when she confronts Mr. Stovall in front of the bank, asking for her money: one can only assume that she gets exactly what she expected, perhaps wanted, from him. Surely she knew that under the circumstances he was more likely to beat her than pay her. Perhaps she thought her own pain, even her death, was a small price to pay for a public humiliation of Stovall. Or was she simply so high on drugs she didn't know what she was doing? There are very many ways in which she deserves our deepest sympathy.

But the chemistry of our sympathy with her is seriously altered when we realize how dangerous it is for her to take the Compson children to her cabin with her to protect her. If Jesus decides to kill her, as she believes he will, does she think he will spare the little ones? Even if she does think he will spare them, if she has thought about it at all, it seems to me by no means responsible for her to try to hide behind them. Does she realize the danger, at any level? If Mr. Compson is the father of her child and so the author of her miseries, does Nancy deliberately, consciously or unconsciously, put them in harm's way to avenge herself on a white world which has wronged her?

I do not know the answers to these questions, and I do not believe that the story itself provides answers. But I insist that the story *asks* these and other questions, and that much of its power is directly related to the complexity of Nancy's characterization and to the complexities of the relationship between Jesus and Nancy. Faulkner's treatment of these two black characters is in very many ways a direct, frontal assault upon racial stereotypes that forces us to the astonishing knowledge that Jesus' and Nancy's feelings are, well, *white:* what we are really astonished at, even if we do not know it, is that those feelings are *human*. Criticism of this story, and of Faulkner's general treatment of blacks, seems stuck at considering them simply tragic victims of white oppression, and so symbols, rather than human beings.

His white characters are also too often read as stereotypes. "Pantaloon in Black" is, for many reasons, generally considered one of Faulkner's greatest stories. Most critics have, in my judgment, misunderstood "Pantaloon" not because of Faulkner's treatment of Rider, but because of their inability to see the deputy of the second part of that story as anything but a stereotypical Southern law man. He is, of course, a redneck deputy, a Southerner with all the prejudices associated with that type. Faulkner deliberately draws him that way. But if that is *all* he is, then "Pantaloon" seems to me an unsuccessful story that rather clumsily juxtaposes the moving story of Rider's love for Manny, his grief, his suicidal murder of the white man, and then his lynching, with the story of the redneck deputy and his crass, unloving wife.

Beyond those ironies, however, lies another story. Why does the deputy continue to tell his wife the story of Rider's lynching, in complete detail, long after she has made it clear that she doesn't care about Rider or about the deputy either? The answer, I think, is that he isn't talking to her at all, but rather to himself. He has just experienced something, Rider's griefstricken and doomed humanness, which nothing in his background has prepared him for, and he is clumsily trying to talk it out, trying to explain to his own mind, using a completely inadequate redneck vocabulary and conceptual system, something it cannot quite grasp. Most have accepted that Faulkner wrote "Pantaloon" to force white readers to go behind the stereotype of the black man. I would argue that he is also asking us to look behind the stereotype of the Southern lawman, even as Nub Gowrie's heartbreak forces Chick Mallision behind the stereotype of Beat Four rednecks: we who have eagerly seen Rider as a misunderstood human being have been unwilling to see the white man as equally human. The deputy is trying to make sense of his actual experience of Rider, which has made that magnificent black man something devastatingly different from the stereotype he has always presumed to think he knows: perhaps this deputy is also somebody devastatingly different from the redneck we have all presumed to know.

Thus that deputy seems to me far more educable than the more highly educated and sophisticated lawyer, Gavin Stevens, whose presence at the end of *Go Down, Moses* has for four decades muddied the racial waters of that novel. For with all the best intentions to be helpful, to demonstrate that he, at any rate, knows something of the civilized world, Stevens is completely blind to Molly's real humanity. Most critics have, of course, noticed this, and many have thought Stevens's paternalism a weakness in the novel. But I would suggest that Stevens is here set in sharp opposition to the deputy of "Pantaloon." Both become privy to grief, to human passion, where they had least expected it, in a Negro. The deputy tries to understand it; Stevens is arrogantly sure that he understands "The Negro" completely. It is thus much more likely to be that redneck deputy who will, one of these days, be able to meet black men and women as individual human beings. I suspect Faulkner would hold that the surer, the long-range solution to racial problems, if there is a solution, lies in the direction the deputy is facing, even if he hasn't yet begun to move forward; and I suspect that, at least as regards the question of race in his real South and in his fictionalized one, that deputy is nearer to Faulkner's position than any other character: he doesn't have any answers, but at least he is beginning to ask the right questions.

NOTES

1. William F. Winter, "New Directions in Politics, 1948–1956," in Richard Aubrey McLemore, ed., *A History of Mississippi* (Jackson: University & College Press of Mississippi, 1973), 2:141.

2. Ibid., 2:144.

3. Edmund Wilson, "William Faulkner's Reply to the Civil-Rights Program," in John Bassett, ed., William Faulkner: The Critical Heritage (London: Routledge & Kegan Paul, 1975), 335–36.

4. Malcolm Cowley, The Faulkner-Cowley File: Letters and Memories, 1944–1962 (New York: Viking, 1966), 110–11.

5. Joseph Blotner, ed., Selected Letters of William Faulkner (New York: Random House, 1977), 285.

6. Patrick Samway, "New Material for Faulkner's Intruder in the Dust," in James B. Meriwether, ed., A Faulkner Miscellany (Jackson: University Press of Mississippi, 1974), 111.

7. William Faulkner, Intruder in the Dust (New York: Random House, 1948), 222, 226, 242. Hereafter cited parenthetically in the text.

8. James B. Meriwether and Michael Millgate, eds., Lion in the Garden: Interviews

9. Joseph Blotner, Faulkner: A Biography, 2 vols. (New York: Random House, 1974), 2:1599. See also James B. Meriwether, ed., Essays, Speeches, and Public Letters (New York: Random House, 1966), 226, and Lion in the Garden, 265. Meriwether's and Millgate's introduction to the Howe interview (257) usefully argues the reasons that one must approach the interview with caution.

10. Blotner, Faulkner: A Biography, 2:1590. In the 1984 one-volume revision (Faulkner: A Biography, 1-vol. ed. [New York: Random House, 1984], 617–18) Blotner omits to mention Commins's presence at the interview.

11. Selected Letters, 381–82.

12. See, for example, "On Fear: Deep South in Labor: Mississippi" and the "Address to the Southern Historical Association" in Essays, Speeches, and Public Letters.

13. Essays, Speeches, and Public Letters, 108, and Blotner, 2:1591.

14. Blotner, Faulkner: A Biography, 1-vol. ed., 535.

15. Faulkner-Cowley File, 111.

16. Michael Millgate, The Achievement of William Faulkner (New York: Random House, 1966), 220.

17. Samway, 111.

18. See, for example, Hodding Carter's Where Main Street Meets the River (New York: Rinehart, 1953) and Southern Legacy (Baton Rouge: Louisiana State University, 1950), and David Cohn's Where I Was Born and Raised (Boston: Houghton Mifflin, 1948).

19. Walter Taylor, Faulkner's Search for a South (Urbana: University of Illinois Press, 1983), 55.

20. "That Evening Sun," in Collected Stories (New York: Random House, 1950), 295.

Light in August and the Rhetorics
of Racial Division

JAMES A. SNEAD

In William Faulkner's novels, race must be discussed, but not
in the sense of Hippolyte Taine's *race, temps, milieu*—or
the "essence" of a particular collection of people. Neither is
Faulkner primarily concerned with the suffering of blacks.
Rather, race enters Faulkner's texts as a practice whereby,
through segregating a certain group of people from the category
of "whiteness," Yoknapatawpha society finds the chief proof of its
authority, integrity, and communal identity. Racial division, racial segregation, and the mythologies surrounding it, collectively
try to outlaw all interracial contiguity, cohabitation, and con-
sanguity. Faulkner's black and white characters, in short, live
under a body of racial barriers and prohibitions that structure the
self-understanding of Yoknapatawpha County. The futility of applying such strictly binary categories to human affairs is the main
lesson of Faulkner's novels, which dramatize the problematics of
division through sensitive white characters such as Quentin
Compson, Darl and Addie Bundren, and Ike McCaslin. By
accident, intelligence, or pure stubbornness these Faulknerian
protagonists reject division, discovering instead those social and
psychological margins where merging, opposition's opposite,
may exist unassailed. Faulkner's narratives utter a truth of merging across social boundaries that his contemporaries found unspeakable. Faulkner himself set this truth in an elusive, complex

Portions of this paper have appeared in *Figures of Division: William Faulkner's Major
Novels* (New York: Methuen, 1986). Used by permission.

discourse of indirection, a literary disfigurement of divisive social figures. In *Absalom, Absalom!* Thomas Sutpen encounters "a land divided neatly up," yet division "had never once been mentioned by name." One Mississippi woman speaks of "'race talk' . . . euphemisms and pretense under certain circumstances," whereby racial ideologies are covered up.[1] Much Faulkner criticism—when dealing with "the Negro," "endurance," "the human heart"—has overlooked, in the manner of "race talk," the systematic social rhetorics that have produced the need for blacks to "endure."

 ⊦Racism in general might be considered a normative recipe for domination created by speakers using rhetorical tactics. These tactics may include both spoken phrases and notions whose effectiveness lies in their remaining unspoken. As recorded and repeated in Faulkner's novels, certain characteristic figures of racial division repeat on the level of phoneme, sentence, and story: (1) diversity produces the fear of *merging*, or identity-loss through syneristic union with the other, leading to the wish to use racial purification as a *separating* strategy against difference; (2) *marking*, or supplying physically significant (usually visual) characteristics with internal value equivalents, sharpening by visual antithesis their conceptual utility; (3) *spatial and conceptual separation*, often facilitated through unequal substitutions that tend to omit and distance a subordinate class from realms of value and esteem; (4) *repetition*, or pleonastic reinforcement of these divisions in writing, storytelling, or hearsay; (5) *invective* and threat, exemplified in random and unpredictable violence to punish real or imagined delictions; (6) *omission* and concealment of the process by a sort of *paralepsis* that claims discrimination to be self-evidently valid and natural.

Faulkner counters these social figures with literary devices of his own. Gérard Genette describes the practice as follows:

> one of the newest and most fruitful directions that are now opening up for literary research ought to be the structural study of the "large unities" of discourse, beyond the framework—which linguistics in the strict sense cannot cross—of the sentence. . . . There would

then be a linguistics of discourse that was a *translinguistics*, since the facts of language would be handled by it in great bulk, and often at one remove—to put it simply, a rhetoric, perhaps that "new rhetoric" which Francis Ponge once called for, and which we still lack.[2]

I would extend these meditations to apply to the author who would both describe and "write against" large-scale ideological concepts encoded in the form of rhetorical narratives. "Translinguistics" would then address figures of *social* as well as *narrative* discourse. The challenge to reigning figures of division emerges in a style that mixes and connects races, classes, and sexes, even as these figures, in their social role, tend to divide and distinguish. Moreover, Faulkner's sequencing of plot unravels rather than fastens the conceptual threads that typically produce neat, coherent endings. Faulkner's discourse of connection employs a variety of effects, including *chiasmus*, an A : B : : B : A figure that conjugates and reverses plot elements (what Robert Penn Warren calls Faulkner's "inversions of roles"); anticipations of plot that effectively reverse causal sequence (*prolepsis* and *hysteron proteron*); plot and character mergings *(syneresis)*; and emphatic repetitions of new conjugations in successive clauses and plot sequences *(anaphora).*[3]

While frequently useful as a general anatomical practice, acts of classification become especially insidious when connected with notions of hierarchy and authority. Although Carl Linnaeus's taxonomy of race in *Systema Naturae* (1758) never implied hierarchy or ranking, it came to be elided with the metaphysical concept of the Great Chain of Being. By accident of timing, in the eighteenth century (within the context of European exploration and colonization of Africa), blacks appeared in the Chain of Being somewhere between man and ape; hierarchies of oppression received the ostensible assent of anatomy and nature.[4] Faulkner's major novels must be seen as an exercise in explicating a certain reality from this tangle. They enjoy the advantage of their locale, a region whose segregationist thinking furnishes us with an extreme case of social classification. Yoknapatawpha's major classifications—white/black, poor/rich, male/female—depend on an obsessive kind of polar thinking.[5] The reality of the human beings thus classified remains absent. Faulkner's narratives mainly concern the effects of these classifications on human sensibilities, white and black, male and female, rich and poor: how can we ever know each other, if our society works through a forced organization into distinct groupings? As Faulkner repeatedly said in interviews, "the white man has forced the Negro to be always a Negro rather than another human being . . . the white man can never really know the Negro."[6] In accepting markings such as skin color, sexual difference, dress, and dialect as significant indices of social value, the trusting reader initially must repeat and reinforce the figures whereby blacks, poor whites, and women have been classified, separated, and dominated. Later, through adopting (at least temporarily) the town's racist perspectives, the reader may discern that the plot of societal division—with every trace of prior preparation and rehearsal removed—suddenly becomes credible and soon seems an indispensable attitude towards reality.

Figures of division fail on two counts: they are binary and as such require the presence of an opposite term in order to signify anything; moreover, absolute segregation, in trying to enforce an unreal polarity, only further agitates the psychic desire to exceed its artificial boundaries. The system of Southern *apartheid* wishes to freeze polar pairs into dominant/subordinate, master/slave terms, yet, as Robert Penn Warren implies, there is a "concealed . . . dialectic progression" in Faulkner whereby the dominant term seems—in the manner of Hegel's master/slave relationship—to depend upon and often to merge with its polar opposite:

> Psychologically and logically, all association implies dissociation, and conversely: the same form which unites various elements into a well-organized whole dissociates them. . . . The two techniques are complementary and always at work at the same time; but the argumentation through which a datum is modified can stress the association or the dissociation which it is promoting without making explicit the

complementary aspect which will result from the desired transformation.[7]

Rhetorical figures of division, particularly when relied upon to underpin a shaky social ideology, prove untrue, contradicting themselves even as they attempt to state truth. The mutuality of separation and merging throws an unexpected shadow, a black one, on the white screen of social normality. "*To divide . . . in order to unite. . . .* Is this not the formula of language itself?"[8]

Since figures of division are at the same time social and linguistic, Faulkner's novels, as literary texts, can examine their invention and demise on both thematic and stylistic levels of analysis. Particularly germane to Faulkner's novels as an instance of actual and stylistic merging is the issue of *miscegenation*. A system of extreme racial division elicits the desire for racial mixing or miscegenation, the South's feared, forbidden, denied, yet pervasive release from societal division. Notions such as "white racial purity," aimed at underpinning the economic order, also underlie the insistence on division. Southern society typically and publicly abhors racial mergings through integration, cohabitation, or miscegenation. Yet Faulkner's narratives repeatedly present a world in which blacks and whites eat, live, and often sleep together despite written Jim Crow laws and spoken categories of racial differentiation. Faulkner's narratives dismember figures of division at their weakest joint, the "purity" notion that seems the requirement for white supremacist logic. White skin could never be the certain signifier of the absence of "black" blood (white racial purity), because white skin, as Faulkner amply demonstrates, can also signify "mixed" blood.

Faulkner presents in *Light in August* a man destined to break all the semiotic codes of society: he is both masculine and feminine, both black and white, a "tragic mulatto," an American double-being. In his novels of the mid–1930s Faulkner seems to be working out the question whether such a reconciliatory, almost mythical figure might transcend in fiction the dire antagonisms of life.[9] Joe Christmas, Charles Bon, and Lucas Beauchamp (the central figures of *Light in August, Absalom, Ab-*

salom!, and *Go Down, Moses*—all mulattoes), far from being ideal reconciliations for racial antagonisms, come to seem exactly those points of chaos that threaten to destroy false serenity. Insofar as Joe Christmas and Charles Bon cannot signify any one thing, they must finally question the very possibility of unitary significance. The tragic realization of these novels may be that a kind of semiotic discrimination is as necessary to reading as it is, deplorably, for the whites of Jefferson, Mississippi.

The early pages of *Light in August* overflow with tropes of domination in the town's common parlance: "Starting in at daylight and slaving all day like a durn nigger"; "Well, maybe some folks work like the niggers work where they come from."[10] Lucas Burch repeats this simile later on, referring to himself as "slaving like a durn nigger ten hours a day" (408). This seemingly offhanded simile, "working like a nigger," is an example of a dividing trope, a figure that would engrave in language by repetition the economic connection between blacks and "slaving"—a relationship whose fixity and reliability has insured the economic stability of Jefferson and, more generally, of American society. Hearsay would write such connections into normality, making them inflexible in the reality of verbal commonplaces. Byron Bunch says of Joanna Burden: "They say she is still mixed up with niggers. . . . Folks say she claims that niggers are the same as white folks" (48). What "they say" may be true or false, but because "they say it," it seems truth.

We have seen just a few examples of significant reference points in Jefferson language. A black is a certain thing; a black does certain jobs. To find these rhetorics in well-socialized speakers is one thing, but it is quite another to find them in the voice of the narrator. Faulkner gives us the choice to be racists in a very cunning way: do we passively accept the truth of the narrator's judgment and thereby ourselves join the town's consensus? Or do we suspend our own judgment for the sake of fairness? There is, for instance, the text's repeated notion that blacks smell differently than whites do: "before he knew it he was in Freedman Town, surrounded by the summer smell . . . of

invisible negroes" (106); "he could smell Negro" (109); "the same
children, with different names; the same grown people, with
different smells" (131). Outrageously the narrator wants bodily
odor here to replace the visual signifier of race that Joe Christmas has now made defunct (dark skin color), but his subterfuge is
transparent. Umberto Eco includes *olfactory signs* among the
possible components of a general cultural semiotics, citing
Baudelaire's notion of a "code of scents," or Peirce's notion of
smell as an "index"—hence olfactory signals are as apt to be
abused by socioeconomic "marking" (presumably, they desig-
nate a "natural" difference) as any other sort.[11] Earlier, we have
read the following sentences:

> He [Armstid] got into the wagon and waked the mules. That is, he
> put them into motion, since *only a negro can tell when a mule is
> asleep or awake.*
>
> None of them knew then where Christmas lived and what he was
> actually doing *behind the veil, the screen, of his negro's job at the
> mill* . . . even the ones who bought the whiskey did not know that
> Christmas was actually living in *a tumble down negro cabin* on Miss
> Burden's place, and that he had been living in it for more than two
> years.
>
> Hightower knew that the man would walk all the way to town and
> then spend probably thirty minutes more getting in touch with a
> doctor, *in his fumbling and timeless negro fashion,* instead of asking
> some white woman to telephone for him. (8, 31–32; 68; italics added)

The italicized statements demonstrate a highly revealing yet
suspect alternation of ignorance and knowledge. The first shows
that "a negro" knows whether a mule is awake or asleep—no
doubt because of a connection "they say" exists between blacks
and the natural world of animals. In the second, "everyone"
ostensibly knows what a "negro cabin" is: the kind of cabin
where a negro would live. But here the narrator even seems to
know more than "they" do. He sees "behind the veil" of a job
that "everyone knows" would ordinarily be a "negro's." In the
third example Hightower knows the future behavior of blacks
already, as if sequence were reversed, and future action had

preceded the present. But these statements, which seem absolutely correct versions of reality, are quite duplicitous. For example, if "only a negro" can really know a mule, then the Negro knows more than both the white narrator and Hightower. In the second example, the narrator does not simply say "job at the mill," but "negro's job at the mill." Joe Christmas hides his "blackness" behind the screen of a "negro's job": he pretends to "slave like a negro" so no one will think he is one. But the very category of "negro" ("negro's job . . . negro cabin") may be seen as a screen, a veil of only apparent difference that society may be using to disguise actual similarities. Therefore, the narrator has yet to see through "negro," even though he has seen through the "job." Possibly the whole white society, like the "white" Christmas, is hiding behind the veil of "negro" (recall Quentin's "a nigger is . . . a form of behaviour; a sort of obverse reflection of the white people he lives among"). One citizen says, "That nigger murderer. Christmas," but says in the next breath, "He dont look no more like a nigger than I do, either" (328). Finally, Hightower, in the third example, predicts that any black will "naturally" hesitate under certain circumstances. Yet he selectively omits to mention that such hesitation comes from the standard consequence—lynching and castration—of a black male "asking some white woman" anything, even "to telephone for him": "Now you'll let white women alone, even in hell," Grimm says over Christmas's emasculated corpse, "flinging behind him the bloody butcher knife" (439). Hightower, typically for Yoknapatawpha, represses society's threats and acts of violence, while highlighting what are blacks' "natural" and "timeless" "fashions." He shows a willed ignorance (akin to Freudian dream censorship) that must ultimately condition all questions of knowledge and ignorance in the novel.

Light in August, *Absalom, Absalom!*, and *Go Down Moses* treat, more informatively than their predecessors, the relationship between language and knowledge. At question is, above all, what the town knows, what it thinks it knows, what it knows but must conceal, and finally what it can never know because that knowledge would imperil its ability to know anything. In *Light in August* Faulkner diverges from Fielding's omniscient narrators or Conrad's and James's unreliable ones by exposing omniscience as unreliability. The unreliability is an active deception. There is no deficiency, either of intelligence or perspicacity: the narrator is actively creating error. Society here turns arbitrary codes of dominance into "fact." To make matters worse, the reader helps accomplish the entire process.

Reading and gossip seem to offer something new to be told, but both operations essentially involve recognizing the old in the new, hence misrecognizing what one sees. *Light in August,* despite its "emphasis on perception," actually is about what people fail to perceive. Perception seems particularly difficult between races and sexes. Martha and her husband, Armstid, for example, seem in different worlds:

> He does not look in that direction; he does not need to look to know that she will be there, is there. . . . He does not watch her. . . He does not need to. . . . He does not look at her . . . He begins to wash, his back to her. . . . Mrs. Armstid does not look around. . . . And he can feel her looking at him. . . . He cannot tell from her voice if she is watching him or not now. . . . And now he knows that she is watching him. (12–14)

Habituation (akin in this context to an optical effect: persistence of vision) tends to obscure whatever it fixes. Lena and her male driver never look at each other; each knows what the other "is": "Apparently he has never looked at her. . . . Apparently she has never looked at him, either. She does not do so now" (24–25). Byron Bunch and Lucas Burch mirror each other when they speak, called "the one" and "the other": "Byron thinks that this is just the reflection of what he himself already knows and is about to tell. . . . He is not looking at the other now" (74–75). At times, distraction, and not habituation, is the culprit. When the young couple stop their car for him, Christmas does not actually register their words: "Christmas did not notice this at the time. . . . Christmas did not hear this either. . . . But again Christmas did not notice. . . he was not even paying attention"

(267–68). But most often, characters remain ignorant either because they cannot look, or because they think they do "not need to look to know." The assumption that omniscience is a real prediction of the future turns out badly. Christmas represents the aporia that comes when real events do not replicate social expectations. All the ways of custom and habit are blocked or at best circular.

Misrecognition, whether caused by oversight or self-delusion, is the central theme in *Light in August,* and the novel shares this concern with *Don Quixote,* which Faulkner invariably listed among those books that had influenced him most. Readers misperceive before anyone else, as at the beginning of chapter 2: "the group of men at work in the planer shed looked up, and saw the stranger standing there, watching them" (27). Our immediate temptation is to think that "the stranger" is Lucas Burch, whom Lena Grove has been seeking in chapter 1. But "the stranger" is Christmas, whom we meet here, unnamed, for the first time. Christmas himself misperceives crucial moments in his life, such as when the dietitian offers him "hush money": "When he saw the hand emerge from the pocket he believed that she was about to strike him. But she did not; the hand just opened beneath his eyes. Upon it lay a silver dollar" (116). Joe seems generally unable to understand the visible and audible signs of society: his foster mother puts "into the can beneath his round grave eyes coins whose value he did not even recognise" (158). Christmas misunderstands Max and Mame: "it was as if they talked at and because of him, in a language which he did not understand" (182–83); "Perhaps he heard the words. But likely not. Likely they were as yet no more significant than the rasping of insects beyond the closedrawn window, or the packed bags which he had looked at and had not yet seen" (201).

Light in August depicts how Joe Christmas resists signification, while showing that we, either as readers or as potential racists, cannot tolerate anything that does not signify. In a similar manner as the citizens of Jefferson itself, Faulkner's readers seem compelled to supply anything that makes Christmas significant, even what is not in the text; he must be "marked" as belonging to one pole or the other. It is as revealing as it is embarrassing to consider how many readers fall into a habit of racist marking, even despite Faulkner's own admonition that Christmas "himself didn't know who he was—didn't know whether he was part Negro or not and would never know." Early critics especially insisted on calling Christmas a "harried mulatto" or a "white Negro." Some credited Gavin Stevens's intentionally ludicrous "blood" theory, discussing "a sinister figure haunted by knowledge of his negro blood." Others described "the conflict in Christmas of the white and the negro blood." Cleanth Brooks is correct to say "we are never given any firm proof that Joe Christmas possesses Negro blood." Indeed, at one point Joanna asks Joe how he knows one of his parents is "part nigger." Joe answers, "I dont know it" (240). The simple basis of "not knowing" about Joe's race (onto which others project would-be knowledge) is the chief rhetorical prerequisite for interpreting the novel.[12] The novel poses a challenge to our own self-reading: do we comply with or resist the signification of Joe Christmas as "nigger"?

Joe resists writing, but he must be written. He cannot be a total absence. He dislikes traces, but he leaves them everywhere. The posse are chasing a "shadow," but an imperfect one: "They could even see the prints of his knees and hands where he had knelt to drink from a spring" (310). In a society in which everyone is part of a "social text," socialization paradoxically means to become white as paper. This fact applies most of all, ironically, to the blacks. The black is a shadow, and Joe is another version of what the white mind thinks a dark mystery. Blacks leave a "mark" or "trace," be it color or smell, even despite society's efforts to erase them altogether, to make their blackness a signifier of what Ellison in *Invisible Man* calls a social "invisibility." Joe senses that he is like blacks as he walks among other blacks:

> In the wide, empty, shadow-brooded street he looked like a phantom . . . before he knew it he was in Freedman town, *surrounded by*

the summer smell and the summer voices of invisible negroes. They seemed to enclose him like bodiless voices murmuring, talking, laughing, in a language not his. . . . About him the cabins were shaped blackly out of the blackness. . . . *On all sides, even within him, the bodiless fecundmellow voices* of negro women murmured. (106–7; italics added)

The effaced black is meant to be the background for society's "writing"—like a carrier wave that you are not supposed to sense, the essential yet unperceived thing that carries the "message." Hence Christmas's flesh is "a level dead parchment color," especially in the scenes where McEachern's voice, "like written or printed words," tries to get him to repeat a catechism, to "mark" him with a definite dogma. Yet Joe rejects being inscribed until the very end. Late in the novel the fugitive can still leave behind, "wedged into a split plank on the side of the church, a scrap of paper." This "pencilled message" is "raggedly written, as though by an unpracticed hand or perhaps in the dark. . . . It was addressed to the sheriff by name and it was unprintable—a single phrase—and it was unsigned" (309)—the last white scrap of Joe's black defiance is still "unprintable" and "unsigned."

As Christmas becomes more "Negro" he becomes less vague, less "parchment-colored." Society flattens him into a back cloth that must become one or the other color:

He watched his body grow white out of the darkness like a kodak print emerging from the liquid. (100)

. . . vanishing as he ran, vanishing upward from the head down as if he were running headfirst and laughing into something that was obliterating him like a picture in chalk being erased from a blackboard. (195)

. . . the black abyss . . . into which now and at last he had actually entered, bearing now upon his ankles the definite and ineradicable gauge of its upward moving. (313)

The townspeople accept Burch's claim that Christmas is a "nigger" mainly because it explains the inexplicable. But the narrator, while sharing this fiction, often needs to call Joe "white": "Sometimes the notes would tell him not to come until a certain hour, to that house which no white person save himself had entered in years"; "Then they saw that the man was white. . . . Then they saw that his face was not black" (245, 305). The vacillation between white and black in the "kodak print" and "blackboard" metaphors is like the confusion in the last example about whether "not black" always means white, or even whether white always means "white." The final misrecognition must be that the "dark complected" (46, 50) Lucas Burch most likely has a darker skin than Christmas, whom he betrays as a "nigger."

Lucas Burch, a criminally and blatantly distorted character, supplies the town with a sense of coherence by introducing at the right time divisive racial classifications. Dividing Joe Christmas from white folks immediately solves the town's problems. He restores the town's sense of identity and thereby escapes his own quandary by intensifying Joe's. Similar to the falsely knowledgeable narrator, Burch pretends to assert his own superior knowledge against the town's stupidity:

> "You're so smart," he says. "The folks in this town is so smart. Fooled for three years. Calling him a foreigner for three years, when soon as I watched him three days I knew he wasn't no more a foreigner than I am. . . . He's got nigger blood in him. I knowed it when I first saw him. . . . One time he even admitted it, told me he was part nigger." . . .
>
> "A nigger," the marshal said. "I always thought there was something funny about that fellow." . . .
>
> "Well," the sheriff says, "I believe you are telling the truth at last." (91–92)

Lucas Burch is Christmas's darker double. He looks more like a "foreigner" and "nigger" and "murderer" than Christmas does (he has a "little white scar by his mouth"—51, 74, 258, 285) and yet Christmas is the "nigger" whom the community sacrifices. In fact, by the time the lynch mob is aroused, actual color makes no difference: The "countrymen . . . believed aloud that it was an anonymous crime committed not by a negro but by Negro and [they] knew, believed, and hoped that she had been ravished too: at least once before her throat was cut and at least once afterward" (272). The intentional humor of this excerpt is matched only by its absolute horror. Following this conclusion through, and given that Joe and Lucas are really each other's "dark doubles," sharing every duty and function, it must follow that the "dark complected" Lucas, and not Joe Christmas, is likely to have "black blood." This assumption would explain why he is so anxious to "darken" and destroy Joe. Lena Grove's child, fathered by Burch, could be another mulatto in a long string of uncertain progeny that here, as in *Absalom, Absalom!*, ravels out into an uncertain future.

White Jefferson constitutes hearsay as authority, and has formed the hearsay into fixed figures to which force lends validity. For Christmas to become part of that society, he has to become one thing or an other. Yet insofar as white males frequently violate their own dividing regimens, producing the category and the reality of the "mulatto," racial divisions of all sorts reveal their true nature as arbitrary and neutral. Christmas, for instance, is neither/nor: neither black nor white, neither male nor female, neither background nor writing—he is, no less than Darl or Addie, conceptually neutral within a society that rejects the neutral as a potentially useful category. Hence he must become the object of a signifying violence. "*We'll see if his blood is black. . . . We'll need a little more blood to tell for sure*" (205), say the men who come to brutalize him; they certainly wish to harm Joe, but their motives are in large part definitional. Yet even their expedient of violence does not help. The more blood is spilled to distinguish black from white blood, the more difficult it is to see the difference; at a considerable price it becomes clear that black and white "blood" are the same.

The fate of Christmas demonstrates that the town signifies "natural" value by force. There is no natural way to know what Christmas is, but this is precisely what annoys the town: "He dont look any more like a nigger than I do. But it must have been the nigger blood in him. . . . He never acted like either a nigger or a white man. That was it. That was what made the folks so mad. . . . It was like he never knew he was a murderer, let alone a nigger too" (331). He has not been socialized; he does not "know" what his "I" signifies. At their moment of outrage, the men of the town choose a murderous sort of coherence, just as in *Absalom, Absalom!* Mr. Compson says of the "white Negro," Charles Etienne Bon, "he was, must be, a negro" (198).

Despite the comic denouement—in which the furniture dealer narrates the farcical encounter between Lena and Byron Bunch—Christmas's tragic death provides the true climax of the novel. Yet, the elegiac description of that death, laced with biblical and romantic allusions, seems strangely coy in supplying the interpretation of the Christmas story that it seems to promise. Even as the narrator would fasten up the conceptual status of Joe Christmas into a neat ending, his prose only seems to proliferate uncertainties. The uncertainties surrounding the meaning of Joe Christmas's murder implicate author, town, and reader in the same web of guilt. We all owe a debt, of sorts, to any victim. Manifestly, in this case, his observers have crucified Christmas (or allowed him to be crucified), and his death will make a good yarn for the public:

> Then his face, body, all, seemed to collapse, to fall in upon itself, and from out the slashed garments about his hips and loins *the pent black blood* seemed to rush like a released breath. *It* seemed to rush out of his pale body like the rush of sparks from a rising rocket; upon that *black blast* the man seemed to rise soaring into their memories forever and forever. *They* are not to lose *it*, in whatever peaceful valleys, beside whatever placid and reassuring streams of old age, in the mirroring faces of whatever children *they* will contemplate old disasters and newer hopes. *It* will be there, musing, quiet, steadfast, not fading, and not particularly threatful, but of *itself* alone serene, of *itself* triumphant. (439–40, italics added)

This long excerpt may be the most important passage in the novel for tracing Faulkner's ambiguous conclusions. At least two things are striking in this tableau of Joe Christmas's martyrdom. In the first place, the various fatal ambiguities concerning

"white" and "black" blood come to a head, without being at all
resolved. What is "the pent black blood"? Whether "black" is
here a "figurative" or "literal" term is crucial, but impossible to
determine. Does this idea of "black blood" share in Calvin
Burden's idea of a curse of blackness "staining their blood and
flesh" (234) or Gavin Stevens's elegant schematics of "white
blood" and "black blood" (424)?

Moreover, the "blood" would seem the antecedent of "it" in
the next sentence. "It" is the "black blast" upon which the figure
of Christmas rises, apotheosized into an elegiac mode of memory. Faulkner has made the scene into a tableau, a "frozen
moment," in which we would preserve in "memory" what he
deems important.[13] This "memory" is above all the written text,
and the lesson, such as it is, has been made at the expense of a
life. Certainly, though, the image that has been "fixed" here as
permanent and self-sufficient ("not fading . . . of itself alone
triumphant") only leads to more instability—particularly in the
interpretation of "black blood." Who are the "they" of this
excerpt? Who actually remembers the death of Christmas?
"They are not to lose it. . . . It will be there, musing, quiet,
steadfast." "They" will certainly refer to the same people as
"their memories." But the memory is as ambiguous as the
"they" who remember. "It" may either be a condemnation of the
inhumanity, or "it" may be a warning to the "niggers" of Jefferson—as such murder/castrations tended to be—about how *not* to
behave with whites in general and white women in particular.
"Pantaloon in Black" gives a similarly striking example of Southern "pedagogy" for blacks, an unwritten education by violence.
After the black hero Rider kills a white man, we find "the
prisoner on the following day, hanging from the bell-rope in a
negro schoolhouse about two miles from the sawmill" (*Go Down,
Moses*, 154). The blacks in Jefferson can be expected to remember every nuance of the Christmas story, including the fact
that he was probably white. "The town," on the other hand,
while remembering the tableau, will probably repress how and
why Christmas died, as Hightower does above. This forgetting

would be in accord with the general style of the town. As Theodor Adorno suggests, "all reification is a forgetting"; Jefferson must forget the truth in order to reify and fix its flattering self-image. For the town, Joe Christmas will always be "the nigger" who slit the "white woman's" throat and "got what he deserved."

In the end, neither the town, which seems "peaceful" and "placid" soon after the murder, nor the narrator chooses between possibilities. The "memory" is only a potentially recapturable trace. Once we extend the possible referent of the "they" to Faulkner's readers, we can perhaps account for the confusion about the meaning and "coherence" of *Light in August*. With few exceptions, investigations that attempt to produce "coherence" remain unsatisfying. Who can describe or define the "it" that Faulkner has promised will not even need justification ("of itself alone triumphant")? The ironic thing—which no doubt did not escape Faulkner—is that if we actually follow his narrator here, who offers a "serene" and "triumphant" recollection of a vigilante murder, then we have but murdered Joe Christmas once again.

NOTES

1. Robert Coles, *Children of Crisis: A Study of Courage and Fear* (Boston: Little, Brown and Company, 1964), 251.

2. Gérard Genette, *Figures of Literary Discourse*, trans. Alan Sheridan, intro. Marie-Rose Logan (New York: Columbia University Press, 1982), 10; French title: *Figures I, II, III* (Paris: Seuil, 1966–1972). Elsewhere, in the chapter called "Order," in *Narrative Discourse*, trans. Jane E. Lewin (Ithaca: Cornell University Press, 1980) 33–85, Genette translates this enthusiasm for large-scale rhetorical analysis of narrative into specific rhetorical terms, such as *prolepsis, analepsis*, and *metalepsis*. I share his enthusiasm but not his terminology, preferring terms customized to Faulkner's rhetorical enterprise.

3. Roland Barthes pioneered the notion of using a linguistic model of syntax to discuss large plot units, without pointing to conceivable political ramifications of discursive reversals and overturnings. See his "Introduction to the Structural Analysis of Narratives," in *Image/Music/Text*, trans. Stephen Heath (London: Fontana, 1977), 79–124; Terence Hawkes, *Structuralism and Semiotics* (London: Methuen, 1977); "Greimas and Structural Semantics," in Jonathan Culler, *Structuralist Poetics: Structuralism, Linguistics, and the Study of Literature* (Ithaca: Cornell University Press, 1975), 74–95.

4. Winthrop Jordan has written the definitive account of how the slave system and Western colonialism justified themselves by falsely applying Darwinism and misappropriating notions of evolutionary anatomy in the second, *marking* phase of racial division. See *White over Black: American Attitudes Toward the Negro, 1550–1812* (New

York: Norton, 1968), 510. See especially chapters 6, "The Bodies of Men," and 13, "The Negro Bound by the Chain of Being."

5. Classical philosophy, and our own, might be said to have been founded on the antagonism between "polarity" and "analogy" that underlies racial perception and sociological organization generally. See G. E. R. Lloyd, *Polarity and Analogy* (Cambridge: Cambridge University Press, 1966).

6. Faulkner, *Faulkner in the University: Class Conferences at the University of Virginia, 1957–1958*, ed. Frederick L. Gwynn and Joseph L. Blotner (Charlottesville: University of Virginia Press, 1959), 211.

7. G. W. F. Hegel, *Phenomenology of Spirit*, Section B, IV A, "Independence and Dependence of Self-Consciousness: Lordship and Bondage." Also Chaim Perelman and L. Olbrechts-Tyteca, *The New Rhetoric: A Treatise on Argumentation* (Notre Dame: University of Notre Dame Press, 1969), 190; French title: *La Nouvelle Rhétorique: Traité de l'Argumentation* (Paris: Presses Universitaires de France, 1958).

8. Genette, *Figures of Literary Discourse*, xii.

9. Faulkner borrows, for the "tragic mulatto" figure, chiefly from abolitionist writers such as Stowe, Hildreth, and Trowbridge. See Walter Taylor, "Faulkner: Nineteenth Century Notions of Racial Mixture and the Twentieth Century Imagination," *The South Carolina Review*, 10 (1977), 59, and also, Judith R. Berzon, *Neither White nor Black: The Mulatto Character in American Fiction* (New York: New York University Press, 1978), 81–98. His enterprise may be a fictional working out of subject/object, master/slave relations in other senses, too. As Theodor Adorno says in his article "Subject and Object," "If speculation on the state of reconciliation were permitted, neither the undistinguished unity of subject and object nor their antithetical hostility would be conceivable in it; rather, the communication of what was distinguished," in Andrew Arato and Eike Gebhardt, eds, *The Essential Frankfurt School Reader* (New York: Continuum, 1982), 499.

10. William Faulkner, *Light in August* (New York: Vintage, 1972), 39. All subsequent quotations from this edition will be cited by page numbers in parentheses.

11. Umberto Eco, *A Theory of Semiotics* (Bloomington: Indiana University Press, 1976), 9.

12. William Faulkner, *Faulkner at West Point*, ed. Joseph L. Fant III and Robert Ashley (New York: Random House, 1964), 83; Irving Howe, *William Faulkner* (1951), 3rd ed. (Chicago: University of Chicago Press, 1975), 201; Robert Penn Warren, "T. S. Stribling," *American Review*, 2 (February 1934, 483–86, quoted in John Bassett, ed., *William Faulkner: The Critical Heritage* (Boston: Routledge & Kegan Paul, 1975), 161; Jean Stewart, "The Novels of William Faulkner," *Cambridge Review* (10 March 1933), 310–12, in Bassett, 150; F. R. Leavis, review, *Scrutiny* (June 1933), in Bassett, ed., 144; Cleanth Brooks, *William Faulkner: The Yoknapatawpha Country* (New Haven: Yale University Press, 1963), 50.

13. Such a "fixing" of a fleeting reality is a standard technique in Faulkner's later fiction, and is certainly inspired by the sensibility of Keats's "Ode to a Grecian Urn." Similar "frozen moments" occur during the river crossing in *As I Lay Dying*, in the death of the bear in the short story of the same title, and in the scene where Henry shoots Charles Bon in *Absalom, Absalom!* See Karl E. Zink, "Flux and the Frozen Moment," *PMLA* (June 1956).

Marginalia: Faulkner's Black Lives

Philip M. Weinstein

Let me begin neutrally, with Webster, who defines marginalia in three related ways: "marginal notes," "extrinsic matters," and "nonessential items." Each definition works by way of a stabilizing opposition: we understand the marginal by opposing it to the central, the intrinsic, or the essential. In what follows I want both to contest and to uphold the claim that the role of black lives in Faulkner's work is marginal.

To contest it because, as Jacques Derrida has eloquently argued with respect to "the supplement," the center does not merely "permit" the margin to exist at its side: rather it is constituted by the very notion of marginality.[1] Take away the margin and you have lost the center: it is that outside the center which allows us to conceive of "center." Faulkner's blacks are in this sense the key to his whites (how could you have whites without blacks to silhouette and make salient their whiteness?).

I want to contest the marginality of marginalia for another reason as well. Like doodling, marginalia may comprise less examined markings: more able to escape the mind's censorship, more likely to accommodate fugitive energies not welcome within the central enterprise. Marginalia may give expression to fears or desires that the legitimate center could not absorb and still remain legitimate. Faulkner's blacks are recurrently the medium through which he imagines—with both longing and repugnance—how it might feel to be not-white.

Yet—though they may serve as a semiotic key for interpreting the center—those in the margins *are* marginal. No amount of deconstructive privileging can transform peripheral lives into central ones. Largely deprived by the narrative of voice, of point of view, of their own past and future (their memories and desires), blacks as represented by Faulkner are truncated figures. These lives may well take on incandescent symbolic importance for the anguished whites viewing them (and this means the white reader and the white novelist outside the novels, as well as the white protagonists within them), but the importance is only symbolic. These figures have no access to their own incandescence; their importance is for *others* alone.

Faulkner's Black Lives: I mean the phrase in both of the senses in which you hear it: the detached lives of the black characters Faulkner's art records, and also the undetached, fantasized black life Faulkner imaginatively projects from within himself as he creates these figures. Faulkner's world is simultaneously *the* world and his alone, simultaneously how things are generally construed and how his remarkable head and heart construe them. Subjective projection is thus continuous in the act of creation, and I want now to claim that its counterpart—subjective introjection—is equally decisive in the act of reading.[2] Faulkner's Black Lives, as he writes them into his art, become our Black Lives, as we read them out of his art. Those of us who are not black undergo blackness the only way in which we can—imaginatively—as we momentarily merge our own psyches with the fictive black ones represented within his work. This subliminal yet powerful identification—we are what we read while we read it—is why the truncation matters, why the marginality needs to be assessed. We need to know what shaping images of blackness we are absorbing, what enabling or disabling traits are being passed on to us in its name.

These, then, are the issues I am concerned with: the covert relations between marginal black and central white, the menace that black "draws off" as well as the eccentric longings it may conceal, the various ways in which Faulkner construes black in order to imagine its intermingling with white, and finally the subliminal images of blackness the reader experiences in the act of absorbing Faulkner's Black Lives. In a word, what is Faulkner doing when he imagines black, and how does the shape of his imagining affect the shape of our own? Because these issues alter significantly throughout the course of Faulkner's career, I shall concentrate on four major novels written over a period of thirteen years: *The Sound and the Fury,* (1929), *Light in August* (1932), *Absalom, Absalom!* (1936), and *Go Down, Moses* (1942).[3]

* * *

. . . I didn't know that I really had missed Roskus and Dilsey and them until that morning in Virginia. The train was stopped when I waked and I raised the shade and looked out. The car was blocking a road crossing, where two white fences came down a hill and then sprayed outward and downward like part of the skeleton of a horn, and there was a nigger on a mule in the middle of the stiff ruts, waiting for the train to move. How long he had been there I didn't know, but he sat straddle of the mule, his head wrapped in a piece of blanket, as if they had been built there with the fence and the road, or with the hill, carved out of the hill itself, like a sign put there saying You are home again. He didn't have a saddle and his feet dangled almost to the ground. The mule looked like a rabbit. I raised the window.

"Hey, Uncle," I said, "Is this the way?"

"Suh?" He looked at me, then he loosened the blanket and lifted it away from his ear.

"Christmas gift!" I said.

"Sho comin, boss. You done caught me, aint you?"

"I'll let you off this time." I dragged my pants out of the little hammock and got a quarter out. "But look out next time. I'll be coming back through here two days after New Year, and look out then." I threw the quarter out the window. "Buy yourself some Santy Claus."

"Yes, suh," he said. He got down and picked up the quarter and rubbed it on his leg. "Thanky, young marster. Thanky." Then the train began to move. I leaned out the window, into the cold air, looking back. He stood there beside the gaunt rabbit of a mule, the two of them shabby and motionless and unimpatient. (106–7)

So much of *The Sound and the Fury*'s rendering of blacks is in this passage. Quentin on a train, disoriented; the black emerging out of nowhere on the road, as if for Quentin's benefit, to give him orientation ("You are home again"); the easy, mutually ratifying verbal interchange, in which Quentin affirms an older and simpler identity (the "young marster" offering "Christmas gift" to a thankful darky); the train moving Quentin away with increasing velocity, while the rooted black man and his mule (as stable and timeless as the hill itself) etch themselves into his mind: "the two of them shabby and motionless and unimpatient." "Unimpatient": Faulkner's urge to emphasize is so great that he invents this word, making us move through the original "patient" (like the hill itself), then through "impatient" (the train, the modern white world Quentin will soon be hurtling toward again), and finally into "unimpatient": an achieved capacity for moving *with* time rather than against or through it: a capacity possessed in this novel only by blacks.

This black man appears as pure symbol, a monument to a certain temporal sanity and mode of social relations that Quentin and his culture used to enjoy. Other blacks in *The Sound and the Fury* may be more prominent, but they are usually deployed in the same manner: as symbols, set pieces, monumental performances. Thus Deacon comes on the stage for five impressive pages in Quentin's chapter, and then is heard no more. Thus the Reverend Shegog is swiftly marshalled into his place in the last chapter, heard in all his eloquence, and then just as swiftly abandoned. These figures, whatever their thematic importance, are marginal to the narrative movement itself. Deprived of the space and time necessary for narrative development (even when they represent "unimpatience"), denied therefore the luxury of becoming themselves, they must perform their essential being in one climactic burst. As such, they appear (like Old Man Job) less as integral figures within the Compson drama than as gnomic counterpositions—enlightening yet narratively unconnected—to the irreversible process of Compson decay.

Dilsey and her family of course operate in another mode: generously developed over space and time, and fully integral to the Compson drama. Indeed Dilsey seems so steeped in the white family's troubles that we never cease to admire her capacity to live a normal life nevertheless. Perhaps the keynote to her success, and to that of her entire family, can be heard in the following interchange with Luster:

"Reckin so," Luster said. "Dese is funny folks. Glad I aint none of em."

"Aint none of who?" Dilsey said. "Lemme tell you somethin, nigger boy, you got jes es much Compson devilment in you es any of em. Is you right sho you never broke dat window?"

"Whut I want to break hit fur?"

"Whut you do any of yo devilment fur?" Dilsey said. "Watch him now, so he cant burn his hand again twell I git de table set." (344)

Every time I reread *The Sound and the Fury* I smile at this passage, and especially at that phrase "Compson devilment." I think I know now why I have been smiling: the phrase is immensely reassuring. So that's all it is that Benjy, Quentin, Caddy, Jason, and Caddy's daughter are afflicted with: "Compson devilment"! "Compson devilment" adroitly transforms idiocy, anguish, and sadism into normal prankishness. And, for the reader, the effect of this tranquilizing counterpoint—this calm black lens, at once comic and normative—is to domesticate, to make more quotidian, the tragic descent of the Compsons. The blacks serve as a powerfully pastoralizing background, a continuous reminder of what survival is like, in the midst of white degeneration. Dilsey, Roskus, Versh, Frony, TP, and even Luster form a sort of chorus of normality. Like trained nurses they enter the sick room without contracting the disease.

What is the disease they do not catch? I submit that it is "the sound and the fury" itself. These black figures are fully self-contained, free of the passion and impatience that afflict the Compson offspring. Presented from without, the black family is conceived in nostalgia, Faulkner's nostalgia. I assume that he had to climb back into his own childhood to find them, and he presents them not as figures drowning in those conflicting internal urges and sanctions of his own (and which he creatively bestowed upon the Compson siblings), but instead as—seen objectively and from a gentle distance—figures of stability, reminders of warm and witty talk, of the saving outward routines of childhood recollected.4 Benjy may keep trying to say, Quentin may think *"Wait just a minute . . . I'll get used to it in a minute"* (140), Caddy and her daughter Quentin may whirl themselves out of the family, Jason may run as fast as he can to catch the stock market and his fleeing niece; but Dilsey's black family stays put. They are "unimpatient"; they know.

Immovably rooted in ancient ways, blacks serve in *The Sound and the Fury* as a sort of benign cultural memory. Their reported conversations take us (as no Compson talk, freighted with portent, can take us) back to pastoral innocence. Quentin's mind lingers on Uncle Louis Hatcher's memories of possum hunts and of riding out the old-time floods (Quentin will soon enough drown in his own flood). More poignantly he remembers Versh's story about a man mutilating himself:

> He went into the woods and did it with a razor, sitting in a ditch. A broken razor flinging them backward over his shoulder the same motion complete the jerked skein of blood backward not looping. But that's not it. It's not not having them. It's never to have had them then I could say O That That's Chinese I dont know Chinese. (143)

To put it in extreme form, when Faulkner imagines black in this novel, the vanishing point he strains toward is Chinese. He imagines a ceremonious life free, precisely, of sound and fury, that is, narratively free of the internal stresses of stream of consciousness, and thematically free of desire itself: a sexless and therefore simplifying antidote to Compson pain. In the novels that follow he was rarely to see black as a simplification of anything.5

*   *   *

His turn came. He entered the shed. It was dark. At once he was overcome by a terrible haste. There was something in him trying to get out, like when he had used to think of toothpaste. But he could not move at once, standing there, smelling the woman, smelling the negro all at once; enclosed by the womanshenegro and the haste, driven, having to wait until she spoke: a guiding sound that was no particular word and completely unaware. Then it seemed to him that he could see her—something, prone, abject; her eyes perhaps. Leaning, he seemed to look down into a black well and at the bottom saw two glints like reflection of dead stars. He was moving, because his foot touched her. Then it touched her again because he kicked her. He kicked her hard, kicking into and through a choked wail of surprise and fear. She began to scream, he jerking her up, clutching her by the arm, hitting at her with wide, wild blows, striking at the voice perhaps, feeling her flesh anyway, enclosed by the woman-shenegro and the haste.

Then she fled beneath his fist, and he too fled backward as the others fell upon him, swarming, grappling, fumbling, he striking back, his breath hissing with rage and despair. (146–47)

What could this be but *Light in August?* Its graphically detailed violence is unmatched elsewhere in Faulkner's work; there is a release in this prose that borders on ecstasy. Though she is the occasion for this violent release, the anonymous black girl counts for very little in herself. Preceded by the dietitian (the smell/sensation of toothpaste), to be followed by Bobbie the prostitute, this girl has no traits of her own. The emotional history she rouses into semiconsciousness is not hers but Joe's. She smells of her entire race and sex. Her eyes betray no personal identity, giving off instead the "reflection of dead stars." Sentient, she screams when kicked, flees from "beneath his fist." She is never seen again.

Her importance lies in what she triggers in the male, not in what she is herself. His foot moves before he knows it is moving; his breath hisses; he becomes a figure of total—almost epileptic—bodily release. She occasions the collapse of Joe's precarious identity, a collapse expressed through ecstatic fighting, the giving and receiving of pain. As elsewhere in *Light in August,* the private act of intercourse between male and female leads to the public act of male to male brawling. Sexuality emerges as that which crosses the culture's codes for maintaining distinctions of race and gender both—distinctions on which the frayed fabric of white male civility depends.[6] And in this book, with some significant exceptions, sexuality is disturbingly connected with black.

The connection is lethal. Black becomes an almost magic fomentor of sexual fantasies and male violence. Pronounce the word nigger and Joanna Burden's murder becomes a rape; the white men's behavior moves into ritual ("'Get me a nigger,' the sheriff said"). There is more beating, more hands laid brutally upon bodies, in *Light in August* than in any other of Faulkner's novels. The beating seems to be both an outraged censuring of sexual release and an illicit indulging in the same release. As always, black in itself counts for nothing; it is needed only as a trigger.

If in *The Sound and the Fury* black is a sanctuary in which the chaos of sexual impulses can be kept at bay, here we have the reverse. (Indeed, that seems to be one of the meanings of the title: this book's fascination with what is on the other side of the light.) Joe's putative blackness lies within him like an inexhaustible toxin, stinging him into ritual forays of sadistic and masochistic beating. It is himself he cannot bear, and his death is surely as much a suicidal immolation at the castrating hands of Percy Grimm as it is a heroic coming to terms with his warring components.

In all of Faulkner's novels characters generalize about blacks, but rarely elsewhere is the generalizing so rabid. The other side of the light is always the *other side*, always ferociously projected from this side. Nathaniel Burden's "A race doomed and cursed to be forever and ever a part of the white race's doom and curse for its sins. Remember that" (239) and Gavin Stevens's "Because the black blood drove him first to the negro cabin. And then the white blood drove him out of there, as it was the black blood which snatched up the pistol and the white blood which would not let him fire it" (424)—both of these crazily polarized abstractions occupy central space in *Light in August*, blinding characters to the flesh-and-blood reality of actual blacks. In fact there are very few actual blacks in this race-obsessed novel. None of those that *are* there is granted even a name, let alone a story of his or her own.[7]

What then does Faulkner imagine when he imagines black in *Light in August?* If we take Joe Christmas as the relevant case, Faulkner clearly isn't imagining black at all. He focuses instead

upon the lifelong nightmare of a white man *imagining* himself
(and imagined by others) to be black. Black is here not the color
of a man's skin but instead a murderously projective state of the
white male mind, that which blasts the community's precarious
chances for mutual acceptance and peace.[8] With respect to
Faulkner and Race, therefore, *Light in August* is the pivotal
novel, the one in which he discovered his white male culture's
(and his own) most deeply seated black preoccupations. He
found that the issues of racial difference, gender boundary, and
sexual desire come together in a single constellation as covertly
appealing as it is overtly appalling: miscegenation.

* * *

It was not the nigger anymore than it had been the nigger that his
father had helped to whip that night. The nigger was just another
balloon face slick and distended with that mellow loud and terrible
laughing so that he did not dare to burst it, looking down at him from
within the half-closed door during that instant in which, before he
knew it, something in him had escaped and—he unable to close the
eyes of it—was looking out from within the balloon face just as the
man who did not even have to wear the shoes he owned, whom the
laughter which the balloon held barricaded and protected from such
as he, looked out from whatever invisible place he (the man) happened to be at the moment, at the boy outside the barred door in his
patched garments and splayed bare feet, looking through and beyond the boy, he himself seeing his own father and sisters and
brothers as the owner, the rich man (not the nigger) must have been
seeing them all the time—as cattle, creatures heavy and without
grace, brutely evacuated into a world without hope or purpose for
them, who would in turn spawn with brutish and vicious prolixity,
populate, double treble and compound, fill space and earth with a
race whose future would be a succession of cut-down and patched
and made-over garments bought on exorbitant credit because they
were white people, from stores where niggers were given the garments free, with for sole heritage that expression on a balloon face
bursting with laughter which had looked out at some unremem-
bered and nameless progenitor who had knocked at a door when he
was a little boy and had been told by a nigger to go around to the
back. (235)

This passage suggests something of *Absalom, Absalom!*'s capacious frame for reading black lives. Rejecting the pastoral

sweetness of *The Sound and the Fury*'s rendering of blacks, *Absalom* is premised upon the same racial violence that suffuses *Light in August*. Unlike that earlier book, however, *Absalom* proposes both to distance and to understand the violence. Here, black is inserted into an extensive social, economic, and historical network. Even as he strikes out at those "balloon faces," Sutpen realizes that it is a *system*, not a *color*, that is wounding him.

Crucially, though, the registering consciousness at this visionary moment is white, not black, and the victim of its insight is white, not black. The passage is built upon the language of perception—of Sutpen seeing through the eyes of the "balloon face," then through the eyes of the plantation owner, seeing himself and his entire family as caught up in an impersonal yet annihilating network of concessions and sanctions. Shaped to the needs of a plantation culture, this network privileges blacks over poor whites. It finds menial jobs for blacks, clothes and feeds them, uses them to maintain its own function and image.

There are in *Absalom* two white classes with but one ideology between them. The ideology is planterly, and although the poor whites share its claim of superiority to blacks, their daily experience of economic irrelevance contradicts the tenets of the claim. This situation of heartbreak—crystallized for Sutpen at the moment of the closed door—might lead either to rebellion or to joining up. Unable to choose between these options, Faulkner seems to choose them both. He has Sutpen join up while he narrates at the same time the collapse (both tragic and justified) of the entire plantation system.

The impact of this system's brutality upon blacks (and not just poor whites like Sutpen and Wash Jones) needs badly to be explored, and *Absalom, Absalom!* would be considerably different if Faulkner *had* explored it. That is, we would have a novel that seriously probed into the systemic damage done not just to poor whites but to blacks as well—their insertion into an alienating network of white powers and sanctions. *Absalom, Absalom!* prepares the way for this inquiry, but Faulkner does not actually carry it out until six years later, in *Go Down, Moses*. Here his principal interest when he imagines black is different—primarily psychological and sexual, it seems to me, and only secondarily economic and class focused.9 Perhaps the simplest way to identify that interest is to call it Charles Bon.

If Charles Bon is another "balloon face" (a container filled by other people's inspiration), he is nonetheless the most compelling figure in *Absalom, Absalom!*—compelling in the sense that no one (not Rosa, Mr. Compson, Sutpen, Henry, Judith, Quentin, or Shreve—and not, therefore, the reader either) can take their eyes off him, or rest with others' versions of him. Charles Bon is the most extravagantly reinvented character in the novel. What does it mean that black in *Absalom, Absalom!* is primarily imagined through him?

Like Joe Christmas, Charles Bon is only putatively black; he *looks* white. But whereas Joe appears to the reader as a white man caught in a nightmare, Bon is genuinely—culturally—different. He is the erotic center of *Absalom, Absalom!* All who see him (except, ironically, his father) or get caught up in the telling or the reading of his story run the risk of falling in love with him. In other words, Faulkner is here imagining the reverse situation of Joe Christmas: a dozen or so white characters in the novel (and countless white readers outside the novel) smitten with one black man. What makes this possible and why might Faulkner be doing it?

Bon's appeal is inseparable from his exoticism. *Absalom* depends for some of its most memorable effects upon exoticism, or another way to put this is to say that *Absalom* can try out through geographic and cultural displacement what it cannot work through on its home space. New Orleans is where it goes to understand sexual and racial ease; Haiti is where it goes to understand racial and economic war; Cambridge is where it goes to understand the stories of Jefferson. Charles Bon, more than any other figure in the book, is the product of Haiti, New Orleans, and Cambridge. Exoticism is another word for his nonprovincial allure; he has been put together out of physical and spiritual traits not available in northern Mississippi.

Thus constituted, thus appealing, thus distinguished from the native black (and white) specimens, Bon can house Faulkner's most audacious fantasy: that black is more beautiful than white, that the unconscious desire for miscegenation lurks deep within the white psyche. Bon represents in his lithe body and unfailing civility the novel's inadmissible desire for racial union, a desire that compels even so recalcitrant a Southerner as Rosa Coldfield so long as his blackness remains invisible and the desire for union be denied its true name.[10] But of course the reverse is equally true in *Absalom, Absalom!:* once identified *as* black, he loses his exotic camouflage, his menace is revealed, and he becomes (despite the persistence of desire) the target of every native code. He becomes anathema.

The contrast between exotic black and homegrown black is pronounced in *Absalom, Absalom!* On the one hand there are (in addition to Sutpen's savage blacks, speaking in incomprehensible tongues) the tragic octoroon, the mysterious Eulalia Bon, her elegantly epicene son Charles, and his emphatically foreign-named son Charles Etienne Saint Velery Bon—all of these figures of physical energy, grace, or pathos. But on the other hand there is the "coal black and ape-like woman" (205) whom Charles Etienne marries to fling in Judith's face: a black woman described more abusively than any other in Faulkner's fiction ("that aghast and automaton-like state in which she had arrived . . . [and] which she seemed to exude gradually and by a process of terrific and incredulous excretion like . . . sweat . . . how he had found her, dragged her out of whatever two dimensional backwater . . . her mentality had been capable of coercing food and shelter from, and married her, held her very hand doubtless while she made the laborious cross on the register before she even knew his name . . . [a woman whom he] kenneled . . . [a] black gargoyle . . . resembling something in a zoo" [205–9]). The offspring of this union, owing apparently everything to the mother and nothing to the father, is Jim Bond.

What is one to make of this genealogy? What has Jim Bond in common with Charles Bon? What does it mean that this black descent, unlike the white one in *The Sound and the Fury* and unlike the white *and* black ones in *Go Down, Moses*, feels both gapped and built wholly of extremes? Faulkner imagines black in this novel with a schizoid intensity, the foreign pole as seductive as the homegrown one is either neutral or repulsive. Another way to put it is to say that in *Absalom, Absalom!* Faulkner can imaginatively desire the union of white and black only by exoticizing black.

Finally there are *Absalom*'s missing narratives. In a novel that richly invents other missing stories, two black ones are crucially absent here: those of Eulalia and of Clytie. One the abandoned wife and the other the illegitimate daughter of Thomas Sutpen, these characters provide the black underweave to the Sutpen design. Eulalia engineers the collapse of that design; her role, only marginally represented, actually matches (and eventually overmasters) Sutpen's point for point in plot import. As for Clytie, she both presides over the repercussions of the collapsing design and sees to it that, when the time is ready, the house burns down too. Beyond her plot function, though, Clytie emerges as the semiotic center of the novel, the foregrounded figure in whom Faulkner's tormented racial imagination fuses a white paternity and a black career, the figure who finally serves for Quentin as the key to the entire enigma.[11] She is a mute key, however, her meaning eloquently residing in the pigment of her skin rather than the quality of her soul. For something of her subjective experience—what it must feel like to be an abused black in the South—we must leave *Absalom, Absalom!* and turn to *Go Down, Moses*.

* * *

"Ah lets hit lay," he said, and cast, and moved as the white man moved, catching the white man's wrist before his hand reached the dice, the two of them squatting, facing each other above the dice and the money, his left hand grasping the white man's wrists, his face still fixed in the rigid and deadened smiling, his voice equable, almost deferential: "Ah kin pass even wid miss-outs. But dese hyar yuther boys—" until the white man's hand sprang open and the second pair of dice clattered onto the floor beside the first two and the white man wrenched free and sprang up and back and reached the hand backward toward the pocket where the pistol was.

The razor hung between his shoulder-blades from a loop of cotton string round his neck inside his shirt. The same motion of the hand which brought the razor forward over his shoulder flipped the blade open and freed it from the cord, the blade opening on until the back edge of it lay across the knuckles of his fist, his thumb pressing the handle into his closing fingers, so that in the second before the half-drawn pistol exploded he actually struck at the white man's throat not with the blade but with a sweeping blow of his fist, following through in the same motion so that not even the first jet of blood touched his hand or arm. (153–54)

If we compare this passage from "Pantaloon in Black" with the passage of Joe Christmas's violence against the black girl, we can see how the luxuriant detail works in each passage to different effects. In the earlier novel the accent is upon pain, upon the brutal and dehumanizing activity of one body pummeling another. Here the stress is upon Rider's exquisite physical grace. There is no pain in this passage, just Rider's flawlessly coordinated strength (Birdsong, the man whose throat he is cutting, has no narrative reality; this is the first page on which he appears). If we further compare this passage with the passage about Versh's story of a man mutilating himself—"A broken razor flinging them backward over his shoulder the same motion complete the jerked skein of blood backward not looping"—we can see how the same gesture has been put to quite a different use. There the move was toward peaceful depletion, here it is toward aggressive fulfillment. Indeed, the real hold this passage from *Go Down, Moses* has upon us comes from its hypnotic illicitness: a black man is, detail by beautiful detail, killing a white man. Placed narratively within his powerful black body, we as readers participate in the act.

I begin with this sequence from "Pantaloon in Black" in order to show that *Go Down, Moses* is fascinated with a variety of illicit moves available to black males. (The black women in this novel have no such instigating power. Rousing desire in others but deprived of it themselves, they rarely escape the tragic—but passive—role of being taken and abandoned by their white lovers.) The other males in question are Lucas Beauchamp, centrally, and Samuel Worsham Beauchamp, peripherally. I continue now with Rider.

"Pantaloon in Black" is unique in *Go Down, Moses* in its abiding focus on a black man's physical prowess. The story is keyed to Rider's body, the sentences moving in mimicry of his powerful motion: "He drank again, swallowing the chill liquid tamed of taste or heat either while the swallowing lasted, feeling it flow solid and cold with fire, past then enveloping the strong steady panting of his lungs until they too ran suddenly free as his moving body ran in the silver solid wall of air he breasted" (148). I do not mean to slight the importance of Rider's mental state—his unmasterable anguish over the death of Mannie—but this mental state is everywhere conveyed not by conceptual abstractions but by Faulkner's lyrical prose of the body in motion. Paralleling Ike McCaslin's painfully won prowess in the wilderness—but never announced as such—is Rider's supreme ease in his natural surroundings.

Lucas Beauchamp has something of Rider's uncanny natural facility—"Then he whirled and leaped, not toward the sound but running parallel with it, leaping with incredible agility and speed among the trees and undergrowth" (40–41)—but this is not the virtue of Lucas that Faulkner stresses most. Rather, Lucas's behavior seems to represent Faulkner's meditation on what a cunning black man does when the things a white man might do are not available to him. Behind Lucas's big bank account lie some stark facts: the land he farms is not his own, the vocation he practices is not a choice, the territory he inhabits may not be escaped.[12] If Ike McCaslin's story is one of precious options, Lucas Beauchamp's is one of given conditions adroitly accepted and exploited.[13]

Lucas is a game-player. He runs an illegal still, he believes in buried treasure, he buys a special machine to find it with. These adolescent maneuvers (one imagines a slightly older Tom Sawyer doing these things) lack the soul-testing seriousness of Ike's drama, and that is their point. A black man living marginally, at the sufferance of the white landowner, with his own options long ago circumscribed, can either release his spirit in harmlessly illicit games or roll over and play by the rules. On the margin there is room only for childish play—Faulkner seems unable to imagine anything else for an established black to *do*—and the usual effect on the reader of these clever machinations in "The Fire and the Hearth" is to convict Lucas of frivolity.

Yet they suggest something more. A traditional man, Lucas nevertheless feels the siren call of progressive capitalism.[14] He alone in *Go Down, Moses* is interested in machines, in renting out equipment, in having his investment return a profit. His secret dream is to find that buried Civil War treasure and to retire: a dream of release from the thralldom of the earth, a dream of unacknowledged revenge against the landed white Southerners whose money would now fall into his enterprising black hands. Faulkner's portrait of this black man is thus poised between manifest admiration for Lucas's fidelity to his ancestry, on the one hand, and latent respect for his unco-opted capacity for a future, on the other. Though Lucas has only games to play, he remains open (unlike the dignified Ike McCaslin) to the fertile possibilities of scandal. He takes his chances as they come, intrepid enough to risk a good deal of trouble, clever enough to get out of it once it arrives.

The black women in *Go Down, Moses* lack the men's aggressiveness, but at least they possess (as compared to the earlier fiction) their own history. It is a history of abuse; and Faulkner passionately rehearses it through the figures of Eunice, Fonsiba, Molly, and the "doe" in "Delta Autumn." Though rarely told in their own voices, it nevertheless registers with much of its emotional fullness intact. Black suffering and white guilt are now inextricably intertwined. Indeed, by the end of *Go Down, Moses* Faulkner is straining to have the entire community bear witness to the sorrow inscribed in black lives.

That final story of an escaped, executed, and returned black man is offered as aftermath, as dirge. Samuel Worsham Beauchamp is dead on arrival, set up for capital punishment the moment we meet him. His life itself has no narrative meaning.

Faulkner's interest is in the traditional community that receives his corpse back into the fold. The organizers of the reception—Miss Worsham and Gavin Stevens—strike a curiously strident note, however. His piety is too officious, hers too assured—the black grief really is *not* theirs—and Faulkner reveals this (with respect to Miss Worsham) unintentionally:

> Now he could hear the third voice, which would be that of Hamp's wife—a true constant soprano which ran without words beneath the strophe and antistrophe of the brother and sister:
> "Sold him in Egypt and now he dead."
> "Oh yes, Lord. Sold him in Egypt."
> "Sold him in Egypt."
> "And now he dead."
> "Sold him to Pharoah."
> "And now he dead."
> "I'm sorry," Stevens said. "I ask you to forgive me. I should have known. I shouldn't have come."
> "It's all right," Miss Worsham said. "It's our grief." (381)

"It's our grief," she says—as though to distinguish her intimacy from Stevens's isolation—but Miss Worsham's voice is not heard in that overwhelming chorus of woe, a chorus uniquely black. The reference goes back to the pariahs, to Jews destroyed by Egyptians, to blacks deformed, uprooted, and executed by whites. These are the marginal people, and they suffer: they are done to. Faulkner can point to their grief, he can be anguished over it, he can quote its voice, but neither he himself nor his white delegates can speak it. Nor can he envisage that those who suffer under it might—through their own activities—escape its burden.

When Faulkner imagines black in *Go Down, Moses*, he imagines a 150-year-long history of oppression (sexual, political, economic, emotional) of blacks by whites of the same family. This is a history that the black women stoically endure and that the black men seek alternately to confront and (in illicit, appealing, and foredoomed ways) to escape. We have come a long way from *The Sound and the Fury*. The blacks and whites—men and women—of this novel emerge as thematically integral to each other's destiny. (How they emerge *narratively* is another question. Their outward stories come to us, but usually not their inner voices.)

Bound to each other through seven generations that begin and end with miscegenation, the blacks see in the whites the conditions they cannot escape, the whites see in the blacks the guilt they cannot assuage. Inescapable because the traditional South is the only place Faulkner can imaginatively endorse, even for his blacks; and unassuageable because the act that Faulkner would have to affirm for his whites to get clear of guilt—the act of miscegenation—remains taboo. The traditional South would, it seems, collapse to its foundations if it were to legitimize such a mixing of the races. And yet on the streets of every town and city of the South the effects of miscegenation are daily visible—inscribed in the pigment of the skin, that silent and eloquent testimony to how things are rather than how they are supposed to be.

Let me conclude by briefly comparing three marginal figures, each one the end of his line: Benjy Compson, Jim Bond, and Samuel Worsham Beauchamp. To set up the comparison is to see where it comes out. In Benjy, Faulkner took a marginal figure and made him central. Not that Benjy can escape his suffering or overcome his handicaps; his future is hopeless. But Faulkner made compelling art out of that hopelessness. Spurred by its silent sound in his own mind, he created the most moving interior voice in all of his work. Benjy is central because he matters. He matters narratively (all of Faulkner's art is in getting Benjy to matter narratively) and therefore he matters to us, his readers. We register his human wholeness.

Jim Bond and Samuel Worsham Beauchamp do not matter in the same way, nor to the same degree. Jim Bond is heard, not felt. Only Clytie is there to care for him, and it is a caring we do not see. He frightens white people; his single recorded interaction with them is to pick Rosa Coldfield off the floor at the end of

Absalom, Absalom! He may have a putative soul, but Faulkner has not created it for him, and so we do not imaginatively credit it.

As for Samuel Worsham Beauchamp, his mistake apparently was to leave Jefferson for points north. This departure has simply undone his identity:

> The face was black, smooth, impenetrable; the eyes had seen too much. The negroid hair had been treated so that it covered the skull like a cap, in a single neat-ridged sweep, with the appearance of having been lacquered. . . . He wore one of those sports costumes called ensembles in the men's shop advertisements, shirt and trousers matching and cut from the same fawn-colored flannel, and they had cost too much and were draped too much, with too many pleats . . . smoking cigarettes and answering in a voice which was anything under the sun but a southern voice or even a negro voice. . . . (369)

Caddy and her daughter can depart from the Compson family and at least survive, if not triumph. Samuel Worsham Beauchamp is sentenced to death for leaving. In this portrait Faulkner proposes a total denaturing, as if the abandonment of his black and white family meant becoming unrecognizable— unrecognizable to Faulkner and therefore to us. All that remains of Samuel Worsham Beauchamp are his urban mistakes—his straightened hair, his overpriced and tacky clothes, his unplaceable voice. The portrait is suffused in disapproval; its subject no longer has a soul.

Samuel Worsham Beauchamp's significance is not intrinsic. It resides in the powerful communal response his returned corpse occasions back home, and it lurks as well in the message being sent to others: Stay at home, grow up by accepting your overwhelming inheritance, by way of endurance. This is the significance, it seems to me, of a marginal character, one whom Faulkner cannot enter as he can enter Benjy Compson, one whom he therefore turns into a symbol. It is no discredit to Faulkner if we say that—despite some remarkable portraits of black beauty, courage, pathos, and cunning—the power of his racial imagination lies elsewhere. It lies in the honest depiction of turmoil and hatred that the notion of black can unleash in the white male mind, and it lies as well in the creative mix of feelings—longing, bafflement, and grief—through which he explores (and therefore permits us to explore) this inflicted pain, this enforced segregation. But Samuel Worsham Beauchamp slips away from him, and it will take another writer, Richard Wright, to see in this denatured corpse the seeds of escape, of Big Boy leaving home.

NOTES

1. The relation of the object to its supplement echoes the relation of the center to its margin. In both cases an independent major term apparently commands a dependent minor one, yet on reflection we see that the dependence works both ways. In thinking through this unstable mutual dependence, Derrida's argument embraces the problematic of language as a whole. On the one hand, signifying language merely supplements the signified thing (object, concept, etc.) it points to (as margin supplements center, black supplements white). The primary thing remains "full," unaltered by its supplement. Yet, on the other hand, the fact that this thing must be supplemented (by being put into language) in order to reach us at all means that the thing in its "original" state was not "full" but lacking. Its independent status is thus belied by its dependence upon a signifying system that can "deliver" it. "For the concept of the supplement . . . harbors within itself two significations whose cohabitation is as strange as it is necessary. The supplement adds itself, it is a surplus, a plenitude enriching another plenitude, the *fullest measure* of presence. . . . But the supplement supplements. It adds only to replace. It intervenes or insinuates itself *in-the-place-of*; if it fills, it is as if one fills a void" (*Of Grammatology*, trans. Gayatri Spivak [Baltimore: Johns Hopkins University Press, 1976], 144–45).

2. The most suggestive account I know of this argument—that reading involves a fantasy-fusion with the text—is that of Charles Bernheimer. In the theoretical introductory chapter of his *Flaubert and Kafka*, Bernheimer, drawing on object-relations psychoanalytic thought, posits that our initial experience of total immersion in an object is with the mother's breast, and that all subsequent attempts at merger seek to replace this absent object. He further claims that our experience of being is itself grounded in these activities: that we sustain the sense of self-presence by an insistent self-immersion in beneficent objects. Not surprisingly, this move that sustains the sense of self in the act of reading is balanced by its opposite: a move toward greater and greater self-fracture, in which alterity reigns—alterity within the text one reads (but can never possess) and within the self that is reading. Drawing on Freudian terminology, Bernheimer calls these two moves that constitute reading (but not just reading) Erotic and Thanatopic impulses. See *Flaubert and Kafka* (New Haven: Yale University Press, 1982), 1–44.

3. I cite from the Vintage editions of *The Sound and the Fury* and *Light in August*, and from the Modern Library editions of *Absalom, Absalom!* and *Go Down, Moses*. Page numbers will appear in parentheses, following the citation.

4. David Minter discusses the personal exposure—deriving from the most painful childhood experiences—that Faulkner imaginatively risked in the creation of these Compson children. See *William Faulkner: His Life and Work* (Baltimore: Johns Hopkins University Press, 1982), 91–100.

5. Faulkner's representation of black as a nostalgic focus of simplified life rhythms is compelling but by no means innocent. The pacifyingly represented black-authored mutilation recalls uneasily a disturbingly real Southern history of white-authored mutila-

tions. *The Sound and the Fury*'s portrayal of black as pastoral is enabled by a series of mirror-projections and distortions—of white reading black as the site of its own fears and desires—that would well repay further scrutiny. I am indebted here and elsewhere to John Matthews for helpful discussion of the ways in which ideology reveals and conceals itself within Faulkner's texts.

6. John Tucker's "William Faulkner's *Light in August:* Toward a Structuralist Reading," *MLQ*, 43, 2 (June 1982), 138–55, reads the novel suggestively as a hive of unstable binary oppositions, of inadequate codes meant to clarify and contain an uncontrollable welter of conflicting human activities.

7. If we leave the foregrounded action of the present scene and drop back to nineteenth-century vignettes, we do find two blacks with names (though dubious gender identifications): Pomp and Cinthy, Hightower's grandfather's faithful retainers.

8. The assertions that Faulkner is not here imagining black at all and that black is not here the color of a man's skin are the beginnings of a further inquiry, even if they conclude this one. For black is, of course, never just skin color, never an essence unto itself. Yet Joe Christmas's way of being black differs significantly from that of a figure with whom he is often twinned: Charles Bon. I develop this difference later in the essay.

9. To say that Faulkner's principal interest is psychological and sexual is not to say that economic and class-focused issues are marginal. It is to say that their impact upon the representation of black in *Absalom, Absalom!* is latent rather than overt, and would require a different analysis from the one I offer here.

10. Eric Sundquist brilliantly argues that *Absalom, Absalom!*, in its way of connecting Rosa with the miscegenation theme, "brings us to the verge of a recognition we are unwilling to make . . . [showing us] the moment that never will be in the certain tragic fullness of what *might have been*" (*Faulkner: The House Divided* [Baltimore: Johns Hopkins University Press, 1983], 115).

11. Peter Brooks's case for construing Clytie as the semiological key to the novel seems to me irrefutable. See his "Incredulous Narration: *Absalom, Absalom!*," *Comparative Literature*, 34, 3 (1982), 247–68.

12. I base my claim of Lucas's nonownership of the land upon the abundant evidence of "The Fire and the Hearth" itself. Of Lucas's coming of age Faulkner writes: "Within the year he married, not a country woman, but a farm woman, but a town woman, and McCaslin Edmonds built a house for them and allotted Lucas a specific acreage to be farmed as he saw fit as long as he lived or remained on the place" (110). Throughout the foregrounded scenes of "The Fire and the Hearth" Cass's grandson Roth acts every bit the long-suffering landowner, chafing at Lucas's pranks, threatening to take matters in his own hands:

> "And remember [Edwards is speaking]. Aunt Molly gets the house, and half your crop this year and half of it every year as long as you stay on my place."
> "You mean every year I keep on farming my land."
> "I mean every damned year you stay on my place. Just what I said."
> "Cass Edmonds give me that land to be mine long as I—"
> "You heard me," Edmonds said. (126)

Edmonds's ownership of the land seems indisputable in these passages, yet in *Intruder in the Dust* Lucas pays taxes on the land, a sure indication that by 1948 Faulkner imagined him to be in possession. I am indebted to James Hinkle and James Carothers for a fuller sense of this issue.

13. Craig Werner, drawing on the work of Robert Stepto, proposes cogently that Faulkner's work in general constrains black narratives within the Euro-American genre of "the narrative of endurance," as opposed to Afro-American genres of "the narrative of ascent" and "the narrative of immersion." Lucas and Rider, like Faulkner's other blacks, remain condemned to "an essentially static pattern for black experience"—or they pay with their lives. See "Tell Old Pharoah: The Afro-American Response to Faulkner," *Southern Review*, 19 (1983), 711–35.

14. Flem Snopes of course has this progressive urge with a vengeance. But Flem's

schemes, though undoubtedly grander, are all egotistical and passionless—as well as accessible to us only through others' speculations (he himself being opaque to narrative voice). He shares nothing of either Lucas's quickness or his ability to interest himself in the "instruments" of progress. Lucas's being black may give him greater latitude than Flem to escape Faulkner's disapproval of his pursuit of nontraditional goals. In any event, his being black prevents him from succeeding enough to disturb the status quo.

Black as White Metaphor: A European View of Faulkner's Fiction

LOTHAR HÖNNIGHAUSEN

It's too fine to doubt. It's too fine, too simple, ever to have been invented by white thinking. A negro might have invented it.[1]

The story too fine and too simple to have been invented by a white imagination is that of Reverend Hightower's grandfather, and one of the major symbolic leitmotifs of *Light in August*. The grandson's glamorized vision of his ancestor's ride through Jefferson and its attribution to a black narrator aptly illustrate our theme—the metaphoric transfer between white and black experience, and Faulkner's sophisticated use of characters as images. In foisting his dream of a glorious past on the innocent Cinthy, Hightower attempts to enhance its imaginative richness and power ("too fine," "too simple"). In doing this he is reemploying a Rousseauistic image of the Negro very similar to that evolved in one of the leading articles in Alain Locke's anthology *The New Negro* of 1925. Albert C. Barnes in "Negro Art and America" calls the "Negro a poet by birth"[2] and, with a vocabulary reflecting an unexpected affinity between the Harlem Renaissance and Herder, Wordsworth and the romantic worship of unspoilt folk art, stresses the poetic nature of black religion: "Poetry is religion brought down to earth and it is of the essence of the Negro soul" (20). Barnes then goes on to compare the Negro with the white man: "The white man in the mass cannot compete with the Negro in spiritual endowment. . . . He has wandered too far from the elementary human needs and their easy means of natural satisfaction. . . . His art and his life are no longer one and the same as they were in primitive man. . . . The Negro has kept nearer to the ideal of man's harmony with nature" (20). This view of the Negro is significant not because it is based on any political, economic, or social black reality, but because it emerges as a contrast and supplement to the decadence of the white imagination. The distinctive feature of the black image is that of a counterimage, black not as fact but as white metaphor.

The deconstructionism of Jacques Derrida has alerted us to the need for a reexamination of our critical assumptions when confronted with framing devices such as Hightower's white story attributed to a black narrator. This is indeed all the more relevant at a time when Southern historians such as George Brown Tindall consider the "mythology and symbolism" of race as much their theme as the so-called facts, and when psychoanalytical critics like John Irwin and Lee Jenkins make it difficult to continue with a simplistic approach to the process of literary character drawing.[3] Richard Wright's critical *bon mot*—"The Negro is America's metaphor"—is, in this respect, more stimulating in its attempt to define a new approach to Faulkner's black characters than Ralph Ellison's criticism in *Shadow and Act*: "Faulkner . . . distorted humanity to fit his personal version of Southern myth."[4] Rightly considered, all literary character drawing as well as all reading implies "distortion" or rather "transfer," "transformation," "stylization," in order to fit the author's and the reader's myth.[5] Certainly, like any writer, Faulkner, even in his most original character depiction, is influenced by the prevailing attitudes and structures of the society in which he lives. Critics should not censure him for this but rather, by distinguishing between "stereotype" in the sense of a neutral sociological term referring to current images or behavior patterns and Faulkner's particular use of them, attempt to define his individual artistic modes and the likely responses they elicit from the reader.

The different reaction of American and European readers, for instance, to Simon Strother and his family in *Flags in the Dust* illustrates how social heritage dictates a reader's response to the metaphoric implications of literary characters. White European readers, remote from the American scene, are exclusively guided by the text itself and therefore tend to appreciate the realism and humor of the carefully orchestrated Strother scenes more than do many race-conscious Americans whose reading process is likely to be disturbed by the impression that Faulkner is exploiting outworn white clichés about blacks. Such racial associations can detract from Faulkner's subtle use of language and the complexity of even his early racial milieu, which results from a unique combination of parodied racial clichés and realistically observed features. If we wish to pursue the implications of "Black as White Metaphor," we must bear in mind not only the transformation of black reality by a white artistic consciousness, but also the inevitable distortions arising from the intervening personality of the black or white reader. Thadious M. Davis acknowledges this in *Faulkner's "Negro": Art and the Southern Context* where she warns present-day readers that "Faulkner never wrote about 'blacks' in the current usage of the term; Faulkner's conception of 'Negro' characters is part of a bygone era."[6] However, the critical question as to whether this concept of Negro should be located exclusively in Southern history is raised by Noel Polk in "Faulkner and Race."[7] As a European, I am inclined to the opinion that there is another equally important image of the Negro emerging from the international modernist movement of the early twentieth century, and this supplementary image is the focus of my paper.

As far as the metaphoric element in character drawing is concerned, psychoanalytical critics like John Irwin and Lee Jenkins have been particularly important because they have examined projection and transformation in addition to mimesis. We should remember, however, that, as psychoanalytical critics, their interest has been directed more to the psychological content than to the esthetics of metaphoric transfer: "The blacks have reality and meaning only with regard to the significance they assume as agents in the interpretation of 'white' phenomena," Jenkins maintains, "and the phenomena in question here are precisely the data of psychic inheritance that the whites have distorted and denied, which in the blacks becomes 'objectified' so that such data might be seen."[8] Although such psychoanalytic interpretation has an undeniable validity, particularly for cases such as *Light in August*, we should refrain from regarding it as absolute.[9] There are other black characters in Faulkner where the metaphoric transfer seems to be more adequately discussed in terms of cultural or intellectual history and where "black" functions not as the sinister image of a suppressed ego but as a symbol of life-giving forces. Accordingly, this paper will not seek out predestination after the gospels of Sigmund Freud and Carl Jung but will focus instead on black images that, emerging from the cultural history of the 1920s, embody the belief in a kind of vitalistic redemption.

Faulkner's references to "Dante's invention of Beatrice" and to the book as the writer's dark twin show the young author already aware of the metaphoric dimension of character drawing. The same is true of a number of his characters; for instance, Bayard Sartoris, who refers to black and white as "two opposed concepts"; or Gavin Stevens, who glibly allegorizes Joe's tragedy in terms of the black and white blood cliché; and Joanna Burden, who has the pathetic vision of a black shadow in the shape of a cross.[10] The special awareness of the metaphoric dimension involved in character drawing is related to a distinctive feature of the inner texture of Faulkner's novels: their symbolist nature, "the novel as poem," as I have termed it in another context.

Quentin Compson's stream of consciousness in *The Sound and the Fury* allows us not only to assess the content psychoanalytically with Jenkins but also to observe a white imagination at work forming black metaphors.[11] The hero, having taken the only vacant seat in a Cambridge streetcar beside a black person, reflects first upon his attempt to adjust to the Northern view of blacks: "I just kept thinking you've got to remember to think of them as colored people not niggers"; and his new awareness of the two different social responses causes him to reflect perceptibly on the metaphoric element in racial communication: "That was when I realised that a nigger is not so much a person as a form of behaviour: a sort of obverse reflection of the white people he lives among" (106). A black person in this definition, instigated in the young Southerner by the experience of the North, appears as "invisible man" and nonperson to the point of being an abstraction: "nigger" for the intellectually conscious Harvard student does not represent any positive or negative individual projection but is taken as an indicator of the moral condition of white society. Faulkner, however, does not let Quentin rest with his generalization. Journeying through Virginia on his way home for the Christmas holidays, Quentin suddenly stops considering how and what Northerners might expect him to think about blacks and affectionately remembers Dilsey and Roskus: "I didn't know that I really had missed Roskus and Dilsey and them until that morning in Virginia" (106).

This momentary recovery from his alienation and emotional paralysis is initiated by the sight of "a nigger on a mule in the middle of the stiff ruts, waiting for the train to move" (106). The scene, closely observed and realistically rendered, has wider metaphoric implications, for Quentin experiences the Negro on the mule like a sculpture or the figures on Keats's Grecian urn freed from time and space as an emblem of home: "How long he had been there I didn't know, but he sat straddle of the mule, his head wrapped in a piece of blanket, as if they had been built there with the fence and the road, or with the hill, carved out of the hill itself, like a sign saying You are home again" (106).

The rare instant of a happy memory briefly alleviating Quentin's profound sadness may lead us beyond the pointless argument as to who among Faulkner's characters is "stereotype" and thus "anti-black," and who is "individual" and thus "humane and pro-black," to a more valid appraisal of character as metaphor.

The black on his mule, his head wrapped in a blanket, has all the authenticity of reality, and yet the view from the train provides focus and represents that element of selection distinguishing the scene from a naturalistic panorama and lending it a metaphoric quality. This is enhanced by the daring comparison suggesting that the rider and his mule are coeval with their surroundings and with them "carved out of the hill." This imagery implies a transfer of the selected piece of reality not only in temporal and spacial terms but, more importantly, in essence. The realistic snapshot of a black rural Southerner, transposed to an imaginative plane, takes on the status of art and, as a consequence of this selection and metaphoric transfer, becomes charged with value. But this piece of black sculpture has a white theme: It suggests to Quentin's homesick, split personality a vision of the South as home, as a social and psychological context in which he can sooner preserve his identity than in the North at Harvard.

The associations and reflections evoked by the image seem to derive more from the author's than from Quentin's mind, although this does not diminish their relevance as regards the use of black as white metaphor. While the qualities assigned to this black image ("shabby and timeless patience, static serenity, childlike incompetence, evasion of responsibility," 107) are hardly consonant with the cultural and social potential of modern black Americans, a careful examination of the context, from which I have extracted only the key phrases, will reveal that Faulkner presents us with a fairly accurate summary of some of the social mores of rural blacks, deriving from Southern history and the social situation between 1910 and 1930.

Certainly, there is no crude racial prejudice apparent in the text but it becomes evident that Faulkner accepts as indigenous and permanent, racial traits or "features" that clearly depend upon a specific situation in social and economic history. Still more significant is that the author appears to delight in these features in a manner irritating to modern readers, black and white, and yet understandable in terms of Faulkner's own historical context. Living in a period of rapid economic change and cynical debunking of all moral order—the kind of experience reflected in the Jason section of *The Sound and the Fury*, the

Mitchell story in *Flags in the Dust*, and the Popeye-Temple plot in *Sanctuary*—Faulkner, like other authors of the period, engages in a quest for relevant values.

Clearly, the creator of the Compsons and the Sartorises is under no illusions about the agony of the old aristocratic South, and yet the same novels demonstrate a profound aversion against modern Yankee commercialism. It is then perhaps inevitable that Faulkner casts about for as yet undiscredited values in the same direction in which many other American and European artists were turning and—as these values were to be equally opposed to those of the ancient regime and to those of an inhuman technocratic future—the syndrome "land, soil, earth" naturally recommended itself.

These "primitivist" ideals are to be found not only in the Agrarianism of the Southern Fugitives but also in Sherwood Anderson's and William Carlos Williams's advocacy of a "local" American art, in Yeats's yearning for simplicity and D. H. Lawrence's hankering after primitivism, and even in T. S. Eliot's *After Strange Gods* with its praise of the indigenous culture of Virginia and the stable social context of the English parish. Certainly there are many traits in Faulkner's black characters, which, although related to the American South, receive additional relevance in terms of the wider context of the international modernist movement. Perhaps a European perspective here can supplement the American view.

Among Faulkner's *New Orleans Sketches* is one entitled "Sunset" which, setting out from the deliberately misleading newspaper quotation "Black Desperado Slain," presents us with the tragic story of a simple black who in his effort to get to Africa symbolizes the yearning of many blacks and whites to return to their roots, to an elementary and therefore authentic mode of existence, but becomes the victim of white brutality and lack of sympathy. "I jest wants to go to Af'ica. I kin pay my way," the black said. "Africa, hell," replied the white man. [12] If one relates this text to "Out of Nazareth" with its primitivist ideals and to "The Kingdom of God" pointing forward to the simples Benjy and Ike, one realizes that Faulkner clearly shares the contemporary fascination with a version of man less developed, less spoilt, and closer to nature. This fascination is seen in Sherwood Anderson's *Dark Laughter,* published in 1925 during the genesis of the *New Orleans Sketches*, as well as in the work of many other prominent modernists, including D. H. Lawrence who, in the preface to *Women in Love,* enthusiastically describes Negro sculpture as "pure culture in *sensation,* culture in the *physical consciousness.*"[13] The modernist effort to gain a new, secular redemption for man by artistically exploring his affinity with the natural world is a common contemporary theme, uniting writers and artists as far apart as Djuna Barnes and the German Expressionists. Hart Crane concludes his poem "Black Tambourine" (1921/1926) with a stanza that is pertinent here:

> The black man, forlorn in the cellar,
> Wanders in some mid-kingdom, dark that lies,
> Between his tambourine, stuck on the wall,
> And in Africa, a carcass quick with flies.

If Hart Crane's comment about the mid-kingdom putting the black man "somewhere between man and beast" strikes us as overtly racist, it is because we fail to relate it to the pastoral tradition in modernism (seen for instance in Expressionism) where closeness to animals, to plants and the soil is an affinity with a more authentic mode of existence.[14]

The scope of this primitivist syndrome within modernism extends to Anderson's *Dark Laughter* and Carl Van Vechten's *Nigger Heaven*, to D. H. Lawrence's comment on Negro sculpture and William Carlos Williams's essay "The Colored Girls in Passenack" and to Eugene O'Neill's *Emperor Jones* (1920), which Faulkner expressly mentions in his O'Neill essay of 1922 stressing "that art is preeminently provincial" i.e., it comes from a certain age and a certain locality."[15]

Until now, Faulkner's return to his "postage stamp of native soil" has always been taken as conclusive proof of his undivided "Southernness." But it is difficult to sustain this theory when one realizes that Sherwood Anderson's interest in regionalism and its importance to Faulkner's credo, along with Williams's propagation of a local American art, are quite in line with a widespread international tendency in modernism, from Béla Bartók's "discovery" of folk music to Kandinsky's fascination with folk art. The discovery of African art, and with it a specific black American culture, should be seen—like that of the American Indian civilization—as part of an international effort to go back and rediscover timeless and essential human values and thus to cope artistically with the uncertainties of a period of extensive political and social upheaval.

In this respect O'Neill's *Emperor Jones* and Faulkner's "Red Leaves" are just two different examples of the contemporary urge to "begin with the beginnings," to return to and probe, in black and red masks, the deep layers or archaic origins of man's consciousness and of man's culture. Before highlighting further modernist features in Faulkner's drawing of black characters, the relevant background must be outlined more fully.

The cultural environment that our formula "Black as White Metaphor" seeks to address is recognizable in these sentences from Carl Van Vechten's novel on the Harlem Renaissance, *Nigger Heaven,* which appeared alongside *Soldiers' Pay* in 1926: "And now the white editors are beginning to regard Negroes as interesting novelties, like white elephants or black roses. They'll print practically anything our coloured writers send in."[16] This novel of the Jazz Age is written with a great awareness of the effect of the discovery of African culture on the development of twentieth-century literature and art, manifest in the references to blues and spirituals and to Gertrude Stein's "Melanctha," a classic example of avant-garde fascination with black characteristics. It is also influenced by African sculpture, the effect of which upon Picasso, Braque, and Matisse is noted by Stein in *The Autobiography of Alice B. Toklas.* A further illustration of the encounter with the black image is the exhibition of De Zayas's collection of African art, photographed by Charles Sheeler (1926), and so important to the New York avant-gardists around Stieglitz and Arensberg. Main events in this tradition were Gauguin's discovery of native art in Tahiti (1891), major sculptures by Picasso (*Dancer,* 1907, and *Bronzehead,* 1909) and Matisse (*Two Negresses,* 1908), and important paintings by the German Expressionists Erich Heckel (*Sleeping Negress,* 1910), Ernst Ludwig Kirchner (*Recumbent Negress,* 1911), and Emil Nolde (*The Missionary,* 1912). The primitive style of folk art appealed particularly to the German Expressionists, and Emil Nolde renders the white missionary as a terrifying Korean mask, against which he sets the harmonious vitality of a "Mother and Child" in the style of a Yoruba sculpture. His observations in this connection are of general interest in revealing one of the key motives of the white avant-garde in their enthusiasm for African art: "Primeval man lives within his nature. He is at one with it and a part of the whole universe. Occasionally I feel that he is the only real human being left, while we are more like marionettes, spoilt, artificial and completely in the dark."[17] In the United States Alain Locke, who is prominent in the Harlem Renaissance and whose anthology *The New Negro* (1925) appears as characteristic of the black image of the twenties as Nancy Cunard's is of the thirties, shows himself fully aware that the "powerful simplicity of conception, design and effect" (258) in African sculpture helped European art to overcome "the exhaustion of imitating Greek classicism" (259).[18] He quotes Roger Fry on Negro Sculpture (259), refers to Matisse and Picasso, Max Pechstein and Franz Marc, to Epstein, Lipschitz, Lembruck, and many other artists, but also to the composers Satie, Poulenc, and Darius Milhaud as well as to the poets Guillaume Apollinaire and Blaise Cendrars, whose *Anthologie Nègre* he calls the bible of this coterie. Locke concludes his article on "The Decay of the Ancestral Arts" by expressing his hope that these European artists "should even now be the inspiration and guideposts of a younger school of American Negro artists. They have too long been the victims of the academy tradition and shared the conventional blindness of the Caucasian eye with respect to the racial material at their immediate disposal" (264).

Carl Van Vechten's use of African art in *Nigger Heaven* is compounded by the same kind of attempt to transfer its attractions to black American culture. Adora, an impressive Negress in Harlem, is portrayed accordingly as "a type of pure African majesty," "beautiful and regal. Her skin was almost black; her nose broad, her lips thick. Her head was well set on her shoulders." (28). In a manner perhaps offensive to a modern black American, Van Vechten emphasizes in his colored heroes and heroines features dear to the avant-garde such as "primitive" (91), "exotic" (163), "savage" (166), "irresponsible like children" (235) and thus achieves a distorted picture of black reality,[19] but one that influenced both black and white artists, as a closer look at the poetry volumes by Jean Toomer (*Cane,* 1923), Langston Hughes's *Weary Blues,* and the anthologies by Alain Locke and Nancy Cunard would reveal. Van Vechten captures the modernism in the spirit of the Harlem Renaissance, when he describes the attempt by the black intellectual, Mary, to rediscover her ethnic roots:

> Savages! Savages at heart! And she had lost or forfeited her birthright, this primitive birthright which was so valuable and important an asset, a birthright that all the civilized races were struggling to get back to—this fact explained the art of a Picasso or a Strawinsky. To be sure, she too, felt this African beat—it completely aroused her emotionally—but she was conscious of feeling it. This love of drums, of exciting rhythms, this naive delight in glowing colour—the colour that exists only in cloudless, tropical climes—this warm, sexual emotion. . . . (89–90)

What Mary seeks, and her ex-lover finds in the black femme fatale Lasca Sartoris, also attracts Bruce Dudley, the split protagonist, and several minor characters in Anderson's *Dark Laughter:* "something primitive like a nigger woman in an African dance."[20] The novel has a significance to our theme far beyond any isolated and random connection of the kind that the influence studies of yore tended to explore, because it brings together the ostensibly separate elements that form the context of Faulkner's use of black as white metaphor.

Bruce Dudley, the ill-adjusted modern hero of the twenties, leaves his wife Bernice, a sophisticated "new woman," because he feels alienated from nature and his own animal self: "all American men are out of touch with things" (52); "men getting away from their own hands, their own bodies too" (80). The cultural background in *Dark Laughter* as in *Nigger Heaven* is again very much that of a modernist novel in which references to Gauguin, Picasso, Matisse, Freud, and Joyce serve as a leitmotif alongside numerous stylistic traces of avant-garde sophistication ("singing voices of the negro deckhands as colors," 88). Bruce's yearning for the lost simplicity of a natural world is the dominant theme, and, like the German Expressionist Emil Nolde, he longs "to be a part of things again" (251). These primitivist values are embodied in two major motif-complexes: the dark laughter and singing of the Negroes associated with the river, and a sensuous existence and love of "the soil, of seed and green things." This pattern of motifs highlights two points also pertinent to the Faulkner texts: (1) "black" for the white avant-garde is not primarily a black racial or social fact but a white cultural concept, or a twenties version of the American Adam; and (2) the black image embodies aspirations strikingly similar to those expressed in the pastoral and agrarian motives of international modernism.

In Faulkner's first novel, *Soldiers' Pay* (1926), as in Van Vechten's *Nigger Heaven* (1926) and Anderson's *Dark Laughter* (1925), the descriptions of Negroes act as a positive, vitalistic metaphor associated with "the passion of spring and flesh" and "something pagan" in the sense of something exotic, vigorous, and subconscious.[21] The darkness of *color* ("from it welled the crooning submerged passion of the dark race," 319), also evident in *Light in August* ("dark and inscrutable," 212) and in Sherwood Anderson's title, tends to become mystified, assuming that Freudian aura to which Faulkner had referred in *Mosquitoes*. His debt to the modernist use of the black image also manifests itself in the structure of his fiction, and the contrapuntal setting of the naturalness and continuity of black life against Donald's paralysis in *Soldiers' Pay* and Bayard Sartoris's war trauma in *Flags in the Dust* clearly identifies its function as a white metaphor. This structural pattern of Faulkner's first two novels is considerably modified in *The Sound and the Fury*, but is nevertheless recognizable—despite Dilsey's highly individual character—in the superiority of her black existence, outlasting the Compsons and achieving mythic timelessness: "I seed de beginnin, en now I sees de endin" (371). The tendency to turn the black image into myth is also apparent in numerous minor stylistic features such as when the blacks and their mule wagon in *Soldiers' Pay* are metamorphosed into "a pagan catafalque . . . carved in Egypt ten thousand years ago" (151). Here the reality of the black rural South assumes a dignity comparable to the Classicist stylization of contemporary industrial reality in the paintings of Charles Demuth and Charles Sheeler.

The groups of Negroes drawn in *Flags in the Dust* more concretely than in *Soldiers' Pay* authentically represent black Southern reality: "young girls in stiff mail-order finery, the young heritage and labor on unaccustomed high heels."[22] But at the same time, the blacks constitute a positive counterimage to the cold violence and emotional atrophy of Bayard's split personality: "He stood for a moment on the sidewalk. . . . Negroes slow and aimless as figures of a dark placid dream, with an animal odor, murmuring and laughing among themselves. There was in their consonantless murmuring something ready with mirth, in their laughter something grave and sad" (127). Similarly, in *Light in August* the anonymity of "the summer voices of invisible negroes" (106) conveys by metaphoric contrast Joe's desperate search for identity. However, the theme of the novel is not black as a positive counterimage but the tragedy of its white metaphorical use, or misuse, a theme recently so competently treated in Lee Jenkins's psychoanalytical study.

Since psychoanalysis depends upon the binary system of a symbolic relationship between the known and the unknown, the conscious and the unconscious, and as black has symbolized the unknown and the dangerous to the white world view, its frequent appearance as a psychoanalytical image—irritating though this must be for a black person—comes as no great surprise. That it does indeed act as a white metaphor is confirmed by its function in *The Unvanquished*, *Absalom, Absalom!*, and *Go Down, Moses* as a replacement for the white twins in the sibling motif of *Flags in the Dust*. A somewhat dubious means of alerting the reader to the metaphoric quality of the black characters is Faulkner's tendency to "editorialize," such as in the debate on black virtues and vices between Ike and McCaslin in "The Bear" of *Go Down, Moses*. The extensive theorizing inevitably draws the reader into a search for the embodiment of the black virtues dear to the author's white heart, and consequently overlooks those features which—as Noel Polk has recently pointed out—may be less flattering, but make Dilsey come to life.[23]

This moralizing tendency and emphasis of representative aspects to the neglect of the concrete, noticeable in "The Bear," become even stronger in the "Sambo" passages of *Intruder in the Dust*. The Lucas Beauchamp of *Go Down, Moses* has here shrunk to an ideological puppet, the object of Faulkner's affirmation and expiation, another example of worthy political intentions leading to inferior literature and an extreme example of black as a white image. What clearly distinguishes *Intruder in the Dust* from *Flags in the Dust* is that, in line with historical developments, the content of the black image is more directly political, whereas in Faulkner's earlier novels, in conjunction with the impact of the Harlem Renaissance, black appears as a cultural metaphor, expressing the modernists' sophisticated yearning for the simple, the archaic, the unconscious. Just how long Faulkner retained this pastoral vision of his formative years can be seen both in its subtle and tragic rendering in "The Fire and the Hearth" of *Go Down, Moses*, and in the affirmative icon of a black ploughman in *Intruder*, reminiscent of Thomas Hart Benton's regionalist painting *Ploughing It Under* (1938).

After having examined specific traces that the modernist concept of the Negro left on Faulkner's drawing of black characters, we should in summing up also clarify the extent of the overall impact that the avant-garde interest in African art and American black culture must have had on the young author. No one who has studied the painstaking exercises of the apprentice Faulkner in fin de siècle and modernist art and literature will doubt his awareness of what the discovery of the black image had meant for the development of modernism. From this he derived encouragement to rediscover as an artist the black environment he had always known, as he had received encouragement from Sherwood Anderson's regionalist gospel to turn to his "postage stamp of native soil." Among the aesthetic beliefs Faulkner shared with other leading artists suffering from the manifold alienations of the period was the fascination with both regional life and black folk culture. Paradox though it may seem, the discovery then of the South and black culture as artistic subjects emerges as a characteristic feature of international modernism. Eventually, in *Light in August* and *Absalom, Absalom!*, he would develop his own intricate and somber vision, leaving the simpler vitalistic Rousseauist Negro image of modernism far behind him, just as Picasso and Matisse had done, although only after the black icons had shaped their imagination. In a wider perspective then, there is neither a paradox nor a true opposition dividing Faulkner the Southerner and Faulkner the Internationalist: As the psychological and artistic confrontation with the black image helped him to articulate and aesthetically form his white identity, the international modernist movement provided the historical context in which it was possible for him to turn the local and regional into world literature.

NOTES

1. William Faulkner, *Light in August* (New York: Random House, Vintage Books, 1972), 458.
2. Albert C. Barnes, "Negro Art and America," in *The New Negro: An Interpretation*, ed. Alain Locke (1925; rpt. New York: Arno Press and the *New York Times*, 1968). Page references in the text are to this edition.
3. George Brown Tindall, *The Ethnic Southerners* (Baton Rouge: Louisiana State University Press, 1976); John T. Irwin, *Doubling and Incest/Repetition and Revenge: A Speculative Reading of Faulkner* (Baltimore: Johns Hopkins University Press, 1975); Lee

Jenkins, *Faulkner and Black-White Relations: A Psychoanalytic Approach* (New York: Columbia University Press, 1981); Irwin, 47–60.

4. Richard Wright, *White Man, Listen!* (Garden City: Doubleday, 1957), 109; Ralph Ellison, "Twentieth Century Fiction and the Black Mask of Humanity," in *Shadow and Act* (New York: Random House, 1953), 25.

5. Failure to reflect upon the nature of this "transformation" is one of the main factors contributing to that "history of misrepresentation" Charles D. Peavy has reviewed in *Go Slow Now: Faulkner and the Race Question* (Eugene: University of Oregon Books, 1964). As far as the nature of the metaphoric transfer is concerned, critical awareness does not seem to have increased much since Peavy's stocktaking and even such a serious contribution to Faulkner studies as Myra Jehlen's *Class and Character in Faulkner's South* (New York: Columbia University Press, 1976), for all its wealth of social and literary insight, shows a certain critical nonchalance as far as the nature of aesthetic transformation is concerned. According to Jehlen, it would seem that "Pantaloon in Black" is such a good story because the Faulkner of *Go Down, Moses* had "extricated his imagination from racial attitudes which had previously bound it to stereotypes" (99) and because "Pantaloon" is "explicitly critical of white men who refuse to see the humanity of blacks." Jehlen's use of the term "stereotype" touches upon an essential part of the complex problem that my title seeks to address. She employs "stereotype" with its connotation of hackneyed literary expression as a matter of content and, in particular, an inadequate social response. As a consequence the borderline between social content and artistic quality of Faulkner's character drawing becomes blurred, leading in turn to the view that the good political intentions of the creator of Lucas Beauchamp in *Intruder* correspond with equally good character drawing. I for one find Caspey the rebellious war veteran— "war showed me de white folks dey cant git along widout de colored man" (William Faulkner, *Flags in the Dust*, ed. Douglas Day [New York: Vintage Books, 1974], 62)—and the efforts of the Strother family to silence him more authentic both in the sociological and in the literary sense. But this individual case seems less important than a caveat against the simplistic generalization that Faulkner's drawing of black characters develops from antiblack stereotype to more individual, lifelike and therefore problack characterization.

6. Thadious M. Davis, *Faulkner's "Negro": Art and the Southern Context* (Baton Rouge: Louisiana State University Press, 1983), 2.

7. Noel Polk, "Faulkner and Race," in *Review*, vol. 6, ed. James O. Hoge and James L. W. West III (Charlottesville: University Press of Virginia, 1984), 1–19. This review essay makes one conscious of the level of sophistication meanwhile characterizing the debate opened by Charles H. Nilon in *Faulkner and the Negro* (Boulder: University of Colorado Press, 1962).

8. Jenkins, *Faulkner and Black-White Relations*, 159.

9. Ibid., 61–105. Before the psychoanalytical critics, Robert Penn Warren ("William Faulkner," in *William Faulkner: Four Decades of Criticism*, ed. Linda Welshimer Wagner [East Lansing: Michigan State University Press, 1973], 94–109) and Heinrich Straumann ("Black and White in Faulkner's Fiction," *English Studies*, 60 [1979], 462–70) had pointed out that the theme of *Light in August* or *Absalom, Absalom!* is not black reality but the complications arising from the white man's black image and that Dilsey is a "metaphor" or "symbol."

10. William Faulkner, *Mosquitoes* (New York: Liveright, 1955), 339, 251; *Flags in the Dust*, 393; *Light in August*, 239. Gavin Stevens, lecturing to his Northern visitor on Joe Christmas as a "typically Southern case," explains: "Because the black blood drove him to the negro cabin. And then the white blood drove him out of there, as it was the black blood which snatched up the pistol and the white blood which would not let him fire it" (*Light in August*, 424).

11. For a different reading of the scene, see Jenkins, *Faulkner and Black-White Relations*, 151–56. References to *The Sound and the Fury* (New York: Random House, Vintage Books, 1956) are cited in the text.

12. William Faulkner, *New Orleans Sketches*, ed. Carvel Collins (New York: Random House, 1958), 77.

13. For the affinity with Sherwood Anderson, see also Davis, *Faulkner's "Negro"*; D. H. Lawrence, preface to the American edition of *Women in Love*, 1920.

14. Hart Crane's verses and remark are quoted from *The Norton Anthology of American Literature* (New York: W. W. Norton, 1979), 2:1354.

15. William Faulkner, *Early Prose and Poetry*, ed. Carvel Collins (Boston: Little, Brown, 1962), 86.

16. Carl Van Vechten, *Nigger Heaven* (New York: Octagon Books, 1926), 49. All page references are to this edition and are hereafter cited in the text.

17. Nolde as quoted in Hans-Joachim Kunst, *Der Afrikaner in der Europäischen Kunst* (Bad Godesberg: Inter Nationes, 1967), 46.

18. See note 2.

19. This is the context in which Faulkner's characterization in *The Sound and the Fury* should be seen: "That blending of childlike and ready incompetence and paradoxical reliability that tends and protects them it loves out of all reason and robs them steadily and evades responsibility" (107).

20. Sherwood Anderson, *Dark Laughter* (New York: Liveright, 1970), 156; hereafter cited parenthetically in the text.

21. William Faulkner, *Soldiers' Pay* (New York: Liveright, 1926), 312; hereafter cited parenthetically in the text.

22. William Faulkner, *Flags in the Dust* (New York: Random House, Vintage Books, 1974), 127; hereafter cited parenthetically in the text.

23. Polk, "Faulkner and Race," 1–19.

Race, History, and Technique
in *Absalom, Absalom!*

FREDERICK R. KARL

Nearly everyone is agreed that Faulkner's public views on race are both difficult to determine and contradictory in what they propose: sometimes enlightened, at other times painful to read.[1] Scholars and critics agree, however, far less on which racial views they should stress, particularly whether the attitudes should be those Faulkner presented as public statements or those he embedded in his fiction. If the former, then we must discriminate among contradictions, ambiguities, fears and hopes; if the latter, in his fiction, then we must seek his racial attitudes amidst a plethora of other, equally forceful, stands on caste, class, social systems. Yet since we are discussing a creative writer, not a sociologist or historian of ideas, it would seem that the most likely place Faulkner's views on race can be discovered and analyzed is in his fiction, in his major fiction. Of what are usually deemed his key novels—*Absalom, Absalom!*, *The Sound and the Fury*, and *Light in August*—all three have strong racial overtones, the first and third most of all. *Absalom, Absalom!*, for one, moves in and out of racial issues from pre-Civil War days to 1909, when Quentin is relating his story—thus it bridges one of the most significant eras in American history. At its core, the novel focusses on attitudes toward race which themselves determine the outcome of the book, which fuel and nourish narrative. Further, the chief narrator is himself shredded by race, although not exclusively by that; and his desire to make his college roommate, Shreve, understand the South is in part the need to explain something about race which cannot quite be explained.

This much can be granted. Yet while *Absalom, Absalom!* moves on several levels, social, historical, personal, it comes at race through secret passageways, by means of hiding necessary information, by using divulgence as a psychological weapon. As a detective story of sorts, it is also a tone poem, employing colors and shadings as a vehicle for thematic material; and this is, for Faulkner, a way of both presenting and commenting on race. What we will consider here is not the obvious point that racial matters are the stuff of this novel, but that such matters are buried in dark rooms, attics, enclosures, most of all in words; so that to extrapolate race we must extract virtually the entire metaphorical meaning of the novel. In one sense, what we are claiming is that race *has been absorbed into technique*. But the matter is even more complicated, for Faulkner has also absorbed race into history, and into a particular view of history. History, in this respect, becomes part of technique; it is "created history," process more than fact. Race lies in *there*, in the creative process itself.

We can argue that the method of narrating the novel, as a modified stream of consciousness, underlies racial matters. For by turning everything into subjective, personalized data—the data of the novel remain buried in commentaries that may or may not be accurate—the novelist has provided a strategical commentary on race itself. That is, as an element that can be approached only from a private point of view, having no substantial qualities beyond those perceived by the holder or speaker. Race is, in a sense, held hostage to the perception of the beholder. It is the great hidden metaphor, the secret god at the center of totem and taboo.

Absalom, Absalom! moves toward forbidden areas by way of a method that disallows divulgation. The narrative transforms what has occurred into a totem, and it transmogrifies Sutpen into a mythical figure who challenges explanation in ordinary language. History, Sutpen, events—all of these have something of the qualities Faulkner associated with racial resonances between black and white, a Caravaggio canvas. Race arises out of shadows, caves, labyrinths. It is part of Sutpen's past, and it brings Charles Bon into the family not only as a future member but as the racial "other half." Yet the physical presence of Bon is not so important as is the textured shadow of the young man, the past as racial avatar. He is the forbidden, the tabooed object, the nasty myths turned into flesh; and his presence begins to dominate the novel less than one-quarter through, although we barely see him. His figure then hovers over the entire novel, which while it doesn't seem to be about him is, in actuality, almost always about him. If Faulkner is recreating the felt texture of Greek drama or an Elizabethan revenge play, the the "American ingredient," so to speak, is race: race and family intertwined, all cast into shadows and depths and enclosures, the contemporary equivalent of the early myths.

History moves through the novel, also, in similar twists. As Faulkner comes at race by way of metaphors of disguise and enclosure, so he comes at history; and the two, race and history, cannot be disentangled. While history in *Absalom* is real, as real as race, it is presented not in its reality, but in its literary dimension as metaphor, as image. Everything appears in the form of something else, as if the novel were itself a gigantic syntactical litotes. When Henry and Bon go to New Orleans, Henry for the first time, Bon preparing him for what New Orleans means to a young man with a mistress-wife and child, Faulkner presents a brief history lesson in terms of sex, class, caste, and race. In speaking of Bon's octoroon mistress and child, he meanders into what kind of women are available to a Southern gentlemen; and here history, social status, sex, and race become intermixed. There are the virgins one marries; there are the courtesans one visits when in cities; and there are slave girls—field hands and house maids, who are accessible and cannot say no. Everything is here, and it is presented as a very complex subculture, which is history as shaped by sexual need, by racial presence, by class and caste considerations. Behind it all is even economics, since marriage to a virgin insures one's line of descent; and it is also political, inasmuch as such a vision preserves white supremacy in all major areas: sexual, racial, social, economic.

Almost in the center of the book, as a kind of arch stone, Faulkner presents one of the many "returns" or duplications that display history as both accretion and flow. Incidentally, many of the points established here had already been made in *Light in August*, where Joe Christmas has foreshadowed the son of Charles Bon. Clytie goes to seek the twelve-year-old boy, finds him in New Orleans, and returns with him on a steamboat. The boy is part-Negro, the result of an octoroon mother (⅛ Negro) and a part-Negro father, Charles Bon, and is, of course, considered Negro. On the boat, Clytie (½ white) and the light-skinned almost white boy sleep on deck with the Negroes. When they arrive at Sutpen's Hundred, Judith tells him to call her "Aunt Judith," while he is put under the care of Clytie, who has herself shared in the household as half-sister. Clytie is Sutpen's daughter, the boy is Sutpen's grandson and Judith's nephew; Judith is half-sister to Clytie and the bereaved of the part-Negro Charles Bon, who was the best friend and potential brother-in-law of his murderer, Henry Sutpen, who is put up to the killing by their joint father, Sutpen. All these crosscurrents of relationships are apparent to anyone who reads the book, but if we examine them in the light of race, we note that Faulkner approached the subject as much by blending as by distinctions.

Further, when the boy grows up, as an act of scorn, mockery, self-hatred, or whatever, he marries a coal-black Negro, and has a part-white dark son. This son is brought up at Sutpen's Hundred, also, chiefly by half-white Clytie. To add to the racial dimension, the grown boy, Charles Etienne, contracts yellow fever, which he transmits to "Aunt" Judith, who nurses him in the big house; she dies before he does from the jointly held fever. Thus, it is, indirectly, race that kills Bon (murdered by Henry when he learns his friend is part-Negro and plans to marry Judith), which is then counterbalanced, as it were, when Bon's son kills "Aunt Judith" with contagious fever. If the play of events is perceived as tragic and not as melodramatic, then the tragic ingredient is not Sutpen's *hubris*, but race itself: race as embedded in historical practice.

Race comes to us so formed by other forces it cannot be disentangled. Further pressing them together so that elements are indistinguishable from each other is narrative, presented as a kind of stream. The stream is in itself a form of history, since it suggests a flow that makes past and present into elements of a single experience. One of the themes of *Absalom* is, of course, that past and present join, flow, remain intertwined. History is not simply past for Faulkner; and, therefore, the substance of history—sexual matters, class, caste, race—has no clear beginning in time or demarcation one from the other. What we are claiming for the novel here is that while such a momentous question as race is affected by Faulkner's sense of history, it is influenced even more by his method of presenting that history with particular narrative strategies. Accordingly, we have not only the modified stream, we have that stream influenced by the use of speakers, who direct and redirect the words that make the stream flow.

If history is subjective, as much speculation as fact, then race is part of that same mind-set; all of it intensified by the particularities of transmission. Racial matters, then, are indistinguishable from narrative sequences, for each transmission of information derives from someone with a racial view different from the one receiving it. General Compson and Mr. Compson appear to have standard racial views, men of their day; but the information they receive from Sutpen and dispense is not representative. Since nothing about Sutpen is standardized, we wonder how much has been distorted. Similarly, information about Sutpen also comes from Rosa Coldfield, who is herself traditional in every respect. The epitome, in Faulkner's depiction of her, of the Southern lady, she is disgusted by the close living of white and black in the Sutpen household. While the material she funnels to Quentin comes with traditional racial attitudes, he is already of a generation breaking from tradition and history, or at least caught on the edge of that break—it becomes his di-

lemma. The transmission of what is for him an archetypal Southern story, with its tragic racial consequences, involves the very
memories and historical sense he cannot deal with—he shivers,
he cries out, he must, like the Ancient Mariner, tell his story.
Shreve, who is the final recipient of information in this complicated daisy chain, is not even an American, and as such has no
connection to slavery, racial questions, or even the historical
matrix in which race is presented.

For Faulkner, in this mélange of information and speculation,
history remains outside definition, in the seams between subjective experience and objective phenomena. *Absalom* consists of
several historical texts, whose primary momentum depends on
the subjective use of words to understand one's relationship to
past and present. Wherever history lies, it is driven by individu-
alized narrative transmission; and embedded in all is race. In the
primary text, Quentin's grandfather, father, Rosa Coldfield, and
Bon's letter are forms of information funneled into Quentin, then
into Shreve, and they tell the reader what happened. Yet what
happened is always secondary to what it all means; words as well
as narrators fail. What it means, history, is associated with
Sutpen, and that aspect is part of the secondary text, in the
seams of the primary, as it were. What Quentin is trying to
explain to Shreve is nothing less than what the South is, and yet
significance goes well beyond any of the details or events as
described by relaying narrators; the true explanation, un-
achieved, lies in what Quentin cannot retrieve from all the words
funneled into him. Meaning or history—and indirectly race—
should be the culmination of language, but turns out to be
embedded in silences between words, in space between lines, in
seams between narrators.

Race, then, like history, becomes inseparable from telling.
Faulkner achieved what the stream intends: that reflection of
levels of consciousness that cannot be quite defined. Unlike
other forms of interior monologue, the stream derives from an
undiscriminated area, somewhere between unconscious and
conscious. It is, therefore, an approximation in language of what

is unreachable; and, therefore, a perfect transmitter of ideas of race as they rush from one generation to another. Before the Civil War, Southern history seemed to have moved slowly, all generations bunched together; but after the war, the time scheme changed, and generations became demarked and moved in smaller time periods—not the twenty years assumed by the Bible, but in five- and ten-year spans. This speeding up was connected in part to race, and what could be a better means of catching this than by use of the stream.

Yet even as Faulkner recognizes the irretrievability of what he is gathering and reflecting, he uses its indeterminacy to present information which, because of the transmission, must be suspect even as it is presented as fact. History becomes so untrustworthy in its transmission that Faulkner after only three pages of *Absalom* locates *his* voice just outside the voices of the narrators. He will be, we suspect, the "voice of truth," but it does not work that way at all, inasmuch as the Faulknerian voice becomes simply another form of dubious history. He cannot disentangle elements, and in that recognition of hopeless confusion, of straying thoughts, of motivations lying beyond explanation, of objectives that go beyond life itself—in all this, race like history resists language.

The two Quentins—the one in the past (the Quentin identified with Henry or with Bon), the one in the present (the Quentin "modernizing" himself at Harvard with Shreve)—recall the two Marcels in Proust's novel; or else the two (or more) Jims in Conrad's *Lord Jim:* young men who live in multiple time frames and upset our very notions of time and history, of information received, of factual bases for anything. Such men and their voices decenter all data. Later, we shall see how whole numbers and fractions in the text reinforce the idea of a nonverbal history, a decentered universe. Those two Quentins move along with Faulkner's "over" voice and Rosa's different set of details. First, the interior narrative establishes the two Quentins, then Quentin takes over and in surges of italicized comments counterpoints Faulkner's voice; inserted into this is Rosa

Coldfield's narrative of events, which nourishes Quentin's narrative and parallels Faulkner's. There is, however, still another dimension, for Quentin responds to Rosa's remarks even as, in italics, he answers Shreve.

Narrative strategies in the revised text of the novel have centralized the key sensibility in Quentin, and that is precisely where Faulkner has located the racial dilemma of the novel. For the others, race is not so difficult to work through: for Sutpen, it counts mainly as something that cannot upset his grand design to establish himself; for Judith Sutpen, it does not seem a dominant factor—she lives with Clytie, would probably marry Bon whatever the makeup of his genes, and dies nursing Bon's son; for Henry, race becomes significant only when Bon insists on marrying Judith—otherwise, he accepts a half-Negro sister in Clytie and he embraces Bon as a friend. Only for Rosa Coldfield are Negroes still slaves, inferior creatures at the service of whites.

Henry's dilemma brings him into Quentin's orbit and makes them, historically, "brothers." They must confront the dilemma of how to respond to what the South demands when it runs counter to what they feel. Even more than Henry, however, Quentin is the one to embrace the full racial dilemma: the knowledge that the Negro should be equal, and yet the feeling that for the white Southerner things are more complicated than that. His tirade at the end of the novel that he doesn't hate the South—"I dont, I dont! I dont hate it! I dont hate it!"—is a display of self-hatred; the result of his inability to link what his mind tells him with what his feelings are saying.

There is, however, more to it than this. One of the major themes in the novel, an offshoot of race, is lack of recognition: Sutpen goes unrecognized when he calls at the "big house" and is turned away by a Negro servant; Bon, according to Quentin's and Shreve's speculation, would give up marriage to Judith if only Sutpen recognized him, however slightly; Sutpen cannot recognize his first wife once he discovers she has some Negro blood; Bon does not recognize his first marriage when he considers bigamy. Yet even as we trace out this theme, which comes at every crucial turn, we see that such "lacks," whatever form they take, are linked to race and are part of a narrative that accentuates absence. The novel works, we have noted, as a kind of litotes, in that it gains its intensity from a negative of contraries; a litotes that is best served by a technique that omits, skips, holds back, bottles up, withdraws.

Faulkner may squirrel away, but the narrative method he employs to bring this about is all words, talk, dialogue—what seems to be the very opposite of withholding. Yet words in this use of stream serve to disguise and shield; not as in detective fiction, where such disguises are connected to plot sequences, but as in more serious fiction where disguise is linked to character and to understanding. Once this occurs, and we as readers accept it, then all information coming through this method has a different life from what it would be in a more objectively framed fiction. If we examine the method further, we note that the verbal stream is also a temporal stream; that voices are divided into subtexts—the way information in an epistolary novel is divided among letter writers. That division means all significance will lie in secondary texts: those areas cutting between voices, not in the voices themselves. For the latter represent persons—whether Compsons or Rosa Coldfield—who play little or no role except as recipients of information. As characters (even Rosa as Sutpen's potential third wife), they serve to pass on what is necessary for our understanding; whereas the active arena lies elsewhere, beyond their words or actions.

Whatever is of consequence in *Absalom, Absalom!* lies in seams—not in what speakers say, not in the stream itself, but in what remains unsaid, what must be left to speculation. An entire area of Faulkner scholarship has grown up around trying to determine who knew what, and when, and how. What Faulkner has done is to bury the intense racial theme (and, by implication, the Southern theme) deep within those seams. He has bypassed questions of fairness, justice, and equality in favor of the historical and traditional role race played in a region that fought and died to preserve a way of life that cannot be glamorized because it included slavery. Faulkner's point, then, is not to present a balanced view, not to argue this advocacy or that, but to freeze a *possible* social and cultural context that created the condition. If we argue over who told whom what, and when he did it, or how he did it, we perform a valuable service, but we also deny a method that presents history as ahistorical, that describes a society as asocial, that defines a subculture as having its own frontiers.

We have, in fact, still another stream, a nonverbal, mathematical stream, and this form of narrative is also connected to matters of race. For example, at the beginnning of part 3, the numbers intensify, even as the voices come at us. Their tale is of time. Rosa moves out to Sutpen's Hundred in '64 (as embedded in Quentin's relaying, in 1909); Rosa was then 20, 4 years younger than Judith, her niece; Rosa had been born in 1845 (which is, incidentally, 64 years before 1909, coinciding with the '64 of her move to Sutpen's Hundred, itself 10 x 10); when she was born, her sister had already been married for 7 years, with 2 children; her mother was "at least" 40. So we have one level, the ages of 20, 4, 7, 40; then the level of dates 1909 (the present), 1864, 1845; finally, the inferred ages, 64 for Rosa, unlisted for the children; and over all, Sutpen's 100 (10 x 10), the original design.

Similarly, at the beginning of part 5, Rosa's grasp of fact becomes shaky, and her mind wanders in terms of numbers: the 12 miles she travels to Sutpen's Hundred, the 2 years since Ellen died, or was it 4 after Henry vanished? or 19 since "I saw light and breathed?" Numbers are repeated: the reappearance of Henry after 4 years, the 12 miles Rosa rode, etc. This numerology is then associated, both directly and indirectly, with purely racial matters, when we begin to figure fractions of what makes one a Negro. Sutpen has married a woman whose family has deceived him about her background—as Bertha's family deceived Rochester in *Jane Eyre*—only here it is racial, some small fractional part of her which is not Spanish, but Negro.

That diluted part, that fraction, dooms her son, Bon, when he seeks acceptance as a Sutpen. That same Bon marries an octoroon, ⅛ Negro, and has a son who is that fraction of Negro that derives from ⅛ Negro plus whatever fraction of Negro Bon is, if indeed he is. Further, Sutpen has Clytie by a Negro slave, which makes her ½ Negro; she is, also, ½-sister to Henry and Judith, and, we may forget, ½-sister to Bon, but a much greater fraction of black than he is. At issue when Bon wants to marry Judith is less that they are ½-siblings than that diluted fraction of Negro blood. In many respects, as Shreve and Quentin reconstruct the confrontation scene between Henry and Bon, the life and death of the characters depend on fractions. It is, ultimately, fractions that destroy Sutpen's grand design. As Sutpen tells General Compson, he can let matters stand—let Bon marry Judith—but *he* will know that his plan has been turned into mockery.

This fraction, then, will lead to Sutpen's own death, inasmuch as once he tells Henry about Bon—in the reconstruction of events in that Harvard dormitory—his first and second family will be destroyed and he will still need a viable heir. When he attempts this, his own death is foreshadowed, at Wash Jones's hands. The circumambient narrative, the secrecy, the withholding of evidence, the squirreling away of fact, the use of a verbal and nonverbal numerological stream all wind back to the racial theme, itself based on fractions; but internally, subjectively posed, without any substantial basis in actuality—nearly all speculation, reconstruction, a mental set. The question of race becomes a question of destruction. If we seek Faulkner's point about racial matters in the novel, we must conclude that he perceived race as heading toward suicide, murder, doom. Sutpen, the man of will, the man of destiny in the American mold, has been doomed by race: that fractional element that has evaded his design. His desire to mold his adult life after the rebuff at the great house is collapsed by forces he cannot comprehend or foresee, no less control.

One further point on the interlocking of race and method, of doom and withholding. Although about one-third through *Absalom* we possess all the facts we need to understand the dramatic situation, the problem is *we do not know* we have all the facts. A by-product of the narrative method and all the numbers and dates is our insecurity about what we already know, what we still have to learn, what later may be revealed. Information manipulates the reader until he is uncertain about what he controls, and experiences in this respect an inverted detective story: not too many details, but an insufficiency. This uncertainty is, of course, a correlative of the question of race, since the characters' apprehension is linked to what they know or do not know about the racial makeup of Bon, Sutpen's first wife, and others. If the characters settle for the surface information and seek no further, they preserve the amenities the culture demands; but if they probe in order to work out the puzzle, then they will discover the very elements of race that will destroy the surface, the design, the family itself.

In that pivotal scene, when Henry shoots Bon, the action takes place in the deepest regions of the novel. It comes as reconstruction, as speculation, and it is cast almost entirely in pauses, what is left unsaid. It is a scene communicable only by silence. Yet everything meets here, history, personal experience, the quintessential Southern confrontation; and it comes to the reader from some primal region of consciousness. Faulkner has layered it in between conscious and preconscious, so that it is history lying outside history, experience forming beyond experience.

Yet even as that terrible event is to take place, the narrative shifts from deep interiority to the external frame of Quentin and Shreve in their room at Harvard. The shot that kills Bon occurs not in his frame, but in the segment associated with the two college students, in the words of Shreve and the speculations of Quentin. Faulkner has refracted the event at least three times: first, as an event at which no witness was present; then to Quentin through a means that is never validated; finally, his words repeated and interpreted by Shreve, a foreigner. A Canadian, for whom the words have least meaning, is the messenger of this information; so that Faulkner has achieved filters within filters, relayers within relayers. History comes to us as this, as a deflected stream.

Quentin's sole response is "Yes," which superficially seems to acknowledge Shreve's view of why Bon switched Judith's picture in the metal case to that of the octoroon and their child. But the "Yes" is a more generalized response to the madness of the situation, to the lunatic history of the South, and, of course, directly to the racial issues underlying that madness. Yet it is all inevitable. One of the by-products of a stream technique is its quality of inevitability; since the stream is subjective, it is final. There can be no external evidence to deflect it. It becomes history, inasmuch as it cannot be argued with. The historical dilemma of race seems finalized by the method Faulkner has chosen to narrate it. If history is transformed into stream, there is no redress from it, even as we attempt to disentangle history from subjectivity, emotional response, feelings of guilt, qualities that relate more to race than to anything else. Further articulation is impossible.

1. Characterizing Faulkner's public statements about race is an anguish equal to Quentin Compson's, in *Absalom, Absalom!* His fullest statement came in his "A Letter to the North," later retitled "Letter to a Northern Editor," printed in *Life* (5 March 1956). Faulkner's position that just as he was once against compulsory segregation he now opposes compulsory integration brought down on him "contumely and insult and threat from other Southerners." In this piece, he addresses the NAACP and asks it and similar organizations to "go slow now." He is clearly on the side of justice for Negroes, but fears that rapid change will destroy the society and inevitably make things worse for the underdog. But interwoven with this gradualist approach is Faulkner's own fear of change, his commitment not only to a region but to an America which must remain recognizable and continuous. What is striking about Faulkner's views on race in the 1950s is how closely they approximate his large sense of himself as an American, who must, somehow, protect the country from the rapid change that permits weakness to leak in. Once we bring the argument to this stage, there is no disentangling racial issues in Faulkner's public statements as a Southerner from everything he said and stood for as an American.

The most famous of his assertions, the intemperate outburst to the English correspondent Russell Warren Howe (published on 4 March 1956 in the London Sunday *Times* and on March 22 in *The Reporter*) was anomalous. In this interview, according to Howe and denied by Faulkner, the latter suggested a reopening of the Civil War if the South were coerced into integration. "If I have to choose between the United States government and Mississippi, then I'll choose Mississippi. . . . As long as there's a middle road, all right, I'll be on it. But if it came to fighting I'd fight for Mississippi against the United States even if it meant going out into the street and shooting Negroes." In a letter to the editor of *The Reporter*, Faulkner claimed that no sober man would make such a statement, and no sane man would believe it. Howe, in his response, said his shorthand notes were verbatim.

"Ah Just Cant Quit Thinking": Faulkner's Black Razor Murderers

HOKE PERKINS

Somewhere, at the bottom, everyone hates everyone.
Ellen Douglas

Knowledge, at the bottom, is acknowledgement.
Ludwig Wittgenstein[1]

I-AM TO I-AM

When Faulkner revised the episode he had published in 1950 as *Notes on a Horsethief* for inclusion in *A Fable*, he excised an interesting passage, one that elucidated the bond between the New Orleans lawyer and his mulatto servant:

> . . . between whom and himself there was a rapport not of mere man to man since flesh is constantly fluctuant or of mere soul to soul since the soul may be beat and battered until it no longer has value even as a negotiable symbol but of I-Am to I-Am: the presence the aura which is the sum of the flagless ruthless unpitying glands which may be vivisected out but even then virulent and defeatless do not die and never surrender.[2]

This peculiar bond results, the narrator writes, because the lawyer had admired the way in which his servant had slit his lover's throat with a razor. Faulkner dropped this passage from his novel, perhaps because he had been so critical of the glands in his Nobel Prize speech four years earlier. He may have excised this passage, but throughout his career Faulkner wrote about black razor murderers, often emphasizing the bond between the murderer and a white character. This study attempts to come to terms with this strain in Faulkner's fiction.

222

Faulkner's bond between lawyer and murderer has its literary precedents, of course, most notably in Dickens's *Great Expectations*, where Jaggers keeps Estella's mother as his personal servant, proudly showing off the scars on her wrists, and harping on the strength in her hands, hands that had strangled her rival for Magwitch's love. Conrad's *The Secret Agent* continually connects police officers with revolutionaries, identifies representatives of the law with miscreants as a way of evoking the bestial ties that fascinate and unite us all.

There is no shortage of black razor murderers in Faulkner's fiction; they show up in *Sanctuary, Light in August*, "That Evening Sun," and *Go Down, Moses*. Whites engage in razor play as well, from Percy Grimm to Uncle Bud. Perhaps this plethora should not surprise us; people do use razors to murder other people. Cullen tells the story of Nelse Patton's murder of Mattie McMillen in Oxford in 1908; she had run seventy-five yards with her throat cut before falling dead.3 This event from Faulkner's eleventh year obviously influenced the description of the mulatto servant's crime in *A Fable*. Ten years ago, as I sat at breakfast in Grove Hill, Alabama, my uncle told of the arrival in the night at the hospital where he worked of two victims of a razor attack. A black woman had found her husband with another woman in the cab of his pickup truck; so, she walked up to them, opened the door, and slit both their throats. My uncle's eyes gleamed with admiration as he recounted the attack, and I believe this audience is also struck, as I was, by the way in which the thing was done. There is thus mere verisimilitude in Faulkner's stories of black razor killings and the way in which whites react to them in the South.

We cannot ignore, however, Faulkner's formulation of the brotherhood of the glands in such a way as to suggest a bonding of men against women. The *Horsethief* lawyer is parallel to the Old General in *A Fable* by several parameters; notably, the Old General has a swarthy Basque chauffeur "with the face of a murderer of female children."4 Both men are representatives of power in male-dominated societies, and their safety is guaran-

teed by complicity with violent male blacks. Dickens's Jaggers, in
his long hypothetical confession of the good he has done for
Molly, says: "Put the case that he took her in, and that he kept
down the old wild violent nature, whenever he saw an inkling of
its breaking out, by asserting his power over her in the old
way."5 For Jaggers the matter is clearly male and female, as well
as lawyer and criminal. Works of literature from *Othello* to *Guess
Who's Coming to Dinner* and *Song of Solomon* reveal that the
problem between the races is partly, if not primarily, a problem
between the sexes. Faulkner's characters use their black dop-
pelgangers to express their most primal urges toward authoritative will and male dominance. Joe Christmas and Percy
Grimm are brothers in this pattern; their razors deny the sex of
the victim, by murder or by castration. They seek to protect
their own position of dominance with their razors. Lacan's discussion of the concept of the phallus as the power of authoritative
language is pertinent here, as we see in Faulkner the bonding of
rhetoricians like the Old General, the lawyer, Percy Grimm, and
even Gail Hightower with razor murderers.6 Those who wield
razors inspire those who wield words. In Faulkner, razor murderers, and those who admire them, are female haters.

Any Faulkner student will counter this picture, I hope, by
citing the example of Rider, from "Pantaloon in Black," a man
who both loved his wife and murdered a man with a razor. I can
only agree, and promise much further discussion of Rider. A
passage in that story, however, does support my view of white
reaction to black crime. Just after the deputy tells his wife the
details of Rider's crime, the narrator says: "The wife passed him
again and went to the dining room. Again he drew his feet back
and raised his voice."7 This does not seem to me an innocuous
passage, particularly since Faulkner went to the trouble to rein-
state these sentences in the setting typescript of *Go Down,
Moses; Harper's,* by accident or editorial decision, had cut the
passage from the original typescript.8 Faulkner may mean us to
think that the deputy watches his wife with murderous intent as
she crosses his path, uninterested in the story that so obsesses

him. There is certainly little love between the two, and the deputy has an odd view of Rider's behavior at Mannie's grave:

> "His wife dies on him. All right. But does he grieve? He's the biggest and busiest man at the funeral. Grabs a shovel before they even got the box into the grave they tell me, and starts throwing dirt onto her faster than a slip scraper could have done it. But that's all right—" His wife came back. He moved his feet again and altered his voice again to the altered range: "—maybe that's how he felt about her. There aint any law against a man rushing his wife into the ground, provided he never had nothing to do with rushing her to the cemetery too." (155)

He cannot conceive of grief being the impetus for Rider's actions, because he lacks such love for his wife; here, too, Faulkner emphasizes her walking across his feet and the change in his voice. Surely the fact that she cheats at cards cements this connection between her and Rider's victim.

There are disturbing biographical parallels that we cannot avoid. Faulkner reacted to news of Hemingway's suicide oddly: "It's bad when a man does something like that. It's like saying, death is better than living with my wife. Hemingway's mistake was that he thought he had to marry all of them."[9] Such a comment tells us more about Faulkner's marriage than Hemingway's. This identification of teller with tale is most obvious in the New Orleans lawyer's view of his servant's act in *A Fable:*

> not that he [the lawyer] held any brief even for the murder of this particular woman, but because of the way it had been done; apparently with the razor already naked in his hand, the man had not driven the woman out of the cabin, but had simply harried and chivvied her through a scene which, as the lawyer imagined it, must have had the quality of ballet, until the woman broke and ran out of the house screaming into the moonlit lane, running without doubt toward the sanctuary of the white kitchen where she worked, until the man without haste overtook her, not to catch, grasp at her, but simply ran past her with one single neat surgeon-like back-handed slash of the razor, running into, then out of, the instant's immobility into which all motion flowed in one gesture of formulated epicene, almost finicking, even niggardly fatal violence like the bullfighter's,

the two of them running on side by side for two or three paces in the moonlight until the woman fell, the man not even spotted and the blade itself barely befouled, as if he had severed not a jugular but a scream and restored merely to the midnight, silence. (182–83)

This description abounds with Faulkner's aesthetic keywords and obsessive imagery, but most important is the fact that it uses his Keats-derived aesthetic of arrested motion not in the interests of love, truth, or beauty, but in the murder of a woman with a razor. Did Faulkner want to cut Estelle's throat? We might as well suggest that all of us want to murder our lovers at one time or another. While I hesitate to make the biographical connection firm, I hope I have shown that Faulkner wrote about black razor murderers not as evidence of racial degeneracy, but as a way of bonding the high with the low, the moral with the immoral, legal rhetoric with bestial impulse. If such a view is bleak, I can only say, "Go slow, now." I have much more to discuss.

BLACK HAMLET

Go Down, Moses everywhere evinces Faulkner's enlightened view of the conflict between blacks and whites in the South, and it is an astounding fact that Faulkner referred to the first four sections of this book as he did. Just after finishing "Pantaloon in Black," Faulkner wrote Robert Haas: "Ober has four stories about niggers."[10] We can cut him some slack, a Southerner in 1940 out to shock his Yankee editors, perhaps infected by the tone of the deputy he had just created. The tone of Faulkner's narration of Rider's ordeal is far different. Mannie's death knocks the chucks out from under Rider's life and sends him on a day-long ride to the buzz saw, a ride seen clearly and compassionately. Looking beyond Faulkner's racial slur, I believe we must make the point that *Go Down, Moses* was conceived as a book about race. The first four sections set patterns for the rest of the book that belie much of the critical attention paid to the wilderness themes. The stories about Tomey and Lucas and Rider preceded "The Bear," and that story, in its complete form, is much more concerned with race than with hunting. "Pantaloon in Black" is a study of the means by which a white man understands and identifies with a black razor murderer.

I have never been satisfied with any explanation for the odd title of the story. Blotner's suggestion—that Pantalone was often a disappointed lover (*Faulkner*, 1038)—has little to do with the story. Pantalone was always an old man, and Rider has nothing in common with him. An East German critic has recently made an interesting suggestion, writing that Rider, "for the representatives of the white establishment is nothing more than a comic and laughable figure, just as was Pantalone in the Italian commedia dell'arte."[11] I have always considered that the reference was less to Pantalone than to the attributes of the commedia dell'arte in general, plays that portrayed man, as Faulkner describes it in his early essay "The Hill": "as though his body had been mesmerized by a whimsical God to a futile puppet-like activity on one spot."[12] Rider, the most fully realized razor murderer in Faulkner's fiction, moves through the story as if already dangling on the rope that is to hang him.

But I must share a further speculation, one provoked by Faulkner's use of the English rather than Italian form of the word Pantaloon. Twice William Shakespeare uses the term: once, in Jacques's famous "ages of man" speech in *As You Like It* where, as in this story, much is made of the piping of an ineffectual voice; and as a passing reference to a foolish old man in *The Taming of the Shrew*. There is no use of the word Pantaloon in *Hamlet*, but I have always thought that Faulkner plays with scenes and ideas from *Hamlet* in "Pantaloon in Black." Here are some parallels and parodies: Hamlet wears black; Rider and Hamlet express grief violently at the graves of their lovers; both are impelled into action by the appearance of a ghost; both turn away emissaries from authority figures with scorn; both have suicidal impulses; both kneel with a female relative who is trying to dissuade them from their purposes; and both, with a blade, kill their adversaries while being cheated in a game, righting old wrongs, and generating their own deaths. The form of the story recalls *Hamlet*'s play within a play, with Rider's story serving as the stage upon which the deputy tries to find himself.

An inventive mind can find parallels between any two texts, and a dolt could find ties between *Hamlet* and any work of art, so capacious, so magnificent is Shakespeare's masterpiece. Whether Faulkner intended the parallel or not, *Hamlet* provides very interesting ways of looking at "Pantaloon in Black" and its place in *Go Down, Moses*. The story is Faulkner's finest, and along with Scott Fitzgerald's "Babylon Revisited," for me the saddest story in American literature. Like *Hamlet*, these stories ground their tragedy in innocence doomed by memory and the palpable presence of the past. They all enact what the German scholar Hans Blumenberg has called "Faulkner's greatest theme: the sorrows of the loss of innocence."[13]

As this essay now suffers an embarrassment of parameters, I'll turn to data. The first section of "Pantaloon" bursts with images of the existence of objects from the past, memory made real in what Faulkner calls "the juncturesless backloop of time's trepan" (152). The first sustained description in the story is of Mannie's grave, which, "save for its rawness, resembled any other marked off without order about the barren plot by shards of pottery and broken bottles and old brick and other objects insignificant to sight but actually of a profound meaning and fatal to touch, which no white man could have read" (135). The narrator here affirms the meaning inherent in seemingly blank objects. Think of Hamlet with Yorick's skull; he uses memory to bring alive a shard at graveside. We begin the story, then, by being instructed to see what we otherwise would not see in the litter scattered on Mannie's grave.

Acey warns Rider that Mannie "be wawkin yit" (136). Rider, nevertheless, turns for home, and Faulkner's narrator shows how it is that Mannie walks the road Rider takes:

> It was empty at this hour of Sunday evening—no family in wagon, no rider, no walkers churchward to speak to him and carefully refrain from looking after him when he had passed—the pale, powder-light,

powder-dry dust of August from which the long week's marks of hoof
and wheel had been blotted by the strolling and unhurried Sunday
shoes, with somewhere beneath them, vanished but not gone, fixed
and held in the annealing dust, the narrow, splay-toed prints of his
wife's bare feet where on Saturday afternoons she would walk to the
commisary to buy their next week's supplies while he took his bath;
himself, his own prints, setting the period now as he strode on,
moving almost as fast as a smaller man could have trotted, his body
breasting the air her body had vacated, his eyes touching the objects—post and tree and field and house and hill—her eyes had lost.
(137)

The paradox of Mannie's being "vanished but not gone" is recon-
ciled through the everyday miracle of shared vision, the leap of
imagination applied to the objects Mannie saw, and Rider sees.
Rider sees Mannie because he sees what she saw on her weekly
trip to town; indeed, routine and simplicity are emphasized as
being the source of imaginative reconstruction. The dog knows
before the man, a pattern of apprehension repeated with
Houston's dog in the Snopes trilogy. Like Houston's dog, Rider's
dog howls at the presence of the dead, once Rider has returned
to his cabin: "But it stopped just outside the front door, where he
could see it now, and the upfling of its head as the howl began,
and then he saw her too. She was standing in the kitchen door,
looking at him. He didn't move. He didn't breathe nor speak
until he knew his voice would be all right, his face fixed too not
to alarm her" (140). This scene does not arise from Rider's sympathetic imagination. The narrator presents her presence in such a
way as to turn Rider's way of seeing into objective reality.
Faulkner's later works are filled with unqualified miracles, and
all are told in this restrained voice, with this level simplicity.
Like Hamlet's father's ghost, Mannie exists. She offers no solace,
however, only an impetus.

Contrast this palpable presence with the walking absence the
deputy's wife represents. Heedless of her husband, she has even
less contact with him in life than Mannie and Rider have in
death. Ironic parallels emphasize this point: she is fixing dinner,
one that will surely lack the symbolic weight of Mannie's "cold

and glutinous peas" (141); and her constant pacing while he speaks plays off Mannie's "wawkin."

The deputy's lack of contact with his wife has its parallel in *Hamlet*, as well. Hamlet must shuck off Ophelia as he gets caught up in his attempt to find retribution. Think also of Ike, who gives up his duties as a husband as part of his own attempt to rework the wrongs of his family's past. All three must channel their virility into their quests, in some ways unmanning themselves. Now, this process contrasts sharply with Rider's case. Part of our, and the deputy's, admiration for him stems from his physical power, his constant concern with using his body, and keeping it free. He wrestles with logs, with the whiskey in his jug, and with the other prisoners as if in a contest with some sort of anima, with the absolute. Ike, as Roth's mistress tells him in "Delta Autumn," doesn't know what love is; Rider is wholly driven by sexual love.

Like Hamlet, and unlike Ike, Rider finds a way to get recompense, and ensure his own death at the same time. The recompense he finds in killing Birdsong may seem impalpable, only part of a suicidal urge, but what he is killing is the unfairness in his world, the injustice that killed Mannie, and that binds him in the straightjacket of his race's place in the South. Birdsong is the God who cheats, Rider the hero who has the hubris to challenge him. His act is meaningful revenge; the Birdsong family ties are mere revenge tragedy bloodshed.

Rider is a new sort of character for Faulkner, an innocent black who can act, who can exercise individual power in the world. Faulkner's earlier novels are filled with innocents who are powerless in the face of those who wish to exercise their will; think of the following pairs in this context: Quentin and Dalton Ames, Charles and Sutpen, Darl and Anse, Hightower and Percy Grimm. Faulkner had begun early in his career to use women and children as characters who can subvert authoritative dominance, with Quentin II, Rosa and Judith, Bayard, Ringo and Grandmother. Successful men in the middle career, like the tall convict and Ike and Gavin and Ratliff, are in substantial ways unmanly. Rider, however, prepares the way for mysterious, but powerful black innocents like Lucas Beauchamp and Tobe Sutterfield. Although these characters are not all razor murderers, they all refuse to work within the structures of white authority and law.

Why does Rider use a razor? The French critic Helene Laurent has said that his razor contrasts with Birdsong's gun, that the razor, "a phallic symbol, is the instrument of death, but also of creation, of liberation for Blacks."[14] This is all well and good, but I like to think of the razor as an instrument that emphasizes the edges, the borderlines between black and white. Think of the Senegalese soldiers in A Fable, standing on the parapet over the imprisoned Frenchmen, stroking their bayonets. They separate the mob of helpless townspeople, who careen purposelessly from place to place, from the division of mutinous soldiers, who have taken the ultimate step in active innocence, passive civil disobedience. The black soldiers stand between men who live controlled by authority and those willing to subvert it. This is Rider's choice in the boiler room, and he chooses to leave the state of mediation to become a revolutionary. In A Fable the general staff uses the Senegalese to assert their power, and uses the black American soldier to execute Gragnon, just as the Old General uses his dark Basque murderer for conveyance. Whites use blacks to subject their own people, and it is Rider's heroism that he refuses to become a part of this brotherhood of the glands. Like Hamlet, he uses his own power to repudiate his false masters.

KNOWLEDGE AND ACKNOWLEDGEMENT

Dirk Kuyk believes that Rider's fate has "entagled" (*sic*) the deputy.[15] This view explains the disturbing narrative structure of "Pantaloon in Black," but it also signals a variation in the pattern we observed earlier in this essay. White characters use black razor murderers as objects in their own psychological dynamics, a process that might best be characterized by Stein's advice to Marlow in *Lord Jim* to submit himself to the destructive element, to find himself by exploring the nature of evil in the world and in himself. The deputy's misogyny ties him to Rider's story, but he seems to seek the source of Rider's violent nature. Noel Polk has said that the deputy is redeemable because, unlike the Maydews, Birdsongs, and his wife, he is "educable."[16] I would strongly argue against Floyd Watkins's view that there is "not a good white man or even a good word or a good action by a white man" in "Pantaloon."[17] I would go further than Polk: the deputy is not merely educable, he is in a state of near empathy. His story is told obsessively, and I believe he feels honest anguish, perhaps greater than Ike's, over his lifelong misapprehension of blacks. His language is that of the ignorant Southern racist; his story is that of a man disturbed to his soul by a mystery he cannot understand. The deputy breaks in upon the narration of "Pantaloon" and wrests the story from the objective narrator, because he must tell it. Rider sees Mannie because he sees her in the objects around him; the narrator of "Pantaloon" tries to force whites to see what blacks can see in Mannie's grave, and the deputy wants to see Rider, wants to know him, but cannot find a way to get this knowledge. Nevertheless, he cannot quit thinking.

A few years after he wrote this story of attempted apprehension, Faulkner explored this issue again, in the published version of *Notes on a Horsethief.* The mystified character in that story is the turnkey, Irey, and the mysterious black man, Tobe Sutterfield. The New Orleans lawyer, whom we have seen living in a dark brotherhood with his servant, tries to bribe Irey into letting Sutterfield go free, but Irey refuses money. He is finally persuaded by the lawyer's reminders that Irey's in-laws, to whom he owes his position, will retaliate if Irey lets the mob get Sutterfield. Before he is talked into this complicity with authority, the turnkey has an awakening in another passage excised from the manuscript of *A Fable*. Irey has shown himself, like the deputy in "Pantaloon," to be a bigot, and he is fascinated by a "nigger's" ability to accumulate $40,000, as he believes Sutterfield has done with the race horse. He has decided not to let

Sutterfield go, however, hoping to protect him from what he sees as a menacing mob of townspeople. The following passage from *Horsethief* chronicles his spiritual awakening:

> not until now standing with a lawyer and the nigger behind the flimsy railing in the very room in the very building which his ancestors and his wife's cousin-in-law's and theirs too who had swept the three of them up and in here had built for this very purpose of not just punishing the evil but of protecting the weak; that once the injured and oppressed reached the inside of the little wooden fence that even a child could throw down with one hand not all the power on earth could touch them until their griefs had been heard and their injuries comforted, looking not at them nor even at the nigger let alone the lawyer but at himself . . . and discovered for the first time between the instant when he snapped the handcuffs and the one when he reached the courthouse something had happened to him: that what he had meant wasnt *what a shame for a nigger to have that much money* but what a shame he has to defend it with only his black skin which itself is the first and deadliest enemy to his keeping it: *and more: that he had known all the time what he meant but had not had the bravery to face it; with shame and grief had known all the time not just the truth but the right too but hadnt had the courage to stand up for it;* but no more shame and no grief now. (46–47)

Irey takes the step beyond the deputy's desire to understand Rider's passion; he acknowledges the humanity of a black man, and decides to stand up to authority and a threatening white community. It is a great shame that Faulkner (or, more likely, Saxe Commins) decided to excise this passage, and ironic that he did so, probably, in reaction to Irey's racist language.[18] Seeing Irey in *A Fable*, we just see Irey as a racist who gives in to pressure from his Birdsong/Maydew-like kinsmen. In *Notes on a Horsethief*, however, he is set in direct contrast to the lawyer who is trying to corrupt him. The lawyer knows only the dark ties of the glands to blacks, only knows blacks from a position of authority and dominance, and therefore knows them not at all. Much is made in *Horsethief* of Irey's position as an underling; he comes to know Sutterfield because he acknowledges their common status as victims.

Wittgenstein writes that we must distinguish between seeing and seeing *as*, and my epigraph reveals his view that we most fundamentally know something when we acknowledge it, and have our view of it acknowledged by others.[19] The "Pantaloon" deputy sees Rider, but cannot find a way to see him as something he can comprehend; part of his problem is that the townspeople and his wife do not share his concern. Irey, in his moment of insight in the courtroom, learns to see Sutterfield as a fellow human, but cannot overcome the racism and greed of his relatives and the lawyer.

I don't believe we can come to any final conclusions about Faulkner and race. A hopeless tangle of conflicting statements, some from his characters, some from his own public speeches and letters, prevents certainty. There is too much history and circumstance in our way, too much world in his art and his life. We can find, however, a measure of growth in his fiction. He begins with a remarkably perceptive view of the way those in positions of authority think of and use black criminals, a psychological pattern grounded, it seems to me, in several other modernist writers.[20] Late in his career he finds a way to show characters who "cant quit thinking" because they are disturbed by their power over blacks. Racism, a knowledge decreed by authority, unnerves the deputy, Ike, Irey, and others. They attempt to negotiate a new view of the politics of race by learning to acknowledge what they see, no longer satisfied to leave the objects on Mannie's grave unexamined.[21]

NOTES

1. Ellen Douglas, *A Lifetime Burning* (New York: Random House, 1982), 66. Ludwig Wittgenstein, *On Certainty*, ed. G. E. M. Anscombe and G. H. von Wright (New York: Harper and Row), 49. This and other quotations from foreign sources are my own translation.

2. William Faulkner, *Notes on a Horsethief* (Greenville, Miss.: The Levee Press, 1950), 58; hereafter cited parenthetically in the text.

3. John Cullen, *Old Times in the Faulkner Country* (Chapel Hill: University of North Carolina Press, 1961), 90.

4. William Faulkner, *A Fable* (New York: Random House, 1954), 230; hereafter cited parenthetically in the text.

5. Charles Dickens, *Great Expectations* (Harmondsworth: Penguin, 1965), 425.

6. For a succinct discussion of Lacan's idea of the phallus, see chapter 8 of Jacques Lacan, *Ecrits: A Selection*, trans. Alan Sheridan (London: Tavistock, 1977).

7. William Faulkner, *Go Down, Moses* (New York: Random House, 1942), 156; hereafter cited parenthetically in the text.

8. I examined Faulkner's reinstatement of this passage in the setting typescript of "Pantaloon in Black" in the Faulkner collection in Alderman Library, accession number 6074, IA:13c.

9. Joseph Blotner, *Faulkner: A Biography*, 2 vols. (New York: Random House, 1974), 1790.

10. William Faulkner, *Selected Letters*, ed. Joseph Blotner (New York: Random House, 1977), 124.

11. Gunter Gentsch, *Faulkner Zwischen Schwarz und Weiss: Betrachtungen zu Werk und Personlichkeit des amerikanischen Nobelprestragers* (Berlin: Akademie-Verlag, 1983), 103.

12. William Faulkner, *Early Prose and Poetry*, ed. Carvel Collins (Boston: Little, Brown, 1962), 90.

13. Hans Blumenberg, "Mythos und Ethos in Werk William Faulkner," *Hochland*, 50, Jahrg. 3 (1958), 250.

14. Helene Laurent, "Pantaloon in Black," in *Le Blanc et le Noir chez Melville et Faulkner*, ed. Viola Sachs (Paris: Mouton et Cie, 1974), 162.

15. Dirk Kuyk, Jr., *Threads Cable-strong: William Faulkner's "Go Down, Moses"* (Lewisburg: Bucknell University Press, 1983), 70.

16. Noel Polk, "'I Taken Taken an Oath of Office Too': Faulkner and the Law," in *Fifty Years of Yoknpatawpha: Faulkner and Yoknapatawpha, 1979*, ed. Doreen Fowler and Ann J. Abadie (Jackson: University Press of Mississippi, 1980), 176.

17. Floyd Watkins, "What Stand Did Faulkner Take?" in *Faulkner and the Southern Renaissance: Faulkner and Yoknapatawpha, 1981*, ed. Doreen Fowler and Ann J. Abadie (Jackson: University Press of Mississippi, 1982), 58.

18. See the setting typescript of *A Fable* (Alderman Library accession number 6074 IA;17d) for Comminss's editorial emendations.

19. Wittgenstein's best discussion of the problem of perspective and aspect may be found in his discussion of the duck/rabbit drawing on pages 194–97 of *Philosophical Investigations*, 3rd ed., trans. G.E.M. Anscombe (New York: MacMillan, 1968).

20. Henry James, for example, has his narrator in "The Jolly Corner," another story about lost love and the search for a shadow self, describe his nightlong hunt for his double in these terms: "It was indeed true that his fully dislocalised thought of these manoevres recalled to him Pantaloon, at the Christmas farce, buffeted and tricked from behind by ubiquitous Harlequin" (*The Complete Tales of Henry James*, ed. Leon Edel [Philadelphia: Lippincott, 1964], 12:213).

21. After I delivered this paper, Pamela Rhodes directed me to John Limon's fine article "The Integration of *Go Down, Moses*," *Critical Inquiry*, 12 (Winter 1986), 422–38. Our essays approach "Pantaloon" from completely different directions, but several times we answer each other's questions, and illuminate each other's arguments. I particularly like his speculation on the title of the story, and his convincing demonstration of the problem of the concept of community in Faulkner. I cannot agree with Limon, however, when he posits that Rider represents a mystery that disintegrates the novel into a series of stories. It seems to me that Rider's place as antimatter in *Go Down, Moses* serves to bring larger issues of racial mystery and communication into coherence in the novel.

Lucas Beauchamp and Jim:
Mark Twain's Influence on William Faulkner

Sergei Chakovsky

Any discussion of William Faulkner and Mark Twain, regardless of its specific purpose, seems to vacillate between the poles of two strong opinions expressed by Faulkner at the beginning and towards the end of his literary career. In 1922 he described Twain as "a hack writer who would not have been considered fourth rate in Europe, who tricked a few of the old proven 'sure fire' literary skeletons with sufficient local color to intrigue the superficial and the lazy."[1] In 1958, however, Faulkner cited Twain among "the masters from whom we learned our craft" and called him quite plainly "all of our grandfather."[2]

In order to accommodate one's general conception of Faulkner, it is easy to hail or dismiss either statement. The first one, which emphasizes "how European was Faulkner's outlook" from the outset, can be interpreted as a "further warning against taking a purely Southern or even purely American view" of him,[3] or seen as the immature bravado of a provincial, imitative poet who as yet does not know what literary "slavery" means, who lacks information about Twain's European fame, and who, ironically, foreshadows what some critics will say about his own work in a decade or so. The second opinion can be seen as a long overdue, explicit tribute to the American tradition of critical realism to which Faulkner was a natural if somewhat whimsical heir; or the comment can be dismissed as the gesture of a writer excessively mellowed with éclat and age who yet reserves recognition for "the clumsy method of Mark Twain and Dreiser"[4] (a comment characteristic of an artist turned "political philosopher").

However paradoxical each of these statements is, and understandably more so when juxtaposed, perhaps the greatest paradox is the degree of their inner consistency. Obviously, Faulkner never ceased to dislike "sure fire" literary tricks, to which his well-known "inverted" theory of artistic success bears witness. To what extent Faulkner's attempts "to put the whole history of the human heart on the head of a pin," in view of the impossibility of the task, really ended in a "magnificent bust,"[5] whether or not he was essentially the "bad" writer of genius, is, of course, another question. The dignity and sincerity of the attempt in view of the problems he had to tackle is of no less importance than the actual result. What is also clear is that the use of the word *clumsy* to describe Twain's daring artistic intrusion into life, even if he like Dreiser had "a terrific difficulty in saying"[6] what he feels called upon to say, is in this context nothing short of praise.

The argument about what kind of influence—European, American, or Southern—played the most pronounced role in the formation of Faulkner's literary individuality is no parlor game. It touches strongly upon the very artistic, ideological, and historical essence of his work. I agree with Michael Millgate, or, for that matter, with Thomas McHaney[7] that no one "exclusively American" tradition will contain Faulkner. Many literary "blood strains" went together to compound him as a writer. Yet wasn't he "taintlessly" American in that too? And wasn't Twain his supreme, if for some time unacknowledged, prototype?

I certainly mean not just Twain the "wild" frontier humorist, the "tall-taler" of the Southwest, or the "local colorist." But also, and perhaps foremost, Twain the philosopher of American "innocence" and the human condition in general, the social thinker and the innovative artist, the greatest "modern" of his time, the daring reformer of literary idioms, who called himself a "jackleg" novelist. Equally misleading, of course, are Faulkner's self-descriptions: a farmer who writes, or a man "uneducated in every formal sense, without even very literate, let alone literary, companions."[8]

Should we elaborate the obvious: that both Twain and

Faulkner were professional writers, well if predominantly self-educated and, certainly, extremely widely read? Yet the "self-made" searching nature of their artistic talents precluded them from consciously emulating any one established literary tradition. On the other hand, it was precisely that originality that gave them the moral gravity, in Faulkner's words, "to rob [one's] own mother" or to "annex" (Alexander Dumas's expression, particularly liked by Twain) the needed material, from whatever source available, be it a newspaper article, European historical or picaresque literature in Twain's case, or the Bible, symbolist poetry, or the stream of consciousness novel in Faulkner's case. What is important is that they did so not for the aesthetic "fun of it," but for the artistic recording of life as they saw it.

Did Faulkner "rob" his "grandfather"? He certainly did. Yet their literary relationship certainly transcends the sphere of pure "intertextuality," a branch of literary scholarship that lately has emerged to give scientific grounding to such acts. It is perhaps true that for every direct or indirect "quotation" from Twain in Faulkner's work one can find ten from the Bible, Shakespeare, other combined European sources, or even Oriental sources—the early draft of the story "Lizards in Jamshyd's Courtyard" was elegantly entitled "Omar's Eighteenth Quatrain." That the title was later discarded is, perhaps, appropriate: the story is built upon the planted money sequence, closely resembling the "salt-a-mine" trick of the West, so vividly described by Twain in *Roughing It.* Surely, Faulkner did not have to read Twain for that and, even if he did, this was too popular a source to acknowledge. It seems likely that from time to time Faulkner himself would pull exactly such tricks on his critics, "salt" the story with imposing "quotations" (just as Twain and Charles Warner did, supplying as epigraphs for *The Guilded Age* excerpts from Chinese philosophers—in Chinese.)

However different individually, Faulkner and Twain were akin in more "substantive" things: the humanistic values that guided their assaults on the social order and their nagging doubts about the essential integrity of human nature; their inbred individualism and organic, communal sociality; their love (or love-hate) for the South, the "patch" of their "native soil" that produced their best works; and simultaneously their aspiration for a cosmic view of universal truth.

What is a writer's grief—to realize that his "tragedy" is "second-hand"—is, of course, a critic's bread. That is why writers do not like critics. Yet, even if Twain's work in general and his artistic treatment of blacks in particular can be seen as a kind of matrix for those of Faulkner's, they are also a good backdrop for the younger writer's quite considerable originality. Let us briefly deal with the "matrix" aspect—the design of *Huckleberry Finn* and Jim's part in it—hoping that it will help to reveal Faulkner's originality as it manifests itself in the portraiture of Lucas Beauchamp in *Go Down, Moses.*

The most interesting aspect of Faulkner's succinct reading of *Huckleberry Finn* at the English Club at Virginia is that, despite its outward whimsicality, it is just as revealing about him (which is more or less true also of his literary judgments) as it is, in my view, about Twain's greatest book. For someone nourished strictly in the symbolic or sociocritical tradition of reading the novel, Faulkner's interpretation would seem at best paradoxical. Was it just his "small size" Huck had to "combat"? Did he really want "to be part of mankind, humanity," which (at least in the Brickville chapters) was already becoming "the damn human race"? Even if this is so, can it be said that "humanity, the human race, would and was accepting him already; all he needed to do was to grow up in it"?[9] Was this interpretation, perhaps, the result of Faulkner's anxieties about the modern "vacuum" of the human race[10] projected—forget Jim, slavery, and all—on the good old times on the Mississippi? I hardly think so. For it is really the human race—an entity we should not altogether ignore in talking about the *race* problem, "Man as part of life," in Faulkner's words—that is really the protagonist of Twain's novel.

Though Huck's "zigzags between raft and shore"[11] (as Walter Blair put it) have been commonly accepted as a structural principle, supplanting the "linear" movement of the plot, it should be pointed out that the border between raft and shore had been virtually nonexistent long before the Duke's and the Dauphin's intrusion. The reason Huck cannot escape from the world is interior rather than exterior: he simply cannot change his irreversibly social self, however "liminal" he may appear. That is why his conscience "takes up more room than all the rest of a person's insides,"[12] striving to embrace the whole world. Yet he has to make a choice between good and bad, which, as he realizes, does not have "color." Had it been otherwise, had the Christian chromatic symbolism (which Jim ironically accepts, musing about the white and the black angels "hoverin'" around Pap Finn), had that symbolism worked, Huck's choice would not have been so important. There would not have been "hoverin'" around him, on the one hand, Miss Watson, "that poor old woman," who "tried to learn you your book, she tried to learn you your manners, she tried to be good to you in every way she knowed how," whose "nigger" he as well as stole himself (*AHF*, 123). And on the other, Jim: "I'd see him standing my watch on top of his'n, stead of calling me, so I could go on sleeping; and see him how glad he was when I come back out of the fog; and when I come to him again in the swamp, up there where the feud was; and such like times; and would always call me honey and pet me" (*AHF*, 271). This interior monologue, which continues for five more lines, renders dramatically vivid the evolution of a "human heart in conflict with itself." This telescoped, "free" sentence, bearing, I believe, the embryo of Faulkner's style (whether Twain acquired this style through the midwife services of Proust and Joyce is not really important now[13]) precedes Huck's crucial decision to tear up the informing letter to Miss Watson and "*go* to hell." Well, he doesn't. In fact, he goes back to "his people," to "the human race," which "would and was accepting him already," whatever the discord that might result from stealing Jim. Why should Twain virtually "start to tell the story again" as he does, beginning from chapter 32? In terms of structure the answer is apparent, for throughout the book Twain repeatedly circles back: the action unfolds in accordance with the principle of repetition with increment (which, of course, was later "rediscovered" by Faulkner). But here something different happens. And it is not just Huck's passing—however important it is—from one stage, one is tempted to say, of Faulkner's "trilogy of Man's conscience" to another: from the "go off into a cave" phase of Ike McCaslin to the "I'm going to do something about it"[14] of Chick Mallison. The author's intentions must have been mixed. On the one hand, he obviously wished (just like Huck, unconsciously) to get the community to recognize Jim's humanity, to get them (at least in the person of Tom Sawyer) to take part in his salvation, that is, to pull them into the orbit of Huck's new knowledge, to save *them* as well. That humanistic intention obviously appealed to Faulkner to such a degree that it was easy for him to condone all the literary "tricks," or "cheating" (to use Hemingway's expression) it took Twain somehow to free Jim again with communal participation.

However, the forced ending of *Huckleberry Finn* leaves many questions unanswered: wasn't it somewhat cruel at least on Tom Sawyer's part to play his "literary" jokes (thus forcing Jim into another, even if more "elevated," set of stereotypes), on a person, he knew, was legally "free"? Doesn't Jim accept too complacently the "roles" forced on him? And isn't the community's admission that "a nigger like that is worth a thousand dollars" (*AHF*, 357) too weak a recognition of Jim's humanity? So, unlike Huck, who after all could still plan "to light out for the Territory," it is Twain who is left "to decide, forever, betwixt two things" (*AHF*, 272). And Twain really seems to have had to "go" to "hell" to decide this issue, as his subsequent novels *Pudd'nhead Wilson, The Mysterious Stranger,* and *Letters from the Earth* would show.

Faulkner, it is generally assumed, seemed to have walked this road in a reverse mode, moving from the "hell" of his own earlier novels to the more "balanced" or "clear" vision of the later ones. So it is easy to envisage Faulkner's movement from the combined heritage of the late Twain, which corresponds to the composition of *Light in August* and *Absalom, Absalom!* to the

style and mood of *Huckleberry Finn* in *Go Down, Moses, Intruder in the Dust,* and *The Reivers.* All this is, of course, gross simplification. Moreover, I, for one, would argue that *Huckleberry Finn* contains "the whole" Twain at least just as much as *The Sound and the Fury* contains the whole Faulkner in nucleus and that Huck's story influences Faulkner—consciously or not—throughout his literary career, or at least from the moment he struck on the idea to let "someone capable only of knowing what happened, but not why"[15] tell *his* story for him. And, of course, Faulkner's movement along the path that Twain had trodden was not linear, let alone retrograde, but rather shuttlelike, eventually taking him considerably beyond where his "grandfather" had stopped. The explosive issue of race, which challenged them both on moral and purely artistic grounds, is quite characteristic here.

In a recently published letter written in 1885, Mark Twain inquired about the cost of tuition at Yale Law School for a black applicant: "I do not believe I would very cheerfully help a white student who would ask a benevolence of a stranger," he wrote, "but I do not feel so about the other color. We have ground the manhood out of them, and the shame is ours, not theirs; and we should pay for it."[16] This, of course, sounds very much like a blueprint of what Ike McCaslin says in section 4 of "The Bear"; or, for that matter, like Faulkner himself, the "theme of the crime, the curse"[17] (to adduce R. P. Warren's authority) being most relevant to his artistic vision of black-white relations. Yet Lucas Beauchamp is "certainly no Nigger Jim,"[18] as Erskine Peters remarks. The "manhood" is not "ground" out of *him.* And so he can proudly proclaim "I'm a nigger. . . . But I'm a man too"[19]—and he lives up to it.

Despite this difference, Faulkner's indebtedness to Twain becomes obvious as soon as we realize that the lyrical theme of love and matrimony is both a unifying element of the novel and a major "testing ground" of black humanity. Lucas Beauchamp's or Rider's dedication to "the fire and the hearth" and the uneasiness it causes their white counterparts recall Huck's observation about Jim: "He was thinking about his wife and his children, away up yonder, and he was low and homesick; . . . and I do believe he cared just as much for his people as white folks does for their'n. It don't seem natural, but I recon it's so" (*AHF*, 201).

Huck's "innocent" perplexity is, of course, essential to Faulkner's mythology of race. As we come to learn in section 4 of "The Bear," it is precisely this dawning doubt about "the awful sacredness of slave property,"[20] to use Twain's expression, that touches off a kind of psychological avalanche on the Southern traditional order. The exchange of entries in the family ledgers between Buddy and Buck McCaslin occurs at about the same time that the action of *Huckleberry Finn* takes place:

> *June 21th 1833 Drownd herself*
> and the first:
> *23 Jun 1833 Who in hell ever heard of a niger drownding him self*
> and the second unhurried, with a complete finality . . .
> *Aug 13th 1883 Drownd herself* (*GDM*, 204)

The deep, "inbred" fear of black humanity at least in part accounts for Zack Edmonds's reaction to Lucas Beauchamp's projected suicide in "The Fire and the Hearth." The "white man" would rather die himself (and he almost does). This theme reaches its violent climax in the finale of "Pantaloon in Black." Just as we have thoroughly identified with Rider's grief over the death of his wife, the deputy sheriff tells his hopelessly inadequate version of the story to substantiate his morbid verdict: "Because they aint human. They look like a man and they walk on their hind legs like a man, and they can talk and you can understand them. . . . But when it comes to the normal human feelings and sentiments of human beings, they might just as well be a damn herd of wild buffaloes" (*GDM*, 121–22).

One has to understand that the deputy sheriff's stance is not just racist. It is essentially *escapist*. The wish to flee the awesome reality of racial conflict is psychologically understandable—even if one has to forfeit his own humanity (a direct implication in regard to the deputy and his wife) or the land of his fathers (which is Ike's option). There is, however, no escape from it—no Jackson Island or the Territory to run to. The whole structure of *Go Down, Moses* with its intermediate "wilderness" theme seems to be predicated on this Twainean idea. Yet it is also at this point, I suppose, when the rift between black and white seems both deadly and insuperable, when the characters (and the author) seem to be vacillating between the extremes of white and black racism, that Faulkner's originality emerges most clearly.

"A house divided . . . cannot stand," said Abraham Lincoln and Eric Sundquist, the latter to trace the varied sociological and artistic implications of this historic phrase in Faulkner's work.[21] Though "division" may really be "at the core of Faulkner's art,"[22] as Thadious Davis says and Sundquist seems to imply, it has to be pointed out that for Faulkner, being an American, a Southerner, and a writer, this could not but be proportionately unsettling. Division with the North, as we know, he more or less could tolerate. As far as inner racial division was concerned (however characteristic it may be of the "traditional" Southern order), it posed a threat not just to the South, but to his whole artistic world, the latter being founded—in a substantive philosophical sense—precisely on the idea of human universality.

A more or less personal digression may clarify the point at issue. The recent choice of topics for Faulkner and Yoknapatawpha conferences, as you have probably noticed, seems to be invertedly following Maxwell Geismar's aphoristic remark concerning "the twin Furies of Faulkner's deep southern Waste Land"—"The Negro and the Female."[23] Having had the privilege to speak at last year's conference on "Faulkner and Women" I then suggested that Faulkner's treatment of the relationship between man and woman could be at least partly attributed to his essentially Platonic view of humanity: as originally whole, "homogeneous," later to become disintegrated, and then awkwardly reassembled again to make man fit, in Faulkner's words, for some "nationally-recognized economic group by profession or trade or occupation or income-tax bracket or, if nothing else offers, finance-company list,"[24] and thus to lose his or her human individuality; in other words, an individual human being is initially one, "androgynous," then later, for its "sins" is "cut" into male and female "halves," doomed forever to search for one another.[25] I then overlooked a rather striking quotation—the words Ike McCaslin says to his hunting companions in "Delta Autumn": "I think that every man and woman, at the instant when it don't even matter whether they marry or not, I think that whether they marry then or afterward or dont never, at that instant *the two of them together* were God" (italics supplied, GDM, 263).

However ambivalent Faulkner's feelings about Ike may be, the character is certainly "reliable" here. Two pages earlier he pronounces something that in a few years would become Faulkner's publicly acknowledged "symbol of faith": "There are good men everywhere, at all times. Most men are. Some are just unlucky, because most men are a little better than their circumstances give them a chance to be. And I've known some that even circumstances couldn't stop" (GDM, 260–61). These words, as you probably recall, elicit a biting retort from Roth Edmonds asking where Ike has been all the time he was "dead." The younger man's "circumstances" as yet unknown, he continues (first explicitly and then subscribing to the third speaker's supposition) with a sort of a paraphrase of Twain's *What Is Man?*: an "animal," if "behav[ing] at all," then "only because folks happen to be watching him." Ike wouldn't agree: "Maybe so," he says, "But if being what you call alive would have learned me any different, I reckon I'm satisfied, wherever it was I've been" (GDM, 261). So Ike is both reliable and, it seems, revealing here. Yet overlooking this quotation was not all that unfortunate, and not only because it gives me something to talk about now.

As the story unfolds itself, the tragic irony of Ike's situation becomes apparent. What if one of the parts in his twin symbol of "God" should turn out to be black (the woman certainly, not the man, the letter would have been not just "tragically ironic" but, perhaps, fatal)? The action mercilessly demands from the hero precisely such an answer. He is soon to meet a woman with whom his "kin," Edmonds, is seriously emotionally involved and who turns out to be colored. Under the unbearable gaze of her "dark and tragic and foreknowing eyes" he first calls her "a nigger" and then lapses into frenzied interior monologue, which combines quite sound social criticism, and—outrageously uncharacteristic of the hero—obviously racist sentiments. *"This land . . . where white men rent farms and live like niggers and niggers crop on shares and live like animals . . . and usury and mortgage and bankruptcy and measureless wealth, Chinese and African and Aryan and Jew, all breed and spawn together, until no man has time to say which one is which nor cares. . ."* (*GDM*, 275).

Granted that these words of Ike's are a sign of his utter moral confusion, a kind of inevitable retribution of "this land" on the one who abnegated it for ostensibly laudable moral reasons. And still, as the last lines obviously stand for the most part as a euphemism for black-white relations, the "thinning" color line between races, one is tempted to pose the unavoidable question: To what extent does Faulkner share Ike's sentiments? Does *he* "care"?

The question is, of course, a brain-wracking one. On the one hand, Faulkner is known to have uttered even harsher statements. Moreover, how can it be conceivably assumed that as a stock Southerner Faulkner was *not* inherently conscious of race; that his mind had *not* wandered among the most fearsome implications of black-white opposition before it struck on symbolist poetry? However, inductive self-evidence may be deceptive. Take, for example, *Light in August*. Just as Faulkner was bringing home to us the awesome reality of racial conflict, what he seemed to be "inexplicably" advocating was the *irrelevance* of race, or "blood," as Gavin Stevens puts it.

Granted, this message was not quite intentional. Originally adduced as "a tool at hand" to illustrate the more general dilemmas of human identity, the race issue turned out to be very much its own master—to very nearly kill not just the pro-tagonist, but also the novel as an integrated whole. Like Ike's symbol of "God," the whole Yoknapatawpha "design" stood in danger of crumbling before it could even acquire full shape. Faulkner simply had to do something about either the design or the problem that challenged its viability. And what was again amazing was Faulkner's persistency. On the one hand, in *Absalom, Absalom!*, he seemed to have granted the race issue enough specificity to build a whole novel more or less around it. On the other, it was precisely the traditional Southern obsession with "race," "color," or "blood" that was being exposed there—on an unprecedented artistic scale—as deadly for man and society.

Original as both novels are, Sundquist is certainly right in viewing them as phases of "Faulkner's stunning exploration of [the] unanswerable question" put by Twain in *Pudd'nhead Wilson*: "Why are niggers *and* whites made? What crime did the uncreated first nigger commit that the curse of birth was decreed for him? And why this awful difference made between white and black?"[26]

However difficult the question, it should be observed that Faulkner did provide some valuable answers: linking racism with fascism in *Light in August* and exposing its economic, moral, and psychological foundation in *Absalom, Absalom!, Go Down, Moses,* and *Intruder in the Dust*. This, however, did not auto-matically provide the answer to the most important question: How to deal with it? For according to Faulkner, as Peters appro-priately remarks, "the path of redemption . . . is not meant to cleanse the Yoknapatawphan of his sins in preparation for heaven. It is meant to prepare the Yoknapatawphan simply to live in Yoknapatawpha."[27] It is this "simple" question that seems virtually unanswerable.

The "seed" metaphor of *Pudd'nhead Wilson*—black and white as "Siamese twins"—is most relevant to *Go Down, Moses*. The half-farcial yet ominous clash between Tomey's Turl and Uncle Buck, the pair of black and white blood relatives in "Was," gives way to a deadly confrontation between Lucas and Zack Edmonds, who also "could have been brothers, almost twins too" (*GDM*, 42). It is here that Twain's metaphor acquires a graphic, almost physically palpable quality of unresolution: "they met over the centre of the bed where Lucas clasped the other with his left arm almost like an embrace and jammed the pistol against the white man's side and pulled the trigger and flung the white man from him all in one motion, hearing as he did so the light, dry, incredibly loud click of the missfire" (*GDM*, 50).

This scene is of key importance to "The Fire and the Hearth" and, I would claim, to the whole novel. The motifs of "embrace" and dissociation, of killing and suicide mold into one—to produce a powerfully symbolic image of a "live cartridge . . . not much larger than a pencil, not much heavier, yet large enough to contain two lives" (*GDM*, 51). And at the same time what kind of "key" is that, except, at least for some critics to the author's anxieties about race, strong and genuine enough to produce a "live cartridge" of a novel, yet which ends, with the "light, dry" and not even very "loud click of a missfire" of the concluding title story?

Granted, in *Go Down, Moses* Faulkner, like Ike McCaslin, is "trying to explain" something which he "ha[s] got to do," which he doesn't "quite understand" himself (*GDM*, 219), and this contributes to the critical complications which the book causes. What is clear, however, is that unlike Ike and the late Twain (at least in his major fiction after *Pudd'nhead Wilson*) Faulkner refused simply to "quit" the race issue. Unlike the old master who seemed to have ended up virtually straddled in the "vacuum of human race," what Faulkner chose was to re-create humanity anew, from whatever scrap there was left. And since the only strip of land he could do it upon was the South, he simply had to enter "the bear country" of the race problem. The black *and* white parts of humanity simply had to be artistically (if not immediately socially) integrated, so as to become—to use his pretty sharp "tool" of a metaphor—"either all people or all horses; either all cats or all dogs."[28] In doing so Faulkner did not seek safe passage, relying on "the compass" let alone "the gun" of preformed conceptions; he did not try to avoid the dormant yet powerfully damaging elements of Southern race mentality; he brought them into the open, into a paradoxical "embrace" with one another to see how much weight they could carry, to match them in fair contest with what *he* thought was right.

It is certainly significant that at the foundation of this "new" Yoknapatawpha, or, rather, Yoknapatawpha made anew, stands the "salt of the earth," the not just black but black *and* white figure of Lucas Beauchamp. Roth Edmonds's observation that most of Lucas's *"blood was pure ten thousand years when* [his] *own anonymous beginnings became mixed enough to produce* [him]" (*GDM*, 61) may be important as a kind of expiatory counterpoint to Gavin Steven's tortured ratiocinations on "black blood" in *Light in August*. Yet, there is much more to the character than such overt (and at least in part "obversely" stereotypical) symbolism could possibly suggest. However important as a metaphoric vehicle, "blood" is hardly the issue in either novel. The very obtrusiveness of the theme can be read as a sign of the author's attempts to conjure it irrelevant by making it tautological. This statement may seem paradoxical in view of what was obviously Faulkner's deliberate intention while reworking the original short stories into a novel. Why should he have made formerly all-black Lucas as well as Tomey's Turl into half-breeds? Why was it necessary to provide Sam Fathers, a mulatto as he was, with a quadroon mother instead of a black slave woman? Was it just because, as James Early suggests, that "Faulkner's most perceptive studies of blacks had previously had men of mixed blood as protagonists"?[29] Can we really envisage Joe Christmas or Charles Bon as "black"? Aside from this commonsense consideration, Early's explanation suggests complement where contrast seems to be a more appropriate relationship. Rather than continue the long-standing literary tradition of the "tragic mulatto" (to which Faulkner and Twain

were important contributors), the younger writer is now appro-
priating its stock situations to put across quite an "unorthodox"
message.

At the core of this message is, of course, the notion of homeland, native "soil" as both a source and a test of human worth-
iness. Incidentally, it is this notion that affords us the possibility
to "transplant" the race issue into one of the most problematic
areas of its potential application, namely the Snopes trilogy.
What I mean is that from the moment of its inception, in 1926 or
earlier, Faulkner seems to have been both social- and race-
minded enough to discern in the ignorant, low-down lot of
Snopeses not just the prospective "political hangers on and professional officeholders and prohibition officers," but "a race that
is of the land and yet rootless, like a mistletoe; owing nothing to
the soil, giving nothing to it and getting nothing of it in return."[30] This line of reasoning later found expression, not just in
the Snopes characterization in *The Hamlet,* but in referring to
the postbellum profiteers swarming the South as to "that third
race even more alien to the people whom they resembled in
pigment" (*GDM,* 221); or to the Gowries and their kind as "not
even . . . a simple clan or tribe but a race, a species."[31] There is,
of course, a kind of "catch" here, for Faulkner's conception of
race, whatever its root form might have been, as it evolved in his
fiction, was far from being purely "racial," let alone confined to
the opposition of "black, white or yellow." This, of course, saves
us the trouble and the attendant critical hazards (of which Sundquist's quite explosive book, if not his somewhat other-directed
stance at the present conference, is so characteristic) of having
ingeniously to discriminate against the bulk of Faulkner's work
that does not explicitly treat the problem of race or, for that
matter, miscegenation. It hardly makes life any easier, though.
In fact, it complicates the critical task to almost historical propor-
tions, if for different reasons.

What makes Lucas Beauchamp a true representative of the
South, of a "house divided," a land "cursed" with racial conflict,
is, to repeat, his being both black and white. What is important,

however, is the author's treatment of his "mixed blood" not just as a disjointing, psychologically and socially crippling element (which is traditional) but also as a unifying force, which yields the ultimate identity to both the character and the land he personifies. Whatever latent fears of miscegenation Faulkner may have entertained, it is only this "mongrel," metaracial, or, in other words, human identity that seems "taintless" and "incorruptible" for him. And it is coming to grips with this identity that makes Lucas Beauchamp one of those rare men (if not *the man* in Faulkner's canon) "that even the circumstances couldn't stop" (*GDM*, 261).

The path to acquiring such an identity is trying for the character since it demands the transcendence of all those deeply engrained racial stereotypes on the compliance with which (since he is black) his very existence is predicated. The path to understanding such an identity is no less exacting for the critic, since it urges him to go beyond the "words," which seem most illustrative of his general argument, that is, if he is willing, for some strange reason, to verify *his* point by that of the author.

As Lucas claims his wife back from Zack Edmonds, challenging him with a phrase, "I'm a nigger. . . . But I'm a man too," it is apparent that, however dignified, his stance is somewhat self-contradictory. Why "but"? Or, rather, can he who calls himself a "nigger" be a "man too"? Every word that follows makes the contradiction more evident. As soon as Lucas alludes to his white blood (and, at that, on the male side of their common ancestry) as a basis of his superior manliness, Faulkner makes him lapse into affectedly "nigger" talk: "I'm more than just a man. The same thing made my pappy that made your grandma. I'm going to take her back." It is this contradiction in Lucas's behavior that Edmonds senses as he perceives what he is being suspected of : " 'Well, by God,' he said quietly. 'So that's what you think. What kind of a man do you think I am? What kind of a man do you call yourself?' " (*GDM*, 42).

What follows this exchange is an attempt—on the part of the author as well as that of the character—to answer that crucial question. The eight-page sequence incorporates not just all of the major themes of the novel, but, I contend, the paradoxical essence of Faulkner's attitude to race. This makes it, I believe, an all-time interpretive challenge. Since my time is short, let me just summarize its more or less obvious implications.

As Lucas manages to recross the flooded Mississippi bringing the doctor for the already dead Zack's wife, the pattern of "emergence" from the river of death and forgetfulness, "a kind of Lethe," "which he entered not for his own sake but for that of old Carothers McCaslin who had sired him and Zack Edmonds both," is accentuated for a good reason. Having narrowly escaped nonexistence in the face of the horribly eerie yet palpable possibility of a wife-swapping conspiracy—"his own wife already established in the white man's house . . . as though the white woman . . . never existed" (GDM, 41)—Lucas starts to think "race." Historically this is more than justified and hence inevitable, whatever the particular relationship between the given black and white men might be. Thus, Lucas's incredulousness regarding Zack Edmonds's keeping Molly solely as a wet nurse for his orphaned child (or because *she* thought it best for Zack's and Lucas's sons) may be more than justified in view of the long-standing tradition of sexual abuse of black women. However, yielding to "circumstances," the accident of one's birth that decrees one's thinking, Lucas, as Faulkner intimates, loses clear sight of the multishaded reality, becoming like Sam Fathers "his own battleground," and almost "the scene of his own vanquishment" (GDM, 129–30). What Lucas fails to realize in the moment of psychological crisis is that Zack Edmonds is *not* "*Old Carothers* [who] *got his nigger bastards right in his backyard*" (GDM, 94); that he is an individual human being, who, perhaps, does not need to see the other as a "nigger" in order not to feel himself one, and whom in the characteristic moments of recurring ancestral rage Lucas "could not even see" (GDM, 42, 50). Yet, unlike Sam, or, for that matter, Ike (the "beyond-color" juxtaposition forming the clearly pronounced imaginative pattern in the novel), Lucas does not "quit." He "endures" the crisis and ultimately prevails—not just over Zack Edmonds (as Zack's son is later to admit), but over his own divided self as well. In the forge of this crisis a whole human being is born, who (unlike his literary predecessors) need not be torn apart to be at once black and man, a "nigger" ("in the world's eye") and a "quintessential" McCaslin; or, to put it simply, a man, irrespective of the ratio of the "white" and "black" blood that flows in his veins.

This fundamental argument was essentially in tune with what Twain thought and said publicly (especially in his later days), yet somehow fell short of fully accomplishing artistically. The paradox is that in order to translate this line of reasoning on race into positive artistic-ideological "action," Faulkner had to amend the older master on certain important issues. But then, perhaps such a relationship is only natural when we deal not only with imitators but with true literary "blood relatives."

NOTES

1. *William Faulkner: Early Prose and Poetry*, ed. Carvel Collins (Boston: Little, Brown, 1962), 94.

2. *Faulkner in the University: Class Conferences at the University of Virginia, 1957–1958* (Charlottesville: University Press of Virginia, 1959), 243, 281.

3. Michael Millgate, *The Achievement of William Faulkner* (Lincoln: University of Nebraska Press, 1978), 292, 291.

4. *Faulkner in the University*, 145. Millgate attributes special importance to the use of the word *clumsy* as a sign of Faulkner's uncertainty (*The Achievement of William Faulkner*, 332).

5. *Faulkner in the University*, 144.

6. Ibid., 234.

7. Thomas L. McHaney, "Faulkner and Modernism: Why Does It Matter?" in *New Directions in Faulkner Studies: Faulkner and Yoknapatawpha, 1983* ed. Doreen Fowler and Ann J. Abadie (Jackson: University Press of Mississippi, 1984), 37–60.

8. *Selected Letters of William Faulkner*, ed. Joseph Blotner (New York: Random House, 1977), 348.

9. *Faulkner in the University*, 244–45.

10. Ibid.

11. Walter Blair, *Mark Twain and Huck Finn* (Berkeley: University of California Press, 1960), 345.

12. Mark Twain, *Adventures of Huckleberry Finn*, Chandler Facsimile Series in American Literature (New York: Harper and Row, 1962), 292. Hereafter cited in the text as *AHF*.

13. In his important article Frank Baldanza quotes E. M. Forster's remark on Proust (in *Aspects of the Novel*) to show that the "rhythmic stitchings" Foster holds to be the basis of the unity of *À la Recherche du Temps Perdu* are also at the core of Twain's "improvisational" style ("The Structure of *Huckleberry Finn*," in *Huck Finn Among the*

Critics, ed. M. Thomas Inge [United States Information Agency, Division for the Study of the United States, 1984], 167).

14. *Faulkner in the University*, 246.

15. Quoted in Malcolm Cowley, *The Faulkner-Cowley File: Letters and Memoirs, 1944–1962* (Harmondsworth, England: Penguin Books, 1966), 39.

16. *New York Times*, 14 March 1985, 1.

17. Robert Penn Warren, "Faulkner: The South, the Negro, and Time," in *Faulkner: A Collection of Critical Essays* (Englewood Cliffs, N.J.: Prentice-Hall, 1966), 257.

18. Erskine Peters, *William Faulkner: The Yoknapatawpha World and Black Being* (Darby, Penn.: Norwood Editions, 1983), 168.

19. William Faulkner, *Go Down, Moses* (Harmondsworth, England: Penguin Books, 1960), 42. Hereafter cited in the text as *GDM*.

20. Quoted in Walter Blair and Victor Fischer," "Foreword," *Adventures of Huckleberry Finn* (Berkeley: University of California Press, 1985), xx.

21. Eric J. Sundquist, *Faulkner: The House Divided* (Baltimore: Johns Hopkins University Press, 1983).

22. Thadious M. Davis, *Faulkner's "Negro": Art in the Southern Context* (Baton Rouge: Louisiana State University Press, 1983), 3.

23. Maxwell Geismar, *Writers in Crisis: The American Novel, 1925–1940* (Boston: Houghton Mifflin, 1942), 164.

24. *Faulkner in the University*, 242–43.

25. See my article "Women in Faulkner's Novels: Author's Attitude and Artistic Function," in *Faulkner and Women: Faulkner and Yoknapatawpha, 1985*, ed. Doreen Fowler and Ann J. Abadie (Jackson: University Press of Mississippi, 1986), 58–80.

26. Sundquist, *Faulkner: The House Divided*, 95.

27. Peters, *William Faulkner*, 162.

28. *Faulkner in the University*, 210.

29. James Early, *The Making of " Go Down, Moses"* (Dallas: Southern Methodist University Press, 1972), 10.

30. William Faulkner, *Intruder in the Dust* (Harmondsworth, England: Penguin Books, 1960), 42. Hereafter cited in the text as *GDM*.

31. William Faulkner, *Father Abraham* (New York: Random House, 1983), 35.

Faulkner and the Vocational Liabilities
of Black Characterization

MICHAEL GRIMWOOD

When William Faulkner bought Greenfield Farm in 1938, he entered the role of a latter-day plantation master, a role that placed him at the very center of his cultural heritage as a Southerner. His "plantation" was only a mule farm, but soon after he acquired it he could enjoy representing himself to an interviewer as a "country squire," who "bosses his cotton plantation near Oxford, Mississippi."[1] A local friend would characterize him as "a plantation man. That's what he was. That's what he was trying to do."[2]

Lewis Simpson, in *The Dispossessed Garden*, defines the plantation heritage as a self-doomed tradition of literary pastoralism. According to Simpson, the Southern imagination early adopted the image of the plantation as a symbol of the South's intellectual "errand." In the writings of Beverley, Byrd, Jefferson, Taylor, Randolph, and Kennedy, he traces two contradictory aspects of that symbol. First, these white Southerners adopted the "idea of the plantation as a homeland of the life of the mind" from the classical pastoral scheme of Theocritus, Virgil, Sannazaro, Pope. According to this ancient vision, the bucolic garden is a seat of intellectual endeavor, in which the writer doubles as a gardener—or shepherd—and in which argricultural labor and mental labor reinforce and complement one another. After Jefferson left the White House, for example, his letters depicted Monticello as a "patrician domain of the mind" where he spent his mornings "in my shops, my garden, or on horseback among my farms" and his evenings in his study reading and writing.[3] Somewhat less splendidly, Faulkner's stepson Malcolm Franklin remembers Faulkner using his pasture as an annex to his writing table: "He would sit at his typewriter for long stretches at a time, there before the window that looked out across the pasture. Quite suddenly he would get up, open the door to his office, reach for his hoe placed conveniently just outside the porte-cochère, and head for the pasture. There he would stay for an hour or more furiously chopping bitter-weed. . . . Then he would return to his typewriter and begin work."[4]

The men who worked Greenfield Farm, however, were its tenants, and they were black. Faulkner's relationship with them embodied the second, more troublesome component of Simpson's plantation eclogue: namely, that the rapid growth of chattel slavery forced the Southern intellectual to assimilate into classical pastoralism an institution that separated the literary gardener from his garden, the shepherd-poet from his flock. This assimilation led to the disturbing awareness that the slave more precisely fulfilled the Southern "mission" than his white owner did, causing a "fear of slavery as being not simply a threat to the social order but of its being a subversion of the very source of order—that is, the mind and imagination."[5]

Thus, according to Simpson, the effort to make the Southern plantation a pastoral environment of the mind failed because it was based upon the premise, later emphasized by proslavery apologists, that the mind could only function if it were *liberated* by black labor from direct contact with the soil. In the 1780s Thomas Jefferson recognized the contradiction: slavery freed him to think and to write, but what he wrote while supervising his black laborers was that "[t]hose who labour in the earth are the chosen people of God, if ever he had a chosen people."[6] His slaves did so labor; he did not. According to Simpson, Jefferson was temporarily able to acknowledge that "[s]lavery not only . . . severs the connection between the mind of the master class and the soil, but it defies the very scrutiny of mind. Slavery destroys the very capacity for rational criticism. It implies the drastic dispossession of the pastoral vision of the plantation as a dominion of mind."[7]

After writing his *Notes on the State of Virginia,* Jefferson voiced few further doubts about the plantation ideal. Few white Southern writers after him expressed misgivings about importing into it a system of black labor that was inherently antipastoral, a system in which the life of the mind was preserved by its thoroughgoing alienation from the earth and from labor. During the nineteenth and early twentieth centuries, a plantation literature flourished in which white writers celebrated the virtues of black labor and the mental incapacity of black laborers, in which the pleasure of both reading and writing derived from the literate person's impersonation of illiterates, and in which the plantation—far from symbolizing the life of the mind—came to accommodate an abdication of intellect.

Only Faulkner has fully addressed the consequences of the tradition's internal contradictions to himself as a writer. In *Go Down, Moses,* written soon after his purchase of Greenfield, he explored the destructive effects of his heritage upon the very vocation it had fostered in him. That book embodies a climax in the evolution of the characterization of black people—not just in Faulkner's writing but in the writing of white Southerners generally. In it, Faulkner shifted his attention most fully from the Negro as a resource for fiction to what Thadious Davis calls "the Negro as an aesthetic problem"[8]—from picturesque depictions of black people to a tortured and fragmented self-portrait.

In his first stories and novels, Faulkner treated his black characters condescendingly or unsympathetically. They resemble the humorous "darkies" in the dialect fiction of Joel Chandler Harris, Thomas Nelson Page, and Roark Bradford. In *Flags in the Dust* (originally published as *Sartoris,* 1929), for example, Simon and Caspey Strother supply comic relief from the unhappy saga of "their" aristocratic white family. Old Simon parrots the unreconstructed opinions of his "master," the elder Bayard Sartoris, on the decline of Southern life: "'De ottomobile,' Simon philosophised, 'is all right for pleasure and excitement, but fer

de genu-wine gen'lmun tone, dey aint but one thing: dat's
hosses.'" His rebellious son Caspey makes an even more
ridiculous figure as a World War I veteran whose military exploits parody those of the younger Bayard. When Faulkner
allowed Caspey to recount his own adventures, in one of the very
rare passages of narration that he ever granted to a Negro voice,
the result was a blackface routine rather than a characterization.
Sitting in the Sartoris kitchen on the morning after his return,
Caspey fabricates answers to the questions of his father Simon,
his sister Elnora, and his nephew Isom.

> "How many you kilt, Unc' Caspey?" Isom asked deferentially.
> "I aint never bothered to count 'um up. Been times I kilt mo' in
> one mawnin' dan dey's folks on dis whole place. One time we wuz
> down in de cellar of a steamboat tied up to de bank, and one of dese
> submareems sailed up and stopped by de boat, and all de white
> officers run up on de bank and hid. Us boys didn't know dey wuz
> anything wrong 'twell folks started clambin' down de ladder. We
> never had no guns wid us at de time, so when we seed dem green
> legs comin' down de ladder we crope up to de een of de ladder, and
> as dey come down one of de boys would hit 'um over de haid wid a
> stick of wood and another would drag 'um outen de way and cut dey
> th'oat wid a razor. Dey wuz about thirty of 'um . . . Elnora, is dey
> any mo' of dat coffee lef'?"[9]

If Faulkner exhibited no qualms in *Flags in the Dust* about
such burlesque portrayals of black people, his next novel reveals
a deep uneasiness. In *The Sound and the Fury* (1929) he began to
display a conscious concern with the special difficulty of describing black characters accurately. In part 2 of that novel, for
example, Quentin Compson experiences a moment of existential
nausea when he notes the instability of his perception of black
people. Deacon, a black man who makes a living by doing odd
jobs for Southern students at Harvard, meets incoming trains
wearing "a sort of Uncle Tom's cabin outfit, patches and all," and
Quentin remembers that when Deacon first talked to him, he
spoke in an obsequious parody of Southern Negro dialect: "Yes
suh. Right dis way, young marster, hyer we is. . . .jes give de old

nigger yo room number, and hit'll be done got cold dar when you arrives." Later, however, Deacon appears as a semirespectable Bostonian in a Brooks Brothers suit, who marches in political parades and speaks standard English. When he momentarily reverts to his slavish demeanor, Quentin confuses him with Roskus, the Compson family's servant back in Mississippi:

> . . . suddenly I saw Roskus watching me from behind all his white-folks' claptrap of uniforms and politics and Harvard manner, diffi-dent, secret, inarticulate and sad. "You aint playing a joke on the old nigger, is you?"
>   "You know I'm not. Did any Southerner ever play a joke on you?"
>   "You're right. They're fine folks. But you cant live with them."
>   "Did you ever try?" I said. But Roskus was gone. Once more he was that self he had long since taught himself to wear in the world's eye, pompous, spurious, not quite gross.[10]

Elsewhere, Quentin reflects that "a nigger is not a person so much as a form of behaviour; a sort of obverse reflection of the white people he lives among."[11] The ambiguity of Deacon's image casts into doubt all of the truisms about Negroes that Quentin has learned in the South. If Deacon's identity seems unclear, then what can be said with certainty about Roskus, or Dilsey, or any of the other Negroes back home among whom Quentin grew up? Do they really love to sing and dance? Do they really like to eat watermelon? Or do they have Brooks Brothers suits hanging in their closets too? What is the true life beneath their conditioned appearance?

Behind Quentin's nausea lurks Faulkner's suspicion about his own ability to see black people—to penetrate appearances—and then to describe the reality within. According to his biographer, Joseph Blotner, "Even toward the end of his life, Faulkner would talk of the difficulty of understanding Negroes' thoughts and feelings. He seemed to feel that not only had they perforce developed a pattern of concealment from white people, but their modes of thought and feeling were often different and therefore difficult for a white person to understand."[12]

Faulkner never exactly defined the ways in which he felt that

Negroes "differed" from Caucasians in their "modes of thought and feeling," though it was a question he posed all his life. But another perceptual shift in *The Sound and the Fury* provides an important clue to his attitude. In part 4, when Dilsey takes her children to Easter services at her church, a guest minister has been invited from Saint Louis to deliver the sermon. As the Reverend Shegog begins to speak, he sounds "like a white man"—"level and cold." But, as he warms to his message, "his intonation, his pronunciation, became negroid"—"as different as day and dark from his former tone, with a sad, timbrous quality like an alto horn." As he moves from a white voice to a black one, something happens to his language that has special significance for any writer. It transcends itself:

> He was like a worn small rock whelmed by the successive waves of his voice. With his body he seemed to feed the voice that, succubus like, had fleshed its teeth in him. And the congregation seemed to watch with its own eyes while the voice consumed him, until he was nothing and they were nothing and there was not even a voice but instead their hearts were speaking to one another in chanting measures beyond the need for words.[13]

A valuable analogy to Reverend Shegog's bilingualism appears in *Along This Way*, the autobiography of the black poet James Weldon Johnson. Johnson, with other black poets of the late nineteenth and early twentieth centuries, had been frustrated by a special literary predicament. To be published, they had had to adopt one of two equally dishonest voices: they could pass for white, writing in a colorless, genteel English, foreign to their own roots; or they could imitate the Negro dialects that had been invented for them by white authors. One of these voices rendered them invisible and unread; the other limited them to self-demeaning expressions of "quaint" humor and pathos. Thus, Paul Lawrence Dunbar could complain to Johnson: "I've got to write dialect poetry; it's the only way I can get them to listen to me." Dunbar continued, throughout his brief career, to practice the art of impersonating his white readers' notion of how black people sounded. But Johnson, declaring that "Negro dialect is at present a medium that is not capable of giving expression to the varied conditions of Negro life in America," called for the discovery of "a form that will express the racial spirit by symbols from within rather than by symbols from without, such as the mere mutilation of English spelling and pronunciation."[14] In 1918 he located one such form when he heard a black evangelist deliver a sermon in Kansas City. At first, Johnson wrote, the preacher spoke from a formal text, apparently intimidated by Johnson's presence. When his audience responded apathetically, however, he suddenly shifted from standard English to the very different rhythms of "the rambling Negro sermon that begins with the creation of the world, touches various high spots in the trials and tribulations of the Hebrew children, and ends with the Judgment Day." In an instant, the congregation responded; and as the preacher "moaned," "pleaded," "blared," "crashed," and "thundered," it "reached a state of ecstasy." As Johnson sat listening, he found a piece of paper and began to write "The Creation," the first of seven verse sermons that comprise *God's Trombones* (1927), his most famous work.[15]

Although they could not have affected each other, Johnson's reminiscence and the scene in Faulkner's novel are remarkably similar. In each a black minister shifts from an explicitly white voice to an explicitly black one to stir a black audience. But they differ even more remarkably. For Johnson, the sermon provided an escape from the literary dispossession black writers had long suffered. It was a verbal resource, which directly stimulated him to write poetry. But for Faulkner the black sermon led to silence. It intimated that black people have a nonliterary way of knowing and communicating—a way that goes "beyond words." Faulkner's imagination of the difference between whites and blacks can most consistently be located in this nonverbal resource.

For the mature Faulkner, the most definitive characteristic of Negroes—certainly more definitive than any mere appearance or custom, and even more definitive than their capacity for "endurance"—was their indifference to literary formulations of experience. Writing about blacks presented Faulkner with Simpson's special case of the literary mode that dominated his work: of pastoralism, or literature about nonliterate people. Except for Quentin Compson, Gavin Stevens, and a few others, his most powerful characters are people who either cannot or do not read. The pool of humanity from which he recruited his dramatis personae were people whom he could not readily conceptualize as an audience for his books about them—a situation that severely limited the degree to which he could experience his writing as a communicative act. The idiots, Benjy Compson and Ike Snopes, are the clearest examples of Faulkner's interest in articulating the experience of inarticulate people, but they are exceptional in the totality of their illiteracy. Writing about poor whites created a more limited sense of communicative barrier in Faulkner. When he wrote *The Hamlet*, he probably did not anticipate that many of the people he regarded as Snopeses would ever read it;[16] but such a possibility was sufficiently strong to affect that book's idiom: through V. K. Ratliff's vernacular narrative voice, *The Hamlet* embodies a controlled conversation between Faulkner and the upwardly mobile "rednecks" he detested.

The possibility that the blacks he knew might read his books about them, however, must have seemed as remote to him as that an idiot might read *The Sound and the Fury*. This is not to say that he believed blacks incapable of literacy. When he won the Nobel Prize, he contributed $3,000 to the college education of James McGlowan, a local black man. Ten years earlier, he had even discussed with McGlowan the possibility of teaching his childhood nurse, the real-life model for Dilsey, how to read. But she never learned, and when he dedicated *Go Down, Moses* "To Mammy Caroline Barr," he did so in the knowledge that it could be a book "to" her in only the most abstract way.[17]

Nor did Faulkner's sense of Negro illiteracy prevent him from creating literate black characters in his fiction. Lucas Beauchamp can read and write, but he does so for only the most practical purposes. Charles Bon goes to a university, but his intellectual refinement is noteworthy because it departs mon-

strously from normality. And Reverend Shegog is clearly a literate man, but he transports his audience *away* from words, away
from intellect.

What is crucial about Faulkner's perception of blacks is the
discontinuity within it between their "modes of thought and
feeling" and the resources of books. Whenever he wrote about
them—as, to a lesser degree, when he wrote about poor
whites—he inevitably felt the incongruity of his sophisticated
analytical intelligence brooding upon what he regarded as direct, instinctual intelligences. No matter how sympathetically
Faulkner approached rustic characters, the constitutional incom-
patibility between their sensibility and his own inhibited his
characterization of them. He was painfully aware of the inhos-
pitality of the novel, as a form, to his subject matter. In the
middle of his career, this awareness helped to precipitate a crisis
of confidence from which he never fully recovered.

To be sure, Faulkner was not alone in his attitude. White
Southern authors since the Civil War generally had depicted the
illiteracy of blacks not only as a defining characteristic, but, more
important, as a positive value. One of the chief assets of the
Negro dialect literature that flourished in the late nineteenth
century was the opportunity it afforded white authors to express
covertly their disenchantment with the virtues of writing. Joel
Chandler Harris, for example, put into the mouth of Uncle
Remus a typical dialect-fiction statement of the evils of erudi-
tion: "W'at a nigger gwineter l'arn outen books? I kin take a bar'l
stave an' fling mo' sense inter a nigger in one minnit dan all de
school-houses betwixt dis en de State er Midgigin. . . . Hits de
ruination er dis country. . . . Put a spelllin'-book in a nigger's
han's, en right den en dar' you loozes a plow-hand."[18] In "Christ-
mas-Night in the Quarters" Irwin Russell extended the case
against books to both races, and he based upon it an invidious
comparison that favors the Negro:

> In this our age of printer's ink
> 'Tis books that show us how to think—
> The rule reversed, and set at naught,
> That held that books were born of thought.

We form our minds by pedants' rules,
And all we know is from the schools;
And when we work, or when we play,
We do it in an ordered way—
And Nature's self pronounce a ban on,
Whene'er she dares transgress a canon.
Untrammeled thus the simple race is
That "wuks the craps" on cotton places.
Original in act and thought,
Because unlearned and untaught. [19]

Julia Peterkin provided a twentieth-century example of the same theme in *Scarlet Sister Mary*. The black heroine of that novel discourages her son from going to school, because she distrusts the white perception of the world: "Instead of reading all the time out of books and papers covered with printed words, he would do better to learn how to read other things: sunrises, moons, sunsets, clouds and stars, faces and eyes. . . . Book-learning takes people's minds off more important things." [20]

Had any of these writers listened to themselves as they wrote, we would not have the books in which they said what they did. Their covert disavowal of literacy constitutes a pose that defines them as pastoral in the traditional usage of the term. For, if a pastoralist really believed in pastoralism, he would quit writing books and take up farming or sheepherding. Like Harris, Russell, and Peterkin, Faulkner was led by his material to the same anti-intellectual postures. But, unlike them, he listened to what he found himself saying. Or rather, he could hear something he had not even yet begun to say, which was so implicit in his subject that it demanded utterance.

When he came to write *Go Down, Moses* in the late thirties and early forties, Faulkner was ready to question the logic of pastoralism—of writing books about people one praises for their superiority to, or immunity from, books. It represents a climactic moment in his career, when his condescension toward his characters backfired, undercutting significantly his will to write about them.

The germ of *Go Down, Moses* was a group of three stories about Lucas Beauchamp, in which Faulkner followed the formulas of contemporary dialect writers, like Roark Bradford, in order to achieve a quick sale to *The Saturday Evening Post* or *Collier's* magazine.[21] But his original version of Lucas, though based on a real man, his servant Ned Barnett, was so stereotypical, so much the comic "darky," that it offended Faulkner's own sense of integrity. Consequently, the next story he wrote, "Pantaloon in Black," is about the difficulty of perceiving black people accurately. A black man named Rider buries his wife Mannie; his grief drives him to a night of violence and drink, and ultimately to the murder of a white man in a dice game. In an epilogue, a white deputy sheriff returns from Rider's lynching to tell his wife a totally inaccurate version of what had motivated Rider. The deputy uses Rider's seemingly inappropriate response to Mannie's death to reaffirm his belief that Negroes have no human feelings. One of the subjects of this story, surely, is its author's guilty need to revise his own literary misperception of black people.

That need became one of the shaping motives of *Go Down, Moses*. When Faulkner revised the earlier stories, he attempted to humanize Lucas Beauchamp by standardizing his speech and by having him defend his pride heroically. But, as the composition of *Go Down, Moses* proceeded, Faulkner's suspicion that black lives are impenetrable to literary scrutiny grew into an anxiety about any writer's power to scrutinize anything. This anxiety exploded in part 4 of "The Bear," one of the central preoccupations of which is writing. In that long and convoluted text, Ike McCaslin and his cousin Cass Edmonds hold a famous debate over Ike's decision to repudiate his racist heritage by dispossessing himself of his family's plantation. At the center of this debate—and by extension, at the center of *Go Down, Moses*—lies a controversy over writing that expresses Faulkner's uncertainty about his vocation. Cass is for writing; Ike is against.

That part 4 of "The Bear" is about writing Faulkner confirmed by filling it with books. It is as replete with manuscripts and published texts as the rest of *Go Down, Moses* is empty of them—a contrast that reinforces an implicit discontinuity between literary and nonliterary experience. The references to books that do appear outside part 4 introduce Faulkner's qualms. In part 3, after the death of the bear, young Ike asks for permission to stay at the camp in order to tend Sam Fathers. Cass, ever an advocate of book learning and other "legacies" from the past, refuses on the ground that Ike should return to school; and Boon Hogganbeck, practically illiterate himself, supports Cass. But General Compson intervenes on Ike's behalf, arguing successfully that the understanding he has gained from the Big Woods surpasses what schools can offer: "If missing an extra week of school is going to throw you so far behind you'll have to sweat to find out what some hired pedagogue put between the covers of a book, you better quit altogether."[22] The opposition between books and life also appears at the very beginning of "The Bear," where Faulkner described the wilderness as "bigger and older than any recorded document" (191). Again, in part 2, Faulkner described the woods as an alternative form of school: "If Sam Fathers had been [Ike's] mentor and the backyard rabbits and squirrels his kindergarten, then the wilderness the old bear ran was his college and the old male bear itself, so long unwifed and childless as to have become its own ungendered progenitor, was his alma mater" (210).

But only in part 4 do bibliographical images begin to accumulate. The plantation ledgers obviously occupy its center, but a host of other manuscripts and published texts crowd the perimeter. The first slave mentioned in the Compson archives, for example, is Percival Brownlee, whom Uncle Buck McCaslin had purchased as a "bookkeeper" (264). Ironically, Brownlee had turned out to be illiterate, and the irony is significant, for the Negro race proves to be the main repository of the knowledge that competes with books. The black man's foreignness to books is emphasized in a later scene in part 4, when Ike discovers the husband of his black cousin Fonsiba reading a book through "gold-framed spectacles" that "did not even contain lenses"

(278). Reading is a technique to which blacks are clearly un-habituated, in Faulkner's imagination, and Ike registers an appropriate sense of incongruity.

Other texts abound within part 4. When Cass retrieves the volume containing Keats's "Ode on a Grecian Urn" from a book-case in the plantation office, for example, Faulkner again casts doubt upon the validity of book experience. Ike tests the poem against his memory of the hunt, and concludes that "[s]omehow it had seemed simpler than that, simpler than somebody talking in a book about a young man and a girl he would never need to grieve over because he could never approach any nearer and would never have to get any further away" (297). Here, and in a spate of other references to "books," "chronicles," "scraps of paper," and many other written records, Faulkner substantiates Gail Hightower's discovery in *Light in August* of "how false the most profound book turns out to be when applied to life."23 To fulfill Hightower's recognition as precisely as possible, the de-bate between Ike and Cass includes an extended discussion of the most profound of all Western books, the Holy Bible. The passage in which this argument occurs comes closer than any other in the novel to encapsulating the knowledge that Faulkner seems to have gained by writing *Go Down, Moses.*

Ike's argument dominates. Although he accepts the Bible's authority and quotes it to support his interpretation of history, he refuses to read it literally, as Cass would have him do. Instead, he presents it as a model of the ideal relationship between an author and his readers, which transcends mere literacy and overcomes all the normal barriers to communica-tion. For a writer as uncompromising with readers—and occa-sionally contemptuous of them—as Faulkner had always been, Ike's explanation of how the Bible transcends its own message is elaborately paradoxical:

> He [God] didn't have His Book written to be read by what must elect and choose, but by the heart, not by the wise of the earth because maybe they dont need it or maybe the wise no longer have any heart, but by the doomed and lowly of the earth who have

nothing else to read with but the heart. Because the men who wrote his [sic] Book for Him were writing about truth and there is only one truth and it covers all things that touch the heart. (260)

The authors of the Bible, Ike says, wrote with a sense of responsibility not only to the meaning they conveyed but to the limitations of their audience as well:

They were trying to write down the heart's truth out of the heart's driving complexity, for all the complex and troubled hearts which would beat after them. What they were trying to tell, what He wanted said, was too simple. Those for whom they transcribed His words could not have believed them. It had to be expounded in the everyday terms which they were familiar with and could comprehend, not only those who listened but those who told it too, because if they who were that near to Him as to have been elected from among all who breathed and spoke language to transcribe and relay His words, could comprehend truth only through the complexity of passion and lust and hate and fear which drives the heart, what distance back to truth must they traverse whom truth could only reach by word-of-mouth? (260–61)

Thus, pastoralism fulfills its natural inclination to self-parody. The writer writing about supposed illiterates naturally discovers that his real subject, all along, has been not their illiteracy but his doubts about his own eloquence. The Moses of the book's title appears here in his role as author of scripture as well as in his role as liberator, and in both roles he "goes down" to defeat. As Faulkner concluded his novel about black people, he praised the virtues of accommodating one's readers—ironically, in the midst of his most notoriously baroque prose. Insofar as he agreed with Ike, then, he was repudiating his own uncompromising practice as a writer.

Just how thoroughly Faulkner was rehearsing the disavowal of his own career, an intriguingly self-allusive passage later in part 4 of "The Bear" makes clear. Ike tries to convince Cass that the War Between the States was God's revenge upon Americans for their failure to renew human history after He had given them a new world in which to do so. Faulkner inserts the titles of his own novels into this treatise on exhaustion:

> . . . He [God] could have *repudiated* them [the American people]
> since they were *his creation* now and forever more throughout all
> their generations until not only that old world from which He had
> rescued them but this new one too which He had revealed and led
> them to as a *sanctuary* and refuge were become the same worthless
> tideless rock cooling in the last crimson evening except that out of all
> that *empty sound and bootless fury* one *silence*, among that loud and
> moiling all of them just one simple enough to believe that horror and
> outrage were first and last simply horror and outrage and was crude
> enough to act upon that, *illiterate and had no words* for talking or
> perhaps was just busy and had no time to. . . . (284, my italics)

Man's "sanctuary" here proves illusory, as it had in the novel of
the same title. "The sound and the fury" are "empty" and
bootless," and followed ominously by "silence." Moreover,
Faulkner's references to his own works occur in the same sentence with a creator considering the repudiation of his creation,
and they immediately precede Ike's prophecy that history will be
redeemed by an illiterate person with "no words."

Of course, Cass Edmonds argues against Ike's negative view of
literacy, but their debate is never resolved in *Go Down, Moses*.
At the end of the novel, Gavin Stevens is returning to his desk
(383) to resume his translation of the Old Testament back into
classic Greek. He has labored upon this project for twenty-two
years (371), the approximate number of years for which Faulkner
had been a published author when he wrote "Go Down, Moses."
On a symbolic level, Stevens's translation may suggest the purity
of Faulkner's intentions as a writer—to recapture the lost Word
of some divine truth. But in reality, Stevens's task—like
Faulkner's?—is quixotic and doomed to failure: were he to suc-
ceed in resurrecting the dead words of Scripture, even fewer
people would be able to read them properly, in classic Greek,
than have actually been able to read Faulkner's own, American
Greek.

Faulkner further undercut Stevens as an affirmative representative of the literary vocation by juxtaposing him with an
illiterate old black woman, Mollie Beauchamp. Although Mollie

cannot read, she insists that her nephew's death be reported in the local newspaper. She does not care to know the literal facts in the case, which are sordid; but she does know, "with the heart," that she must fulfill the obligations of human kinship. Although her knowledge of Scripture is imprecise, she quotes its spirit accurately; and it is from her illogical utterances, not from Gavin Stevens's book-learning, that the whole novel derives its title. In the end, Faulkner's attribution of illiteracy to blacks subverted his own literacy. The successive waves of Shegog's voice ultimately whelmed Faulkner too.

NOTES

1. James B. Meriwether and Michael Milligate, eds., *Lion in the Garden: Interviews with William Faulkner, 1926–1962* (New York: Random House, 1968), 39.

2. A. I. Bezzerides, *William Faulkner: A Life on Paper*, ed. Ann Abadie (Jackson: University Press of Mississippi, 1980), 71.

3. Lewis P. Simpson, *The Dispossessed Garden: Pastoral and History in Southern Literature* (Athens: University of Georgia Press, 1975), 12, 23, 32.

4. Malcolm Franklin, *Bitterweeds: Life at Rowan Oak with William Faulkner* (Irving, Texas: Society for the Study of Traditional Culture, 1977), 84.

5. Simpson, *The Dispossessed Garden*, 22–23.

6. Thomas Jefferson, *Notes on the State of Virginia*, ed. William Peden (New York: Norton, 1972), 164–65.

7. Simpson, *The Dispossessed Garden*, 30.

8. Thadious Davis, *Faulkner's "Negro": Art and the Southern Context* (Baton Rouge: Louisiana State University Press, 1983), 214.

9. William Faulkner, *Flags in the Dust*, ed. Douglas Day (New York: Random House, 1973), 53–54, 221.

10. William Faulkner, *The Sound and the Fury* (New York: Vintage 1963), 120, 123.

11. Faulkner, *The Sound and the Fury*, 106.

12. Joseph Blotner, *Faulkner: A Biography* (New York: Random House, 1974), 2:1038–39.

13. Faulkner, *The Sound and the Fury*, 366, 367, 368.

14. James Weldon Johnson, ed., *The Book of American Negro Poetry*, rev. ed. (New York: Harcourt, Brace & World, 1959), 35–36, 41, 42. See also Louis D. Rubin, Jr., "The Search for a Language, 1746–1923," in *Black Poetry in America: Two Essays in Historical Interpretations*, by Blyden Jackson and Louis D. Rubin, Jr. (Baton Rouge: Louisiana State University Press, 1974), 1–35.

15. James Weldon Johnson, *Along This Way: The Autobiography of James Weldon Johnson* (New York: Viking, 1933), 335–36. See also Rubin, "The Search for a Language," 20–23.

16. In 1924, nonetheless, Faulkner actually presented a copy of *The Marble Faun* to Joe Parks, a probable model for Flem Snopes (Louis Daniel Brodsky and Thomas Verich, *William Faulkner's Gifts of Friendship: Presentation and Inscribed Copies from the Faulkner Collection of Louis D. Brodsky* [Oxford: University of Mississippi, 1980], item 4).

17. Blotner, *Faulkner*, 2:1026, 1094, 1370–71.

18. Joel Chandler Harris, "As to Education," in *Uncle Remus: His Songs and His Sayings*, ed. Robert Hemenway (Harmondsworth, England: Penguin, 1982), 216.

19. Irwin Russell, *Poems*, intro. Joel Chandler Harris (New York: Century, 1888), 4.

20. Julia Peterkin, *Scarlet Sister Mary* (Indianapolis: Bobbs-Merrill, 1928), 196–97.

21. Blotner, *Faulkner*, 2:1036–37.

22. William Faulkner, *Go Down, Moses* (New York: Modern Library, 1955), 250. Subsequent references to *Go Down, Moses* will appear within the text.

23. William Faulkner, *Light in August* (New York: Harrison Smith and Robert Haas, 1932), 455.

Requiem for a Nun
and the
Uses of the Imagination

KARL F. ZENDER

It is scarcely an exaggeration to say that *Requiem for a Nun* poses more severe problems for interpretation than any other novel by Faulkner. This is so for both thematic and formal reasons. Thematically, the novel resists interpretation because of the odd character of its central action. To suggest, as Faulkner apparently does, that Nancy Mannigoe can only preserve Temple Drake's marriage by murdering her youngest child commits an outrage, in Michael Millgate's words, "not simply upon our moral sensibilities but on our credulity." Yet to attempt to overcome this outrage by interpreting Nancy as a murderess rather than as a martyr, as Noel Polk has done, would seem to reverse the difficulty without resolving it.[1] When approached in formal terms, the novel presents an equally knotty problem, in that the interconnections between the dramatic and narrative sections are so few in number and so general in character as to prevent us from answering satisfactorily the question of the novel's coherence. After we have noted these interconnections, we are left agreeing with Cleanth Brooks, when he says that the structure of *Requiem for a Nun* "constitutes the most daring but perhaps the least successful solution of the structural problems attempted by Faulkner in any of his novels."[2]

Before we accede entirely to these judgments, though, we ought to consider the possibility that they may arise more from our way of reading than from the novel itself. Interpretations of

Requiem for a Nun created under the aegis of New Criticism exhibit New Criticism's strengths, but also its limitations. They explore quite well those features of the novel that are consistent with a view of it as an autonomous formal artifact; but they are almost entirely silent about the novel's expressive dimension.[3] Yet as Joseph Blotner, Carvel Collins, David Minter, and Judith Bryant Wittenberg have all taught us, it is always dangerous to ignore the expressive element in Faulkner's art. His own disclaimers to the contrary, Faulkner is perhaps the most intensely personal of all major American writers—not in the sense that his novels provide a direct transcription of the events of his life, which they rarely do, but in the sense that his universal, public meanings always have at their core a meditation on some aspect of his psychic life or of his relation to the world.

If we read *Requiem for a Nun* with the intention of allowing its personal meanings to emerge, then a number of features of the novel immediately demand our attention, all of which have to do with Faulkner's understanding of himself as an artist. That this matter should have been of concern to Faulkner at the time he wrote *Requiem for a Nun* will scarcely surprise us if we recall the circumstances out of which the novel arose. Shortly before writing the novel, Faulkner underwent the longest period of artistic silence in his career, one extending from his completion of *Go Down, Moses* in late 1941 to his writing of *Intruder in the Dust* in 1948. The narrative and dramatic sections of *Requiem for a Nun* enact, in different but related ways, Faulkner's attempt to work through the implications of this period of creative blockage. In both parts of the novel, Faulkner places extraordinary emphasis on acts of reading and writing; in both, he explores the relation between imagination and time; in both, he depicts a change, or an attempted change, from one way of understanding and using the imagination to another. My purpose in this essay is to examine this process of working through, in the hope that I will add to our appreciation of *Requiem for a Nun* as a work of art and to our understanding of the important place it occupies in Faulkner's career.

*   *   *

In the dramatic sections of *Requiem for a Nun*, Faulkner's act of artistic self-scrutiny takes the form of a struggle between two views of the function of the imagination, one of which is embodied in Temple Drake, the other in Gavin Stevens. The nature of the view embodied in Temple will become apparent if we reflect for a moment on the relation between the letters she wrote in the Manuel Street bordello and her sexual experiences with Alabama Red—experiences engaged in, we recall, under the gaze of Popeye Vitelli. "I would write one," she says, "each time—afterward, after they—he left, and sometimes I would write two or three when it would be two or three days between, when they—he wouldn't—."[4] In this comment, we can detect three properties of the imagination as Temple understands it. For Temple, the imagination is transgressive, libidinal, and memorial. Its function is to permit one to reexperience lost and forbidden pleasures by reconstituting them in words. As Temple says in explaining why she hired Nancy Mannigoe, the illicit nature of her life with Red meant that once "it was all over . . . it had to be as though it had never happened." But the disappearance into silence of the memory of Red, she says, "was even worse" than the loss of Red itself (153). Hence she hires "an ex-dopefiend nigger whore" (158) to help her reanimate her forbidden but treasured memories.

Turning from Temple Drake to Gavin Stevens is like turning from night to day. Faulkner suggests that it may be useful to think of Stevens in relation to the imagination in his first stage direction, when he says that Stevens "looks more like a poet than a lawyer and actually is" (49). How this poet understands the function of the imagination can be inferred from the whole course of his interaction with Temple. His view contrasts with hers on a point-by-point basis. Where she associates the imagination with libidinal pleasure, he associates it with ethics and morality; where she uses the imagination to return to the past, he insists that it be used in the service of the future; and where she assumes that the purpose of the imagination is to preserve and renew desire, he assumes that its purpose is cathartic.[5]

The contrast between Temple's and Gavin's views gains significance when we realize that they constitute two dimensions of Faulkner's own understanding of the function of the imagination, and that these dimensions exist in chronological relation to one another. If we wish to find views of the imagination similar to Temple's, we turn, as John T. Irwin has taught us, to *Mosquitoes* and to the two unpublished introductions to *The Sound and the Fury* that Faulkner wrote in 1933. In *Mosquitoes*, for example, Dawson Fairchild says that "about all the virtue there is in art" is that "it reminds us of youth" and hence permits us to "remember grief and forget time."[6] Elsewhere, Fairchild describes the artist as the person who is more willing than other people to enter "the dark room" that Havelock Ellis and Sigmund Freud "have recently thrown open to the public" (248, 251). And throughout the novel, as in his reminiscence of his childhood encounter in the outhouse with the girl with the blonde curls, Fairchild associates beauty and artistic creativity with tabooed thoughts and activities. But to find statements of Gavin Stevens's view of the imagination, we must turn from the works of the 1920s and 1930s to the public pronouncements Faulkner was making around the time of *Requiem for a Nun*—pronouncements such as the Nobel Prize Speech (1950), the Foreword to *The Faulkner Reader* (1953), and the Address to the Graduating Class at Pine Manor Junior College (1953). In the Nobel Prize Speech, for example, Faulkner specifically proscribes the association of the imagination with libidinal pleasure—here called "the glands"—and instead insists on associating it with the heart, the soul, and the spirit. Here too, he turns the imagination away from the past and toward the future, first by saying that the artist who writes of the glands "will write as though he stood among and watched the end of man," and then by saying that "the poet's voice need not merely be the record of man, it can be one of the props, the pillars to help him endure and prevail."[7]

The emergence of this uplifting view of the function of the imagination is of course a familiar fact about the second half of Faulkner's career. For a variety of personal and cultural reasons—advancing age, the creative blockage already alluded to, the challenge posed to the modernist ethos by the postwar world—Faulkner evidently felt the need, in Hemingway's phrase, "to [move] in on the side of the strongest battalions"[8] But the evidence of the Nobel Prize Speech notwithstanding, the emergence of this ethical emphasis does not mean that Faulkner wished to repudiate his earlier, libidinally oriented view. In fact, he believed that both views had always been present in his art. As he says in the Foreword to *The Faulkner Reader*, the desire "to uplift men's hearts" was not absent from his earlier work but latent in it. When "the blood and glands and flesh still remained strong and potent," he says, the hope that his books might inspire people "was unimportant . . . as measured against the need to get them written" (180). But when "the blood and glands began to slow and cool a little," he suddenly saw that this hope had been present in his art "all the time." Conversely, the emergence into prominence of this hope does not mean that he is "trying to change man" or that his art has become any less "completely selfish, completely personal." Rather, trying to lift up men's hearts is simply a new way of doing what he had been trying to do in his earlier art, which is to "say No to death" (181).

In effect, then, in the early 1950s Faulkner was hoping to establish a complementary relation between the libidinal and the ethical dimensions of his art. He was searching for a way to allow the view of the imagination associated with Gavin Stevens to emerge into prominence without at the same time repudiating the view associated with Temple Drake and with his own earlier career. In his speech to the graduating class at Pine Manor Junior College, Faulkner describes the form that such a complementary relation might ideally take. The backbone of the speech is an abbreviated creation story centering on a "splendid dark incorrigible" angel (137) who embodies the spirit of rebellion. The innovation that Faulkner brings to this story consists of splitting the dark angel's rebelliousness in half and of distinguishing between the effect on human history of the two halves. One of the halves—the dark angel's ambition—produces human woe, for from it springs "the long roster of the ambition's ruthless avatars—Genghis and Caesar and William and Hitler" (137). The other half, which Faulkner identifies as "the temerity to revolt and the will to change," produces human glory, for out of it comes "the long annal of the men and women who have anguished over man's condition . . . the philosophers and artists . . . who have reminded us always of our capacity for honor and courage and compassion and pity and sacrifice" (137–38).

In depicting the philosopher and artist as descendants of a primal act of Lucifernic rebellion, Faulkner echoes William Blake's interpretation of the fall as the story of humankind's attempt to recover the power of the imagination from a jealous God. But the purpose to which Faulkner directs this Blakean myth measures the distance he had travelled since his own youthful romanticism. In contrast to Blake's Imaginative Man, who is inherently transgressive, Faulkner's artists and philosophers serve surprisingly conservative ends. They do not direct their rebellion at God or nature or political institutions but at the fears and anxieties that prevent people from living comfortably in the world. Our aim in allowing "the poets and philosophers to remind us . . . of our capacity for courage and endurance" (138), Faulkner tells his audience of young women, is not to learn how "to be Joans of Arc with trumpets and banners and battle-dust" but to learn how to live happily within "the normal life which everyone wants and everyone should have" (139–40). If we devote our energies to achieving this normal life, which Faulkner here calls "home," we will find that we have overcome completely the dark angel's "ruthless and ambitious split-offs" (141–42).

The argument of the Pine Manor Speech provides an almost exact synopsis of the second act of *Requiem for a Nun*. Very nearly the whole objective of Gavin Stevens's long struggle with Temple Drake is to have her tell the story of her life in a new way, one that will not renew her illicit memories but will instead purge her of them, and hence make it possible for her to reassume her familial responsibilities. Central to this struggle is the name "Temple Drake." Toward the end of the first act of the play, Gavin and Temple discuss whether "Temple Drake" or "Mrs Gowan Stevens" will visit the Governor. Temple wishes it to be "Mrs Gowan Stevens" because "Temple Drake" is, in her view, the secret part of herself who "liked evil" (135) and who sought out opportunities to reconstitute her bordello experiences in language. Temple wishes to exempt this secret self from the conversation with the Governor because she cannot believe that retelling her story in an environment so alien to her former way of telling it can result in anything other than humiliation and suffering. Gavin Stevens, by contrast, wishes to involve "Temple Drake" in the conversation as fully as possible, for in his view only if Temple undergoes a cathartic reenactment of all of her shameful experiences (including the experience of reenactment itself) will she be able to transform herself into a willing wife and mother.

At first, the struggle between Gavin Stevens and Temple Drake seems to result in Temple's conversion to Gavin's way of seeing. This transformation occurs in three stages, the first of which begins with a dance of psychological evasion in which Temple engages during the first half of her visit to the Governor's office. In all its elements, this dance reflects Temple's resistance to Stevens's way of understanding the function of the imagination. Temple enters the Governor's office saying that the retelling is "not for anything." It is "just suffering," and its effect will not be cathartic but emetic, "like calomel or ipecac" (152). Similarly, she treats every incidental detail of her encounter with the Governor as a symbol of her despair, converting the offer of a cigarette into a joke about a firing squad, and viewing a handkerchief extended in anticipation of her tears as if it were a blindfold for the execution this firing squad is about to perform. Also, she treats her own identity in this same despairing way, pretending that "Temple Drake" is a separate being, to be referred to in the third person, as "Temple Drake, the white woman, the all-Mississippi debutante" (120) and "Temple Drake, the foolish virgin" (130).

Yet despite the ingenuity of her effort at evasion, Temple undergoes a slow shift in outlook as she tells her story. Like a patient in a therapeutic session who attempts to recount a traumatic event without emotion, Temple gradually loses her defensiveness and her capacity for self-alienation as her story advances. First she accepts the cigarette and handkerchief; then she begins speaking of herself and "Temple Drake" as if they were the same person; and finally she moves, hesitantly but inevitably, to an account of the core secret on which her self-loathing is founded. Significantly, this secret does not consist of her rape, or of her perjury against Lee Goodwin, or of her experiences with Popeye and Alabama Red, but instead of her hiring Nancy Mannigoe to help her relive her libidinal memories. Other than the account of her child's murder, this is the fact about her past that Temple evades telling longest and that she recounts with the fullest amount of emotion. A moment's reflection should convince us of the rightness of Faulkner's decision to place this secret at the end of the initial stage of Temple's development. All of Temple's other secrets are simply events from the past, and can presumably be retold repeatedly without altering the emotion—whether of pleasure or of loathing—that accompanies them. But Temple's reliving of her sexual experiences in her conversations with Nancy is not simply an event *from* the past but a way of relating *to* the past. Recounting this secret, then, opens to the possibility of change not just the content but the structure of Temple's imagination. This Temple herself indicates, both in her inchoate resistance to voicing this secret and in her reaction immediately afterwards, when for the first time in the novel she speaks of the possibility of a cathartic function for the imagination, saying that the Catholic Church had the right idea in inventing the sacrament of confession (159).

Once Temple shows herself to be receptive to the possibility of catharsis, the second and third stages of her development follow in rapid succession. The second consists of Gavin Stevens's replacement of Temple as speaker. Early readers of the novel tended to view Stevens's interruptions of Temple as attempts by an inexperienced dramatist to distribute essentially narrative material among his characters. But the line of argument I am following here suggests that Stevens's emergence as speaker has a thematic function. His voice replaces Temple's because she has developed to the point where her outlook is ready to merge with his. Stevens's earlier attempts to interrupt and guide Temple had been greeted with objections by the Governor, but after Temple tells of her conversations with Nancy, the Governor invites Stevens to speak. As he does, a new, redemptive version of Temple's story comes into being. In this version, "The letters were not first. The first thing was the gratitude" (161). Seemingly secure in her role as wife and mother, Temple had actually been trapped inside a spiralling obligation to display gratitude to her husband for having been gentlemanly enough to marry her. When this fact is taken into account, Stevens suggests, Temple's behavior can no longer be interpreted as the product of an innate affinity for evil. Instead, it must be seen as noble, even heroic, for she has managed to hold together her family for six years while juggling "three glass bulbs filled with nitroglycerin": the need to offer atonement, the need to receive forgiveness, and the need to offer gratitude in response to the forgiveness (164–65).

As we might expect, Stevens's reinterpretation of the meaning of Temple's past encompasses even her recounting of her illicit memories. Far from being tawdry, semipornographic acts of self-titillation, Temple's conversations with Nancy must be viewed as attempts to "slough away the six years' soilure of struggle and repentance and terror to no avail" (170). Indeed, these recollections can even be construed as acts of love, for Temple's experiences with Alabama Red are the closest that her sorry history ever permitted her to come to "honeymoon" and to "the similitude of being wooed" (169–70). From this radical reinterpretation of the meaning of Temple's acts of recollection, it is an easy step to the final stage of her transformation, which consists of the flashback scene depicting the events surrounding the murder of her infant child. This scene completes Temple's turn toward catharsis both in its content, which presents a much more sympathetic view of Temple than she had presented earlier, and in its form. As Temple's completion of the scene in her own voice indicates, the flashback must be understood to be a dramatic enactment of her response to Gavin's final words: "Now tell him" (172). In shifting representational modes in this way, Faulkner creates a formal analogue for Temple's transformation in outlook. Underlying this shift is the assumption, common to our culture, that drama stands in a more immediate and authentic relation to experience than narrative. Hence replacing Temple's voice with a dramatic enactment of the content of her speech symbolizes the completion of her journey toward self-renewal. Beginning with evasions, lies, and acts of self-alienation, Temple here arrives at a moment of self-integration and self-acceptance, a mystical fusion of voice and action, past and present, memory and imagination.

*   *   *

Read as I have read it here, the struggle between Gavin Stevens and Temple Drake reveals itself to be a meditation on the imagination, how impaired and restored. There can be little doubt that the climax of this meditation, with its promise of an integration of libido and superego, spoke to a very deep need within Faulkner himself. Yet the second act of the novel does not end with Temple's flashback, but instead returns to the present time of the story and to the revelation that Temple's husband, rather than the Governor, had listened to her confession. As this scene develops, evidence rapidly accumulates that the supposed cathartic function of the flashback scene has at best been incompletely realized: Temple emerges from the flashback saying "still no tears" (195) and alluding once again to a cigarette as an emblem of an impending execution; and at the end of the scene she and Gavin Stevens revert to the idea, expressed earlier by Temple, that her future will consist of repetition without progression when Temple says "tomorrow and tomorrow and tomorrow" and Stevens responds "he will wreck the car again against the wrong tree, in the wrong place, and you will have to forgive him again, for the next eight years until he can wreck the car again in the wrong place, against the wrong tree—" (206).

The reason Faulkner carries the action of the drama in this direction is not far to seek. Touching as it is, Temple's turn toward a cathartic view of the imagination is radically incomplete, for it does not carry the question of the purpose of catharsis beyond merely short term, utilitarian considerations. If the dramatic portion of the novel stopped at the end of the flashback scene, we would be left with a superficially appealing but ultimately unsatisfactory view of the imagination as simply the handmaiden of therapy—as nothing more than a way of arriving at a condition that Faulkner elsewhere in the novel dismissingly calls "eupepsia" (145). The whole tendency of Faulkner's mind, his insistence on pressing his thought beyond conventional limits and on exposing its ultimate, even eschatological, implications, argues against his ability to rest content with such a limited notion of the function of the imagination. If the cathartic view of the imagination is to justify itself, it must do so under more severe conditions than those provided by an easy, optimistic appeal to the idea of mental health.

Faulkner depicts these more severe conditions in the third act of the play, in Temple's and Gavin's visit to Nancy Mannigoe. As I suggested in my introduction, it is difficult to arrive at a satisfactory overall interpretation of Nancy's role in *Requiem for a Nun*. But her function in relation to the theme I am exploring here is entirely unambiguous. She signifies the dream of a life free of the imagination—free, that is, of the need to exist in a mediated relation to either a past or a future condition of pure being. Faulkner indicates that Nancy carries this significance in three aspects of her characterization: her illiteracy, her blackness, and her religious faith. Throughout his career, Faulkner associates the idea of pure being with illiteracy and preverbalism. In *Mosquitoes*, for example, Dawson Fairchild says that "when you are young, you just be. Then you reach a stage where you do.

Then a stage where you think, and last of all, where you remember." When a person reaches this last stage, he says, "you don't have thoughts in your mind at all: you just have words in it" (231). Later in his career, Faulkner challenges Fairchild's view, instead inclining toward the belief, à la Jacques Derrida, that the notion of pure being itself has no existence outside language.9 But he never loses his inclination to associate this idea (whether viewed as reality or as illusion) with illiteracy and preverbalism. Furthermore, perhaps because of the relatively high incidence of illiteracy among blacks in the premodern South, Faulkner frequently expands the association to include blacks as well. Time and again in his fiction, we see him toying with the notion that black experience—wordless black experience—may be more authentic than white experience, and that blacks may have access to "a Oneness with Something, somewhere" that is denied to whites.10

This set of associations receives its fullest expression anywhere in Faulkner's fiction at the moment when Temple emerges from the flashback scene and begins to contemplate the question of what she is to do with her future. She immediately draws a lengthy contrast between how people react when a white person and when a black person enters "a jail or a hospital" (196). In the case of the white person, Temple says, "before you even know it, you have sent them books to read, cards, puzzles to play with." But when the patient or inmate is black, "You dont even think about the cards and puzzles and books. And so all of a sudden you find out with a kind of terror, that they have not only escaped having to read, they have escaped having to escape" (197). The implication of Temple's contrast (and its application to her situation) should be clear. White people read, she suggests, because they are doomed to the Sisyphean task of attempting to reconstitute in words a lost condition of being. But blacks, by virtue of their illiteracy, have never fallen into the world of representation; they have escaped having to escape. Hence they are "serene and immune to anguish." When you look up at the window of the jail, Temple says, if the hands you see are white, they will be "tapping or fidgeting or even holding, gripping the bars." But if they are black, they will "just [be] lying there among the interstices, not just at rest, but even restful" (197).[11]

Illiteracy and blackness, then, are two of Temple's names for the dream of pure being. When this dream is projected into the future, beyond the life of representation, it of course carries another name. Then it is called "heaven." In the third act of *Requiem for a Nun*, in Temple's conversation with Nancy Mannigoe, Faulkner poses the hard question of whether the cathartic imagination can carry Temple forward into this condition, or at least into a secure enough belief in its existence to make her life bearable. The key term here is "belief," which Faulkner places in tension throughout the third act with the word "hope." One might expect that a conversion from despair to hope, could Temple achieve it, would be sufficient confirmation of the efficacy of the cathartic imagination. But in ultimate terms, such a conversion in outlook would simply reverse the direction of Temple's dilemma; it would merely shift the focus of effort and expectation and desire, to use Wordsworth's definition of hope, from the past to something evermore about to be. This Nancy Mannigoe fully understands. Hence her insistence on associating hope with sin. "Hoping," she says, is "the last thing of all poor sinning man will turn aloose." "You mean," says Gavin Stevens, "when you have salvation, you dont have hope?" "You dont even need it," says Nancy. "All you need, all you have to do, is just believe" (272–73). Nancy does not say why the believing individual can dispense with hope, but we can readily supply the reason. The believer does not need hope because he or she exists outside time and beyond desire. Like "heaven," "belief" is a name we give to the dream of oneness with God—which is to say, to the dream of pure being imagined as a future possibility.

In setting Temple on a quest for an existence free of the need for hope, Faulkner makes an extreme demand on the idea of catharsis. Not satisfied with a notion of catharsis as an occasional period of release within an ongoing dialectic of desire, Faulkner requires that the concept justify itself in ultimate terms, by enabling the imagination to encompass itself, consume itself, and free the mind of itself. One suspects that a desire for this sort of imaginative self-transcendence was a frequent visitor to Faulkner's mind during the early 1950s. We see traces of it in his recurrent assertions (the first in his career) of belief in God, in his concern (also new) with the relation between art and immortality, and in his frequent statements that he wished to break the pencil and cease writing.[12] But however strong this desire might have been, it was outweighed by an even stronger sense of skepticism. Neither Faulkner's belief in God nor his concept of immortality is personal in nature, and his most frequent term for the state of the individual beyond death is not "heaven" (or "hell") but "oblivion." Similarly, his most deeply held view of the purpose of the imagination is not that it should conduct us to an other-worldly condition of pure being but that it should, in the phrase already quoted, "say No to death." The artist, he says, is "everyone . . . who has tried to carve . . . on the wall of that final oblivion beyond which he will have to pass . . . 'Kilroy was here.'"[13]

Faulkner's skepticism has two effects on the dramatic sections of *Requiem for a Nun*. The first is that it causes him to leave Temple's quest for pure being in a state of unresolved ambiguity. Temple seeks the answers to three questions in the last act of the play: whether she can believe, what she is to believe, and how she is to act. Nancy Mannigoe offers no practical help in answering any of these questions. In response to Temple's desperate final expression of doubt—"suppose tomorrow and tomorrow, and then nobody there, nobody waiting to forgive me" (283)—Nancy simply repeats her insistence that Temple must enter into an absolute condition of unqualified belief. But whether Temple—or anyone other than Nancy Mannigoe—can manage this feat, Faulkner does not tell us. At the end of the novel, he shows us Temple saying that without belief she is doomed and damned, but he does not show her saying that she has attained belief.

Instead, he suggests, in her last line—the single word "coming," spoken to her husband (286)—that she may simply be reentering without alteration the world of effort and expectation and desire.

The second, and for my purposes more important, effect of Faulkner's skepticism is that it prevents him from ever completely subordinating his transgressive, backward-looking view of the imagination to his ethical and progressive view. Had we known to look, we could have seen Faulkner rescuing the first of these views from incorporation into the second in the flashback scene itself. In the middle of this scene, Pete, Alabama Red's brother and Temple's lover, offers to return to Temple the packet of letters that has served as the basis of his blackmail. Temple takes the packet to the fireplace and threatens to burn it. The whole logic of the cathartic movement of the play demands that Temple fulfill her threat, for the letters are the play's central symbol of the attitude she must relinquish if she is to integrate herself into home and family. But Temple instead returns the packet to the table. With this gesture, the letters evade assimilation into the cathartic labor of regeneration and renewal. Slightly later, Faulkner carries the symbolism of the decision not to burn the letters a step further, when in a stage direction he says that "Pete . . . goes to the table . . . and with almost infinitesimal hesitation takes up the packet of letters [and] puts it back inside his coat" (180). Pete then passes out of the room and out of the novel. We never see him again because he has completed his role in Faulkner's meditation on the function of the imagination. With his departure, Temple's letters—and, we may add, "letters," writing, art—return to the possession of the outlaw, while the labor of catharsis looks forward only to tomorrow and tomorrow and tomorrow.

* * *

But what was this backward-turning imagination to feed on? This question required Faulkner's attention in the early 1950s for both internal and external reasons. Internally, as my argument suggests, the question arises because of Faulkner's fear that the libidinal subject matter of his earlier art—the "blood and glands"—was receding into inaccessibility. Externally, it arises from his sense that his other great subject matter—the sights, sounds, smells, and customs of his native region—was also disappearing. Faulkner had anticipated this second disappearance fairly early in his career: in a note written around 1931, he said that *Sartoris* originated in a desire to "bind into a whole [a] world which for some reason I believe should not pass utterly out of the memory of man"; and in one of the introductions to *The Sound and the Fury* written in 1933, he said that the South he had inherited from his ancestors was being replaced by "a thing known whimsically as the New South."[14] By the time Faulkner came to write *Requiem for a Nun*, these statements must have seemed like prophecies whose time of fulfillment had arrived. In the postwar world depicted in this novel, Faulkner says, the idea of the South as "one last irreconcilable fastness of stronghold" has become little more than "a faded (though still select) social club or caste"; it is a "form of behavior" that one only remembers to observe "on the occasions when young men from Brooklyn, exchange students at Mississippi or Arkansas or Texas Universities, [vend] tiny Confederate battle flags among the thronged Saturday afternoon ramps of football stadia" (246–47).

The prose sections of *Requiem for a Nun* combine an elegaic account of this second, external disappearance with an exploration of its implications for Faulkner's art. Central to both these concerns is an elaborate array of images of language. In all three prose sections, Faulkner depicts the disappearance of the South as a descent from an original Edenic condition into a debilitating and destructive modernity. This descent has several starting points, so that at various times we are shown the destruction of the South as the fall of the wilderness into civilization, as the fall of the settlement into the town, as the fall of the pre-Civil War into the post-Civil War world, and as the fall of the nineteenth into the twentieth century. Accompanying the descent in all its phases is a contrast, similar in significance to the contrast between Nancy's illiteracy and Temple's literacy, between an unfallen and a fallen language.

It should not surprise us to find that the unfallen half of this contrast consists of signs etched directly into the surface of the world. The external equivalent of the dream of pure being is the dream of an unmediated interfusion of the self and the world. Like his romantic forebears, Faulkner tended to express his interest in this dream in images of inscribed writing. Throughout his fiction, he repeatedly invokes a representational hierarchy in which signs incorporated into the surface of the world—whether in the form of words or of nonverbal signifiers—are accorded greater force and authenticity than either speech or handwritten or printed writing. (One thinks, for example, of the many tombstones and signposts in his fiction, and of the high place he assigns sculpture in comparison to the other arts.) These observations explain why examples of inscribed language appear so prominently in the descriptions in *Requiem for a Nun* of each of the beginning stages of the South's fall into modernity. In prehistory, inscribed language appears as the "recessional contour lines" left behind by the ice age on "the broad blank midcontinental page" (99–100); later, it appears as the "toed-in heelless light soft quick long-striding print" of the Indians' moccasins in the "dusty widening" that will become Jefferson (215, 220); and still later, it appears as "the fragile and indelible signature" etched by Cecilia Farmer on the jailhouse window in 1861 (229).[15]

As the South descends into the modern age, this original, unfallen language gradually comes to be supplanted by a debased alternative. Faulkner depicts this change in two ways. The first consists of a series of acts of erasure and overwriting. Time and again in the prose sections, Faulkner suggests that the march of history erases or washes away the unfallen signs originally inscribed on the surface of the South, and that new signs are continually being written over the old ones. Thus the advance of white civilization replaces the print of the Indians' moccasins wilth insignia of its own, first by allowing "the pioneers, the long hunters" to step "into the very footgear of them they dispossessed," then by requiring the Indians to wear "the alien shoes" sold at the general store, and finally by encouraging the arrival of a steadily accelerating steam of "land speculators and . . . traders in slaves and whiskey" who print "deeper and deeper the dust of that dusty widening, until at last there [is] no mark of Chickasaw left in it any more" (218–20).

The second way Faulkner depicts the shift from an Edenic to a fallen language is through an overlapping series of associations between fallen writing and imprisonment. The disappearance of the Indians from the South occurs not only because of their physical departure for Oklahoma but because of their enclosure in a text. Among the "miniscule of archive" (3) housed in Ratcliffe's store is "a ruled, paper-backed copybook . . . in which accrued . . . in Mohataha's name . . . the crawling tedious list of calico and gunpowder . . . drawn from Ratcliffe's shelves by her descendants and subjects and Negro slaves" (21). Once the Indians become inscribed in this book, their physical departure is virtually assured. Long before Faulkner depicts this departure, though, he creates a further association between writing and imprisonment, by saying that the documents pertaining to the dispossession of the Indians are enclosed in "a sort of iron pirate's chest" (3). From this association further associations follow, as the iron chest disappears inside the lean-to courthouse attached to the jail, and Alec Holston's "ancient monster iron padlock" (3) undergoes a "transubstantiation" (9) into the new, permanent courthouse. So finally the world symbolized by the Indians (along with their ability to inscribe their experience directly onto the surface of the South) can be said to be enclosed in a text that is inside a chest that is inside a building that is itself a transformed version of a lock.

Faulkner's equation of the South's descent into modernity with the erasure, overwriting, and imprisonment of an unfallen language suggests an obvious parallel to his own situation as a recently blocked artist. Perhaps surprisingly, it also points toward a liberating alteration in his understanding of his art that was taking place in the early 1950s. To see how this is so, we need to compare the attitudes toward time expressed in the prose and the dramatic sections of the novel. The prose sections lack the intense fascination with an ameliorative view of the future that we found in the dramatic sections. In the dramatic sections, Gavin Stevens and Temple Drake struggle over the question of whether Temple is journeying through a tunnel or into a barrel, up a hill or toward a precipice. In the prose sections, the answer to this question is never seriously in doubt. In the short term, Yoknapatawpha County and the South are heading mindlessly toward complete assimilation into the "W. P. A. and XYZ" of an anonymous federalism (243). In the long term, the nation as a whole is heading with similar mindlessness toward apocalypse: America, Faulkner says, is a "towering frantic edifice poised like a card-house over the abyss of the mortgaged generations" (247); driven by "a furious beating of hollow drums toward nowhere" (4), it is whirling "faster and faster toward the plunging precipice of its destiny" (226).

The extreme pessimism of this view of America's future explains why the prose sections of the novel do not include any significant attempts to alter the course of history. With only minor exceptions, Faulkner depicts no public, collective acts of resistance to the juggernaut of modernity. He does, however, depict a private form of resistance, one that grows in the course of the third prose section into a metaphor for the change occurring in his art. This private form of resistance consists of the defiant nostalgia with which single individuals or small groups of individuals greet each major step in the modernization of the South. First Alec Holston turns his face toward the wall during the founding of Jefferson and the departure of the Indians for the West; then a group of "aging unvanquished women" defy reconstruction by "facing irreconcilably backward toward the old lost battles, the old aborted cause" (239); and finally a few "irreconcilable Jeffersonians and Yoknapatawphians" insist, in the mid-twentieth century, "on wood-burning ranges and cows and vegetable gardens and handymen who [have] to be taken out of hock on the morning after Saturday nights and holidays" (251).

Faulkner's central symbol for this defiant nostalgia is the jail, which he depicts as possessing the ability to watch, remember, and record the history of Jefferson. For most of the third prose section of the novel, the jail's nostalgia appears as unlikely as that of Alec Holston and the other irreconcilables to stem the tide of modernity. But as I have argued elsewhere, the last third of "The Jail" depicts a countermovement in which the "rush and roar of . . . progress" (248) is not merely stemmed but dispelled. [16] This countermovement begins when Faulkner suggests that the jail survives change better than the rest of Yoknapatawpha County. Whereas change affects the rest of the county as an obliterating flood, Faulkner says that the "ephermerae of progress and alteration" merely wash across the surface of the jail "in substanceless repetitive evanescent scarless waves" (250). Because of this ability to resist change, the jail is able to carry undamaged into the modern world, and hence make available for a liberating act of reading, a fragment of unfallen language—the signature of Cecilia Farmer inscribed on one of its windows. The reader of this signature is "a stranger, an outlander" who comes to Jefferson "to try to learn . . . what has brought [his] cousin or friend or acquaintance to elect to live here" (252). The lesson the stranger learns exceeds his expectation, for his communion with the signature teaches him "that there is no time: no space: no distance" (261). "All you had to do," Faulkner says, addressing the stranger in the second person, "was to look at [the signature] a while; all you have to do now is remember it." Do either, and Cecilia Farmer's "clear undistanced voice" will repeat once again its original, unfallen, undying message: "*Listen, stranger; this was myself: this was I*" (262).

In effect, then, the prose sections of the novel espouse the same view of the relation of the imagination to time as the dramatic sections: in both, Faulkner rejects an ameliorative, progressive view and reaffirms his original association of the imagination with the past. At first glance, this reaffirmation might appear to answer by force of will the question I posed earlier about what Faulkner's backward-turning imagination was to feed on. In a limited sense, this impression is correct: in assigning an act of reading the power to overcome time, Faulkner implies that it might be possible to recreate by fiat the Southern culture whose passing he had chronicled. But Faulkner was too clear-sighted an artist to devote his energies for very long to this sort of antiquarian project. Instead, he searched for and discovered a more workable way of allowing his imagination to remain allied to the past.

The nature of this more workable way can be inferred from a change that occurs midway through the stranger's act of reading. When Cecilia Farmer's signature first begins to stir the stranger's imagination, he asks for an account of the few facts still known about her life. The account he receives causes him to engage in an act of historical reconstruction, as he finds himself "watching and hearing" Cecilia's husband-to-be on the occasion of her first glimpse of him (256). But this reconstitutive use of the imagination, compelling though it is, reveals its inadequacy almost immediately. First the stranger feels the need to go beyond the few known facts about Cecilia by supplying a color for her hair. Then he rejects the conventional interpretation of her subsequent history as a "long peaceful connubial progress toward matriarchy." Although he knows that Cecilia left Jefferson with her husband-to-be, he decides that "bridehood, motherhood, grandmotherhood, [and] widowhood" are "nowhere near enough" for the person he has begun to see in his mind; this person, he says, is "fatal instead with all insatiate and deathless sterility; spouseless, barren, and undescended"; she is "demon-nun and angel-witch; empress, siren, Erinys: Mistinguette, too" (258–60).

Implicit in this startling reinterpretation of Cecilia's story is a new way of viewing the relation of the imagination to the past. By interpreting Cecilia's story as freely as he does, the stranger suggests that he is less interested in her signature as a historical record than as a fictional text. He is not content simply to use Cecilia's act of writing as a way of recovering the experience it encodes (if indeed this is even possible); he wants to read the signature in a "writerly" fashion, to use Roland Barthes's term.[17]

He wants to read it in a way that will foreground the availability of the signature—the text—to multiple, even contradictory interpretations. As we see in the stranger's equation of Cecilia with Mistinguette, who was not even born until 1875, this writerly form of reading does not reject meanings that could not have been intended when the text was written. Refusing to privilege the relation of a past text to past experience, the stranger views Cecilia's story as something that lives and grows in time, accruing new meanings as it comes into contact with new experiences and new readers.

As with the stranger, so with Faulkner himself. In 1945, midway through his long period of creative blockage, Faulkner wrote the addendum to *The Sound and the Fury* called "The Compson Appendix." In the Appendix, Melissa Meek, the Jefferson town librarian, discovers a photograph depicting Caddy Compson in the company of a German staff general. After keeping the picture locked away in the library for a week, Melissa journeys to Memphis to ask Dilsey Gibson to help her save Caddy. But Dilsey, who in *The Sound and the Fury* had said "I've seed de first en de last . . . I seed de beginnin, en now I sees de endin" (371), refuses to look at the picture, saying "My eyes aint any good anymore . . . I cant see it."[18] On her way back to Jefferson, Melissa understands the real reason Dilsey did not look at the picture. It is because Caddy, the character Faulkner always spoke of as if she were his muse, *"doesn't want to be saved hasn't anything anymore worth being saved for nothing worth being lost that she can lose"* (420). So Melissa, presumably still carrying the picture, returns to the library, where "life [was] lived too with all its incomprehensible passion and turmoil and grief and fury and despair, but here at six oclock you could close the covers on it and . . . put it back . . . on the quiet eternal shelves and turn the key upon it" (419).

In *Requiem for a Nun* Faulkner accepts the vision of his artistic future he had glimpsed in "The Compson Appendix." He allows his art to enter the library. In turning his imagination back toward the past, Faulkner was not seeking to recreate a lost

Southern culture, or even his own past libidinal experiences. He was attempting to renew his creativity by engaging in a writerly reading of a group of literary texts. These texts are his own earlier works of fiction. In *Requiem for a Nun*, for the first time in his career, Faulkner makes his own past artistic achievement the subject of his art—in the dramatic sections by making Temple's story an extension and revision of *Sanctuary*, and in the narrative sections by retelling parts of the Sartoris, Compson, and Sutpen stories and by reusing some of the language of *Go Down, Moses*. In turning to this subject matter, Faulkner discovered the central artistic strategy of the final phase of his career, for in *The Town*, *The Mansion*, and *The Reivers* he repeatedly makes similar use of his earlier fiction. The elegaic tone of *Requiem for a Nun* suggests that Faulkner did not willingly choose this artistic strategy: only a fragment of unfallen language speaks at the end of "The Jail," not a full text, and the message it whispers is *"this was I,"* not *"this is I."* And certainly, as many critics have told us, this strategy entailed a risk, not always as successfully overcome as in *Requiem for a Nun*, of self-parody and self-repetition. But in comparison to the alternatives exercised by so many of his artistic coevals—suicide, alcoholism, silence—Faulkner's decision to enumerate old themes can be seen to be life-affirming—even, if I may hazard the term, therapeutic. O joy! that in our embers is something that doth live.

NOTES

1. Michael Millgate, *The Achievement of William Faulkner* (1966; rpt., New York: Vintage, 1971), 223; Noel Polk, *Faulkner's "Requiem for a Nun": A Critical Study* (Bloomington: Indiana University Press, 1981), passim. Although my reading of *Requiem for a Nun* is in some ways diametrically opposed to Polk's, I am indebted to him for his willingness to challenge the moralistic interpretations prevalent in the 1950s, 1960s, and 1970s.

2. Cleanth Brooks, *William Faulkner: The Yoknapatawpha Country* (New Haven: Yale University Press, 1963), 140.

3. The most important studies in English of *Requiem for a Nun* are Panthea Broughton's "*Requiem for a Nun*: No Part in Rationality," *Southern Review*, n.s. 8 (1972), 749–62; the chapter on the novel in Olga Vickery's *The Novels of William Faulkner: A Critical Interpretation* (Baton Rouge: Louisiana State University Press, 1959); and the

chapter by Millgate and the book by Polk cited above. See also the essays in French by André Bleikasten, Michel Gresset, Jacques Pothier, and Jean Rouberol in RANAM 13 (1980).

    4. William Faulkner, *Requiem for a Nun* (New York: Random House, 1951), 148. Subsequent references to *Requiem for a Nun* are to this edition.

    5. The contrast between Temple's and Gavin's views corresponds in a general way to the contrast between a romantic and an Aristotelian understanding of the function of the imagination. For a discussion of this contrast that was influential during Faulkner's formative years as an artist, see Irving Babbitt, *Rousseau and Romanticism* (Boston: Houghton Mifflin, 1919).

    6. William Faulkner, *Mosquitoes* (1927; rpt., New York: Liveright, 1955), 319. Subsequent references to *Mosquitoes* are to this edition. Faulkner's introductions to *The Sound and the Fury* are reprinted in "An Introduction for *The Sound and the Fury*," ed. James B. Meriwether, *Southern Review*, n.s. 8 (1972), 705–10, and "An Introduction to *The Sound and the Fury*," ed. J. B. M. [James B. Meriwether], *Mississippi Quarterly*, 26 (1973), 410–15. For Irwin's discussion of these materials, see *Doubling and Incest/ Repetition and Revenge: A Speculative Reading of Faulkner* (Baltimore: Johns Hopkins University Press, 1975), 158–72.

    7. William Faulkner, "Address upon Receiving the Nobel Prize for Literature," in *Essays, Speeches, and Public Letters*. ed. James B. Meriwether (New York: Random House, 1965), 120. Subsequent references to the Foreword to *The Faulkner Reader* and to the Address to the Graduating Class at Pine Manor Junior College are to this edition.

    8. Ernest Hemingway, *Selected Letters, 1917–61*, ed. Carlos Baker (New York: Charles Scribner's Sons, 1981), 807. For discussions of the challenge posed to modernism by the postwar world, see Alfred Kazin, *Bright Book of Life: American Novelists and Storytellers from Hemingway to Mailer* (Boston: Little, Brown, 1973); Harry Levin, "What Was Modernism?" in *Refractions: Essays in Comparative Literature* (New York: Oxford University Press, 1966), 271–95; and Ricardo J. Quinones, *Mapping Literary Modernism: Time and Development* (Princeton: Princeton University Press, 1985). Quinones argues that "the very negativity that marks so strongly the preliminary phase of modernism looks to future growth." Modernism, he says, is a "break-up" that looks forward to a "break-through" (8–9). The disappointment of this expectation by the Great Depression and World War II forced modernist writers such as Faulkner to rethink—and to make more explicit—the ethical bases of their art.

    9. Jacques Derrida, *Of Grammatology*, trans. Gayatri Chakravorty Spivak (Baltimore: Johns Hopkins University Press, 1976), 141–64.

    10. William Faulkner, *Soldiers' Pay* (1926; rpt., New York: Liveright, 1951), 319. The association of blackness and illiteracy with authenticity and pure being was common in the first half of the twentieth century. See, for example, Sherwood Anderson, *Dark Laughter* (New York: Boni & Liveright, 1926), and William Alexander Percy, *Lanterns on the Levee: Recollections of a Planter's Son* (New York: Alfred A. Knopf, 1941). The American Negro, says Percy, has an "obliterating genius for living in the present. . . . He neither remembers nor plans. The white man does little else: to him the present is the one great unreality" (23; quoted in Kazin, 65). For a discussion of the pernicious political implications of the myth of an innate link between blackness and illiteracy, see Henry Louis Gates, Jr., "Editor's Introduction: Writing 'Race' and the Difference it Makes," *Critical Inquiry*, 12 (1985), 1–20. This issue of *Critical Inquiry* is subtitled "'Race,' Writing, and Difference"; it contains several articles pertinent to an understanding of Faulkner's use of racial motifs.

    11. It should be emphasized that Faulkner presents Temple's view of blacks as a trope, not as an assertion about reality. In commenting in Japan about the "foolish, silly things" people believe about blacks, Faulkner said, "They would tell you that a different kind of blood runs in the Negro's veins from the white man's veins. Everybody knows that blood's blood. Any student in biology could tell them that" (Interviews in Japan," in *Lion in the Garden: Interviews with William Faulkner*, ed. James B. Meriwether and

Michael Millgate [1968; rpt., Lincoln: University of Nebraska Press, 1980], 143). In *Requiem for a Nun* itself, Faulkner makes clear the metaphoric status of Temple's comments by following them with a retelling of the story of "Pantaloon in Black," in which Rider, a black, dies an anguished death in the Yoknapatawpha County jail because he "cant quit thinking" (199).

12. *A Fable*, the novel Faulkner was laboring on during much of his period of creative blockage, can be read as an outgrowth of his desire for imaginative self-transcendence. Like the Bible (the source of the novel's central allegory), *A Fable* aspires to be a book beyond books, a book with a meaning so universal and all-encompassing as to exist outside time. Faulkner said that his purpose in writing the book was "to shape into some form of art [my] summation and conception of the human heart and spirit." Speaking of the agonizingly slow composition of the novel, he said, "I'm doing something different now, so different that I am writing and rewriting, weighing every word, which I never did before; I used to bang it on like an apprentice paper hanger and never look back" (*Selected Letters of William Faulkner*, ed. Joseph Blotner [New York: Random House, 1977], 261, 188).

13. For a discussion of the centrality of the idea of defying death to Faulkner's understanding of his artistic vocation, see Robert W. Hamblin,"'Saying No to Death': Toward William Faulkner's Theory of Fiction," in "*A Cosmos of My Own*": *Faulkner and Yoknapatawpha, 1980*, ed. Doreen Fowler and Ann J. Abadie (Jackson: University Press of Mississippi, 1981), 3–35. The comment about Kilroy is taken from Faulkner's acceptance speech for the National Book Award (*Essays, Speeches, and Public Letters*, 143).

14. Joseph Blotner, "William Faulkner's Essay on the Composition of *Sartoris*," *Yale University Library Gazette*, 47 (1973), 124; "An Introduction to *The Sound and the Fury*," 411.

15. For a discussion of the romantic and symbolist antecedents of the idea of an unmediated relation between the self and the world, see Geoffrey Hartman, *The Unmediated Vision: An Interpretation of Wordsworth, Hopkins, Rilke, and Valery* (New Haven: Yale University Press, 1954); for a discussion of the relation between this idea and inscribed language, see John T. Irwin, *American Hieroglyphics: The Symbol of the Egyptian Hieroglyphics in the American Renaissance* (New Haven: Yale University Press, 1980).

16. Karl F. Zender, "Faulkner and the Power of Sound," *PMLA*, 99 (1984), 99–100.

17. Roland Barthes, *S/Z*, trans. Richard Miller (New York: Hill & Wang, 1974). For an illuminating discussion of the importance of "writerly" and "readerly" ways of reading in Faulkner's fiction, see David Krause, "Reading Bon's Letter and Faulkner's *Absalom, Absalom!*," *PMLA*, 99 (1984), 225–41.

18. William Faulkner, *The Sound and the Fury* (1929; rpt., New York: Vintage, 1954), 371, 418. I have used this edition rather than the corrected edition (Random House, 1984) because the corrected edition does not contain the Compson Appendix.

Contributors

Sergei Chakovsky is a research fellow at the A. M. Gorky Institute of World Literature in Moscow. He specializes in Faulkner studies as well as literary theory and the depiction of blacks in American literature. As part of a joint USA-USSR project on William Faulkner, he has lectured at four Faulkner and Yoknapatawpha Conferences and presented a paper at a Faulkner symposium held in Moscow. His publications include "William Faulkner in Soviet Literary Criticism," "Word and Idea in *The Sound and the Fury*," and "Women in Faulkner's Novels: Author's Attitude and Artistic Function."

Thadious M. Davis studied at Xavier, Southern, and Atlanta universities and received her Ph.D. from Boston University. Among her many awards are two grants-in-aid from the American Council of Learned Societies, three grants from the National Endowment for the Humanities, and fellowships from the Rockefeller and Ford foundations. She has taught at Boston University, the University of Massachusetts, and the University of North Carolina at Chapel Hill, where she is currently Professor of English. Her many contributions to Faulkner scholarship include "The Other Family and Luster in *The Sound and the Fury*," "The Yoking of 'Abstract Contradictions': Clytie's Meaning in *Absalom, Absalom!*," and *Faulkner's "Negro": Art and the Southern Context*. At the University of Mississippi's November 1985 symposium on Richard Wright she presented a paper on "Wright, Faulkner, and Mississippi as Racial Memory."

Michael Grimwood received M.A. and Ph.D. degrees from Princeton University and has taught at North Carolina State University since 1975. His articles and review essays on Faulkner have appeared in *The Southern Review, Notes on Mississippi*

Writers, American Literature, Modern Language Review, and other journals. His *Heart in Conflict: Faulkner's Struggles with Vocation* was recently published by the University of Georgia Press. Professor Grimwood is currently working on a study of Southern dialect literature.

Lothar Hönnighausen is Professor and Chairman of English and American Literature at the University of Bonn. Among his books are *Der Stilwandel im dramatischen Werk Sir William Davenants, Präraphaeliten and Fin de Siècle,* and *Grundprobleme der englishen Literaturtheorie des 19. Jahrhunderts.* His *William Faulkner: The Art of Stylization* will soon be published by Cambridge University Press in the series entitled Studies in American Literature and Culture. Professor Hönnighausen is also the author of numerous articles, including "The Role of Swinburne and Eliot in Faulkner's Literary Development" and "Faulkner's Poetry." He presented a slide lecture on "Faulkner's Art in Historical Context" at the 1982 Faulkner and Yoknapatawpha Conference.

Blyden Jackson received his M.A. and Ph.D. degrees from the University of Michigan and taught at Fisk and Southern universities before moving to the University of North Carolina at Chapel Hill in 1969. After his retirement from Chapel Hill in 1981, he has been a fellow at the National Humanities Center, a visiting professor at the University of Delaware, and Ford Foundation Professor of Southern Studies at the University of Mississippi. His publications include *Black Poetry in America, The Waiting Years: Essays on American Negro Literature,* and more than eighty journal articles, book chapters, and review essays. A senior editor for *The History of Southern Literature,* he serves on the editorial advisory board of the *Southern Literary Journal* and is writing a history of Afro-American literature. At the 1975 Faulkner and Yoknapatawpha Conference he spoke on "Faulkner's Depiction of the Negro" and "Two Mississippi Writers: Wright and Faulkner."

Frederick R. Karl was educated at Stanford and Columbia universities and taught at City College of New York for twenty-four years. He has been Professor of English and American Literature at New York University since 1982. In the spring of 1986 he was Visiting Professor at the University of Mississippi, where he absorbed background for a biography of William Faulkner on which he is now engaged. Professor Karl has held Guggenheim and Fulbright fellowships and grants from the National Endowment for the Humanities, the American Council of Learned Societies, and other agencies. His numerous books include three on Joseph Conrad, one of which, *Joseph Conrad: The Three Lives*, was a Pulitzer Prize finalist. Among his other books are *American Fictions, 1940–1980* and *Modern and Modernism: The Sovereignty of the Artist 1885–1925*.

Hoke Perkins received his first B.A. degree from the University of Alabama and his second from Oxford University after spending two years at Oriel College as a Rhodes Scholar. As a graduate student at the University of Virginia, he wrote "Fleeing and Speaking: Authority and Narrative in William Faulkner's Later Career," a dissertation directed by Douglas Day. Professor Perkins has worked as a researcher on Faulkner manuscripts for Garland Publishing Company and has taught at Davidson College since the fall of 1986.

Noel Polk is Professor of English at the University of Southern Mississippi. His publications include *Faulkner's "Requiem for a Nun": A Critical Study; William Faulkner: "The Marionettes"; "Requiem for a Nun": A Concordance to the Novel; "Sanctuary": The Original Text;* and *An Editorial Handbook to Faulkner's "The Sound and the Fury."* Professor Polk recently prepared new editions of *Sanctuary* and *The Sound and the Fury* for Random House and coedited four Faulkner novels for the Library of America. He is also series editor of the Garland Faulkner Casebooks, a member of the editorial team for Garland's Faulkner Manuscripts project, and on the editorial board of *The Faulkner Journal*.

Pamela E. Rhodes taught in Sixth-Form Colleges in Hampshire and Shropshire, England, for several years and has been Lecturer in English and American Literature at the University of Durham since 1984. She earned a Ph.D. degree from the University of Keele, where she wrote a dissertation on aspects of narrative in Faulkner's works of the 1920s. She has reviewed critical works on Faulkner for the British *Journal of American Studies* and *The Library: The Transactions of the Bibliographical Society* and is the author, with Richard Godden, of "*The Wild Palms*: Degraded Culture, Degraded Texts," published in *Intertextuality in Faulkner*.

James A. Snead is Associate Professor of English and Comparative Literature at Yale University. After receiving his B.A. from Yale in 1976, he studied for three years at St. John's College, Cambridge University, and completed his Ph.D. in English Language and Literature there in 1980. In addition to presenting a paper at the James Joyce Centennial Symposium in Dublin, Ireland, he has lectured on Faulkner's *Light in August* at the Free University of Berlin, Oberlin College, and the University of Pittsburgh. Professor Snead is the author of "Repetition as a Figure of Black Culture," an essay in *Black Literature and Literary Theory;* book reviews in *Black American Literature Forum*, the New York *Times*, and the Los Angeles *Times;* "Recoding Blackness: The Visual Rhetoric of Black Independent Film," written as guest curator for an exhibit of the same title at the Whitney Museum of American Art; and *Figures of Division: William Faulkner's Major Novels*, a book published by Methuen in the fall of 1986.

Eric J. Sundquist was educated at the University of Kansas and Johns Hopkins University and has taught at each of those schools. He is currently Associate Professor of English at the University of California, Berkeley. He has held three fellowships, including one from the American Council of Learned Societies, and recently received a grant from the National Endowment for the Humanities for "Race and Slavery in American Literature," a summer seminar for college teachers. His book *Home As Found: Authority and Genealogy in Nineteenth-Century American Literature* won the Gustave Arlt Award from the Council of Graduate Schools in the United States. Other books

by Professor Sundquist are *American Realism: New Essays,
Faulkner: The House Divided*, and *New Critical Essays on Uncle
Tom's Cabin*.

Walter Taylor, a native Mississippian, received his B.A. from
the University of Mississippi and his Ph.D. from Emory University. He has taught at Louisiana State University, the University
of Southwestern Louisiana, and the University of Texas at El
Paso, where he is Professor of English and a past chairman of the
department. Among his most important contributions to
Faulkner scholarship are "Faulkner: Social Commitment and the
Artistic Temperament" in *The Southern Review*, "Faulkner's Pantaloon: The Negro Anomaly at the Heart of *Go Down, Moses*" in
American Literature, and *Faulkner's Search for a South*, published by the University of Illinois Press in 1983.

Philip M. Weinstein was educated at Princeton University, the
Sorbonne, and Harvard University, where he taught for three
years after receiving his Ph.D. in 1968. He has been a member
of the faculty at Swarthmore College since 1971 and served as
Chairman of English Literature from 1980 until 1985. His publications include *Henry James and the Requirements of the Imagination, The Semantics of Desire: Changing Models of Identity
from Dickens to Joyce*, and several journal articles on Faulkner
and other authors. At the 1985 Faulkner and Yoknapatawpha
Conference he presented "Meditations on the Other: Faulkner's
Rendering of Women."

Craig Werner received his B.A. from Colorado College and
his Ph.D. from the University of Illinois. From 1979 to 1983 he
taught at the University of Mississippi. Since 1983 he has been at
the University of Wisconsin, Madison, where he is Associate
Professor of Afro-American Studies. Among his publications are
articles on James Baldwin, Amiri Baraka, Gwendolyn Brooks,
and other black authors in journals and reference works; "Tell
Old Pharaoh: The Afro-American Response to Faulkner" in *The
Southern Review;* "Beyond Realism and Romanticism: Joyce,
Faulkner, and the Tradition of the American Novel" in *The
Centennial Review;* "The Old South, 1815–1840" in *The History*

of Southern Literature; and *Paradoxical Resolutions: American Fiction Since James Joyce.*

Karl F. Zender received his Ph.D. from the University of Iowa. After teaching at Washington University from 1966 until 1973 he joined the faculty at the University of California, Davis, where he is now Associate Professor of English. In addition to publishing articles on Faulkner in *Studies in Short Fiction, Mississippi Quarterly, The Southern Review,* and other journals, he has written annual reviews of Faulkner criticism for seven volumes of *American Literary Scholarship.* Professor Zender is now completing a book-length study of continuity and change in Faulkner's fiction.

Index